ETHNICITY IN THE EAST AND NORTH-EAST INDIA

ETHNICITY IN THE EAST AND NORTH-EAST INDIA

Editors

Sanjay K. Roy

Rajatsubhra Mukhopadhyay

GYAN

ISBN : 978-81-212-1255-7

Price : ₹ 875

First Published, 2015

Published by

Gyan Publishing House
23, Main Ansari Road, Darya Ganj
New Delhi-110002
Ph. : 23282060, 23261060
Fax : 011-23285914
E-mail: books@gyanbooks.com
Website : www.gyanbooks.com

Laser Typesetting : Gyan Print (AB-I), Delhi
Printed at : G. Print Process, Delhi

Cataloging in Publication Data—DK
Courtesy: D.K. Agencies (P) Ltd. <docinfo@dkagencies.com>

National Seminar on 'Modes of Ethnic Identity Construction in India' (2012 : Department of Sociology, North Bengal University)
Ethnicity in the east and North-East India / editors, Sanjay K. Roy, Rajatsubhra Mukhopadhyay.

pages ; cm
Includes bibliographical references and index.
ISBN 9788121212557

1. Ethnicity—India—Congresses. 2. Ethnicity—India, Northeastern—Congresses. I. Roy, Sanjay K., editor. II. Mukhopadhyaya, Rajatsubhra, editor. III. University of North Bengal. Department of Sociology.organizer. IV. Title.

DDC 305.800954 23

Dedicated to:

Professor Nirendra Chandra Choudhury (21st January, 1924 and 18th October, 2013), our beloved teacher, who founded the Department of Sociology and Social Anthropology in North Bengal University

Contents

SECTION–III

ETHNICITY IN NORTH-EAST INDIA

List of Contributors

Rajat Kanti Das, Professor (Retired), Department of Anthropology, Vidyasagar University, West Midnapore, West Bengal.

Jayanta Sarkar, Superintending Anthropologist (Retired), Anthropological Survey of India, Kolkata.

Biswajit Ghosh, Professor, Department of Sociology, Burdwan University, West Bengal.

Arun K. Jana, Associate Professor, Department of Political Science, North Bengal University, Distt. Darjeeling, West Bengal.

Rup Kumar Barman, Associate Professor, Department of History, Jadavpur University, Kolkata.

Kanchan Mukhopadhyay, Superintending Anthropologist (Cultural), Anthropological Survey of India.

D.C. Roy, Associate Professor, Department of Economics, Kalimpong College, West Bengal.

Dipak Piplai, Writer and Social Activist.

Rajib Nandy, Research Fellow, Institute of Social Studies Trust, New Delhi.

Nandini Basistha, Department of Political Science, Allahabad University.

Sanjay K. Roy, Professor, Department of Sociology, North Bengal University.

N.K. Das, Former Dy. Director and currently Visiting Fellow, Anthropological Survey of India, Kolkata.

Surajit Kumar Pal, Anthropologist (Retired), Anthropological Survey of India, Nagpur.

Aparajita De, Assistant Professor, Department of Geography, Delhi School of Economics, Delhi University.

Acknowledgements

The present volume on *Ethnicity in the East and North-East India* is an anthology of the papers presented in a National Seminar on 'Modes of Ethnic Identity Construction in India' organised by the Department of Sociology, North Bengal University, on 9-10 March, 2012, under the Special Assistance Programme (SAP) of the UGC. After the seminar, we persuaded the paper presenters to revise their papers in line with the discussion/critical observations that followed their presentations in the seminar. Most of the paper presenters revised their papers, although there have been a few casualties. Notwithstanding a few hitches, we are finally able to bring out the present anthology on a subject which bears high relevance in comprehending the contemporary social and political dynamics of the Eastern and North-East India. There have been many books on ethnicity and ethnic conflicts in North-East India but there are a very few on the ethnic problem in Eastern India and here lies the specialty of the present volume. There is one paper discussing ethnic conflict in Gujarat, which, needless to say, falls outside East and North-East India; yet, we included the paper in the present volume in order to give the readers a comparative perspective. The contributors in this volume are from different social science disciplines, namely, history, sociology, anthropology, economics, political science and geography and, therefore, one could drawn an interdisciplinary perspective on the subject of ethnicity.

Many institutions and individuals have helped in making this volume possible. We would extend special thanks to UGC which had given us generous financial support in organising the seminar. Prof R.K. Bhadra, the Co-ordinator of the SAP (DRS-I) in the Department, had taken keen interest in having the seminar organised and has encouraged us to work for the volume; we are extremely thankful to him. Prof Jeta Sankritayana, the Dean, Faculty of Arts, Commerce and Law had delivered the Keynote Address and Prof B.P. Mishra had given the valedictory address. The scholarly insights of both the senior scholars enriched all those who participated in the seminar with a greater understanding of the subject of ethnicity in the contemporary social and political locale of the region. We thankfully acknowledge their kind patronage. Other colleagues in the Department, Dr Saswati Biswas, Dr Mita Bhadra and Dr Swatasiddha Sarkar, who worked selflessly in holding the seminar, deserve special thanks. The tireless and hard work of the student volunteers in organising the seminar and the enthusiastic participation of the students and scholars of the Department make us hopeful about the future of the discipline of sociology.

Sanjay K. Roy
Rajatsubhra Mukhopadhyaya

Introduction

I

The impact of Western enlightenment and scientific rationalism on social science discourses all over the globe has been enormous. The impact has been so vivid that at one point of time, there seemed to be a growing consensus in social sciences that the life of the people in modern times would be guided solely by modern rationalism and scientific spirit and the social institutions, groups and organisations based on traditional norms and bonds, like caste, clan, kinship and religious groups, would lose their relevance. Sociologists like Durkheim, Simmel, Tonnies, Weber and many others endorsed this view of social change in modern times. Marx and many Marxists went to the extent of maintaining a clear distinction between 'consciousness' (based on class relations) and 'false consciousness' (based on traditional relations and ideologies) arguing that the former would defeat the latter in moulding the praxis of life, culture and politics. Max Weber left a note on the growing penetration of rationalism in all walks of modern life and the resultant disappearance of values based on tradition, emotion and sentiments. The idea of rational-calculative one-dimensional man captured the imagination of some of the members of the German Critical School in the pre and post War II periods. The Italian school of sociologists (Pareto, Mosca and Gramsci), however, explored the relevance of culture, emotion, sentiments and passions even in modern life arguing that besides logic and rationalism, the traditional social and cultural space is craftily cultivated by the modern day rulers as a part of their hegemonic strategy. In his interpretation of history, Weber, unlike Marx, refused to relegate religion, values, and other elements of culture to the less significant zone of superstructure or 'false consciousness' but explored their significance in guiding people to a particular mode of action. He explored the political economy of shared values drawn out of religion and traditions.

The long tradition of critical thinking in Germany, France and Italy and later in England (especially the culture study group) squarely unraveled the mediation and reproduction of culture by the dominant economic interests and power elite combine. Although developed out of Western experience the methodological significance of the discourses on 'hegemony' (Gramsci), 'culture industry' (Adorno), 'ideological state apparatuses' (Althusser) or ideas like 'mass culture' or 'popular culture' in understanding the non-Western contexts, especially the process of mediation of culture by the bourgeois-hegemonic forces, could hardly be ruled out. The universal nature of the economic and power interests and the similarity in the 'governmentality' (Foucault) make this parallel possible.

'Ethnic consciousnesses', appropriation of culture in political praxis by both the hegemonic and counter-hegemonic forces and ethnic politics, have co-existed class consciousness and class-line movements. These two alternative modes of political mobilisation are rooted in contesting political ideologies – liberalism and Marxism, at the global level (during the period of cold war) and at the national and local level, particularly in the post-World War II period. Some scholars believe that ethnicity is found mostly in developing world because of cracks and strains in the secular sphere (Phadnis, 1989). For others, ethnic politics is very much a Western phenomenon as well. Rattansi, for example, has observed: 'The spectre that haunts the societies of the West is no longer communism, but… a series of racisms and ethnocentrisms' (1994:1). Thus, to identify West with rationality and class and the non-West with tradition, primordiality and ethnicity would be too naïve and, therefore, untenable. The alternative and conflicting modes of drawing consciousness and mobilisation equally apply to East and West, North and South.

In Europe and America, ethnic movements surfaced in no insignificant scale from the 1960s. The downfall of Soviet Union in 1991 has only encouraged the trend. More than 70 years of communist experiment in erstwhile Soviet Union could not resolve the issue of sub-nationalism, based on religion, region, language, race and culture. The ideology of communism, or at least the way it was applied to overrule other forms of identity construction and consciousness, did not succeed in its mission to integrate distinct nations and cultures into one unified entity. The unity of communist Soviet Union now appears to have been 'forced' from the above rather than based on voluntary and 'natural' alliances. With the withdrawal of armed forces the nations fell apart and their distinct cultural identities resurfaced; communist ideology, which was forced, got replaced by resurgent religious and regional nationalism in the Central Asian and European parts. New nations emerged out of the wreckage of the erstwhile Soviet Union. New nations based upon dominant ethnic affiliation have been recognised since 1990s in other parts of the globe as well. Other fitting illustrations of the argument could the breakdown of communist Yugoslavia of Czechoslovakia into smaller nations in the recent past.

Culture and other elements of superstructure in Marxist frame are the means to a capitalist end; they are appropriated for reproduction of the capitalist mode of production, the capitalist relations of production in particular. Taking a look at the modern day art of governance (or 'governmentality') it can be said, following the interpretations of Gramsci, Althusser, Habermas and Foucault, that power continues to be mediated through culture and other elements of civil society, and through the body of knowledge and discourses produced from the above. But the appropriation, cultivation and reproduction of the elements of culture in a liberal order cannot be the monopoly of the ruling forces; the forces with political ambitions, which may not be a part of the ruling hierarchy in a given point in time, may also appropriate and 'cultivate' culture as means to capture power, although for the latter it is very difficult to find a 'free space' and maintain it. Driven by a fear of losing cultural identities the ethnic communities can also make efforts in the form of mobilisation and movements to resist the larger systemic efforts to appropriate and 'discipline' cultures and identities. The global and national forces of homogenisation are met with resistance as peoples (or cultural communities) make efforts to defend their cultural rights, identities and autonomy. Cultural 'place', thus, becomes a site of war and contestation between the hegemonic and counter-hegemonic forces. Again, there can be strategic shifts in the positions of those who consciously cultivate the cultural place for power. Thus, the forces that appear counter-hegemonic in one context may turn hegemonic in another context and time or they can go the other way around as well. For example, the Gorkhaland movement in Darjeeling hills has essentially been counter-hegemonic vis-à-vis Bengalis and the state of West Bengal but the Gorkhas work as a hegemonic force vis-à-vis the minority Lepchas or Bhutias in Darjeeling Hills. Similarly, before the takeover by the British the Ahom kings were looked at as 'hegemonic' by the neighbouring hill tribes in Garo, Khasi, Naga or Mizo hills or by the plains tribes like Bodo and Rabha but later the Ahoms found hegemonic forces among the neighbouring Bengalis or in the Indian Union, a feeling that found expression in Assam movement of 1980s or in the 'freedom movement' spearheaded by the United Liberation Front of Assam (ULFA) in the 1990s.

The Indian union is multi-ethnic and multicultural. Politically, it is not a federation of states the way America is. We have rather a strong central government with a mission to integrate the cultures and peoples in the name of nationalism and liberalism (socialism has been dropped from the ideological package), liberalisation, globalisation, modernisation, consumerism, development and welfarism. These forces are bound to have some leveling impact on the cultures, especially on the vulnerable cultures, shared by small populations or communities. Rephrasing Pareto's famous dictum 'human history is the graveyard of aristocracies', one can perhaps say 'human history is the graveyard of small and vulnerable cultural forms'. Roy (2013) has argued that cultures and knowledge forms are not only engaged in an unending dialogue (as Sen, 2005 argues) but they are unequally placed in a power relation, in a relationship of domination and subordination and in the process the stronger cultural forms (shared by a majority and patronised by the power) survive and thrive while the weaker ones (which are shared by a small group and are out of favour of the power) face extinction. Smaller languages and art forms, thus, wither away to make room for the languages and art forms that represent the majority. The cultural forms that manage to weather off the cultural invasion end up conceding territories and 'places' and accept the given space by the invader and make significant adjustments in order to survive. Material and power interests reproduce the relationship of dominance and subordination in the cultural fields although culture and the emotive power it can generate, alone can be a 'real' base of identity formation and conflict.

In India, the mainstream political parties, the Hindu Rights and the centrist Indian National Congress, try to enforce their ideologies of nationalism (Hindu nationalism and Indian nationalism) over the diverse populations who lived as distinctive nations with distinctive cultures and states for centuries. The politics of 'difference' at the sub-national level questions the hegemony of the unitary ideologies. This finds reflection in regional ethnic movements, ethnic formation of the distinctive cultural communities as they look for a 'place' of their own in the body of Indian democracy. The sub-national movements in Assam, Nagaland, Mizoram, and Kashmir are some of the ones that take positions against the mainstream accounts of nationalism and the state-created identities. While challenging Indian union and its integrationist 'nation building' package these 'sub-national' or 'anti-national' populations get into occasional dialogues with the mighty Indian state to make adjustments. In other words, ethnic movements are means to bargain for a political place in a democracy which is willing to redistribute political space along the 'pre-modern' or 'post-modern' ethnic considerations. It is often argued that identity politics of the minorities is contextualised in a modern global context because they challenge national narratives of social cohesion and homogeneity (Appadurai, 2006).

The ethnic question in India, or in the region of our present concern or elsewhere, essentially centres on the praxis of culture. The cultural praxis can happen at different layers and levels, both from the below (from the side of the people or community) and from above (from the side of the national and global orders). From the below, culture can be shared and reproduced at the levels of consciousness and interaction in everyday life, at the level of a collective movement for the protection of culture and against the forces of invasion, in the form of appropriation of culture and cultural symbols for an ethnic movement for finding a political 'place', either within or without the existing arrangements. From above, on the other hand, the dominant economic and political interests mediate through culture for securing an ideological unity of the people across classes by spreading the 'desired' knowledge forms or by promoting different forms of mass culture ('bourgeois culture' in the guise of 'popular' or mass culture). The varying interest groups take the ethnic route to 'politics' or praxis of culture both from the above and from below because it provides an already existing foundation of emotive unity at the community level. In other words, the ethnic route to political mobilisation 'naturally' follows from the pre-existing cultural unity and 'conscience collective' which tends to negate the internal tensions and conflicts. The Indian democracy, from colonial times, has set a strong tradition of appropriating the cultural field for political ends. The categories like religion, caste, and tribe have been recognised by the state as means of distribution of rights and privileges, thus consolidating the foundation of these primordial institutions. The state has often diluted the definition of secularism to accommodate the aspirations of the religious interests and interfered in religious matters, which should have been left to the civil society. In post colonial 'secular' India, thus, much of civil society has been transformed into 'political field' which, in turn, promotes ethnic consciousness and ethnic politics.

However, it is not culture alone as an independent variable that influences peoples' shared perceptions and collective actions in the form of dissent, mobilisation and movement. Loss of control over resources, denial of material rights often prompts a sense of deprivation and injustice which also finds expression in cultural or ethnic movements. The populations and communities that take the cultural route to ethnic mobilisation and fight the perceived injustices, perpetrated on them by the system, often fail to appreciate the fact that it is the market driven liberal democratic order which is essentially modeled to further the interests of the classes that control the productive resources, is the root of all inequality and injustice. The mechanisms of exploitation are essentially systemic and they can be understood only in terms of unequal control of resources and 'surplus value' generating class relations. The categories like caste or tribe appear 'real' because they are the means to legitimise certain types of class relations, because they justify unequal distribution of productive resources and exchange of labour. However, they also appear 'autonomous' and 'real' because they enforce certain type of social consciousness and social relations, both at the individual and collective levels, legitimised in terms of certain value systems, and reproduced in the customs, rituals and practices. The market-driven liberal social order, thus, reproduces inequality while marginalising the sections or classes that do not have much control over the productive resources, material or human. The continuous loss of control over the productive resources and marginalisation in the economic, social, cultural, and political levels create a psychological rupture between the 'marginalised' and the dominant systemic forces. A 'political or ideological void' and a sense of alienation, thus created, sometimes lead the marginalised to try their hands in various modes of anti-state mobilisation combining class exploitation and social exclusion. A large section of *adivasis* in parts of central and eastern India seem to be into this kind of anti-state protest, using both constitutional and extra-constitutional means for some time now. The irony, however, is that the ethnic political 'places' created through ethnic movements (e.g., states, autonomous councils, scheduled districts or territorial administrative units) continue to follow the language and politics of the liberal democratic order and this could be the key reason why solution to fundamental problems like marginalisation, inequality, and injustice eludes them.

Another common feature of ethnic mobilisation is the construction of the 'other' by the ethnic population, united by a sense of 'self'. There could be a mix of 'reality' and arbitrariness in the construction of both self and the other. In construction of self or a culture-based identity the ethnic populations try to downplay the internal micro-ethnic differences and also construct the 'other' as a united whole. In case of Jharkhand statehood movement in the 1980s and 1990s, or in the ongoing *adivasi* autonomous council movement in North Bengal the *adivasis* forget about their individual tribal identities (such as Santal, Oraon, Monda, Kharia and so on) and construct a united *adivasi* self. Similarly, the 'other' can be a conglomeration of the state, administration and one or more than one ethnic communities which are perceived to be a source of threat. The construction 'diku' as the 'other' is permanent in the consciousness of the *adivasis* of central India.

Every region of the Indian union has its unique history, populations and cultures, level of development and underdevelopment, level of modernity, tradition of movements and protests, level of integration and dissent, and so on. The Eastern region, Bengal, in particular, is distinguished for its early contact with the British colonisers, early industrialisation, and urbanisation. Calcutta was the capital of colonial rule until 1912, it was the epicenter of modernist and anti-colonial movements, place from where Marxism had spread. It saw the rise of the middle-class, the reform movements, led by Rammohun and Vidyasagar, which had spread the messages of modernism, secularism and universal fraternity across the primordial boundaries. It has a long tradition of social reform movement, peasant movements and working class movements. A long legacy of universal values, and three and a half decades of Left rule in recent past had at least partially checked communal passions and parochialism in civil and political societies. But there should be no denying that the class-line mobilisation and delivery of social justice in class line, which seem to have been attempted by Left Front Government in the State, could not kill the caste, community, religious and other forms of primordial consciousness, since the members of the subaltern castes and communities continue to nurse a strong sense of backwardness and a sense of deprivation in comparative terms. When a sense of alienation, real or perceived, captures the collective conscience the members of such communities mobilise their people in the name of caste, tribe or community. After establishing some degree of ethnic unity these groups go for a hard bargain in the power sharing arrangement. Most of the ethnic movements end in political alliances and 'compromises' with the ruling forces, benefitting only the ethnic elite and not the ethnic populations. Thus, a sense of otherness and alienation continues to be reproduced in the everyday life of the underprivileged communities in their economic, social, political and cultural life even after some political settlements. This is what has been happening to the leading movements in contemporary Odisha and West Bengal.

Religion was a big divider of political landscape of colonial Bengal, the partition of Bengal in 1947, the communal violence and the migration of refugees had their serious repercussion on West Bengal. However, unlike in Bihar, caste had never occupied the centre stage in the social and political consciousness or praxis in Bengal. The mainstream politics controlled by the Indian National Congress and the Left parties did not take the caste route to political mobilisation. Caste-based movements, for example, the movements by the Namasudras in South Bengal or Rajbanshis in North Bengal, in colonial and post-colonial periods were primarily social movements. However, the caste based social movements seem to have developed political ambitions, as they now want a share of the political space, either an exclusive space (as in case of statehood movement by the Rajbanshis) or in the form of power-sharing arrangement with the ruling party (as with the case of the Matuas). Apart from their shared backwardness and distinctive cultural symbols the factors that have sustained the 'otherness' of these communities are: (a) the failure of the mainstream political parties to develop enough organic leadership in these communities, (b) failure to address the systemic forces that keep them socially and economically backward, (c) to offer an ideological order and a system of symbols which could have integrated these communities into their organisational orders.

Apart from the divisions on caste lines there is also a dividing line between the dominant mainstream and the marginalised *adivasis,* in all the states in the East, namely, Bengal and Orissa, Bihar and Jharkhand. The *adivasis* have supported the mainstream political parties for many years and for generations, yet they are the poorest of the poor and their control over the social, economic and political 'place' has been minimal. This has been the case despite their territories being rich reserve of natural resources, which have now been colonised by the aggressive global and national capital. While taking away their resources, with full support of the state, the bourgeoisie have put in place a mechanism to extract surplus value out of *adivasi* labour.

They are now responding to the injustices perpetrated on them by taking the Naxalite route (in Odisha, Jharkhand and in some districts of West Bengal) or taking the ethnic route to political mobilisation (as in the Terai and Dooars regions of North Bengal).

Extending the discourse to the North-East one cannot help but see a process of ethnicisation of society, both in everyday life and in social, cultural and political praxis. In terms of governmentality, in the subnational (e.g., Assamese), sub-sub-national (Bodo, Rabha and other hill and plains tribes) and anti-national (e.g., ULFA and NSCN fighting for creation of independent Assam and Nagalim respectively) movements, everywhere, one can see the omnipresence of ethnic consciousness and assertion of ethnic identity. The people in North-East India and the State and Central Governments – all – seem to be the permanent prisoners to ethnic consciousness, as they do not see anything but 'ethnic' solution to the problems of the region. This appears to be permanent trap that people in the region seem unlikely to tear apart and try alternative modes of mobilisation and movement. The solution to more fundamental issues that define the existing backwardness, marginalisation or injustice, are thus lost in the mist of ethnic-political compromises with the state or the systemic forces. The worrying fall-out of all this is the endless fragmentation and atomisation of the populations and the unending violent ethnic conflicts among the 'marginals'. There seem to be no takers, except in Tripura, of the message of class-line mobilisation and universal brotherhood among the oppressed (for more details of the argument see Roy, 2005).

II

The articles in the volume have been arranged in four sections, namely, (i) *Perspectives on Ethnicity*, (ii) *Ethnicity in Eastern India*, (iii) *Ethnicity in North-East India*, and (iv) *Ethnicity in Gujarat*. The first section has three papers which deal with some conceptual issues relating to ethnicity. Drawing from Indian experiences the papers make attempts to critique Western concepts.

The first paper 'Modes of Ethnic Identity Construction' by Rajat Kanti Das, an eminent anthropologist, begins by defining 'ethnicity'. Ethnicity, for Das, refers to a group identity formed on the basis of a set of common and distinctive characteristics, which constitute a substantive core of the ethnic group. Das argues that since ethnic group identity is a subjective construct certain degree of arbitrariness is unavoidable in its construction. Ethnicity presupposes a level of shared consciousness on the part of the members of an ethnic group. The consciousness may be based on caste, tribe, community living, territoriality, religion, sect, language, race, nation, common cultural traditions, all of which may not be equally effective at a particular point of time but may be inducted depending on the need of the concerned peoples and strategies adopted by them. Das maintains a clear distinction between 'ethnic group' and 'ethnicity'; while the former is formed on the basis of common cultural core or history and is essentially apolitical the latter is a construct based on a core shared culture and history and is essentially political, with power interest at its core. Ethnicity always has a sense of 'we' and 'they' and a sense of injustice and therefore involves a course of mobilisation to restore some sense of justice. Referring to post-colonial context of ethnicity in India Das argues that before the globalisation began ethnic movements had a bargaining point in the nation state but after globalisation and the consequent decline of the nation state the ethnic movements have to look for new strategies and bargaining points. Referring to the on-going Naga-Kuki ethnic conflict Das argues that despite the best efforts by the State and Central governments the conflict remains unresolved because there are foreign hands involved in the conflict.

The second paper in this section 'Modes of Ethnic Identity Construction: Some Observations' is by another senior anthropologist Jayanta Sarkar. The most important part of identity formation for a group, according to Sarkar, is to identify the distinct social, cultural, political and mythical markers and then conscious collective efforts to maintain ethnic boundary. This applies to the religious groups, caste groups and the tribes in the Indian context. The ethnic groups, defined at the cultural level, can potentially take the political turn, and thus gets engrossed in a praxis called ethnicity. At the conceptual plane, therefore, Sarkar takes a similar stand as that of Rajat Kanti Das. Sarkar draws our attention to the dynamism with which the Bhil sub-groups in Rajasthan maintain their distinct identities by imposing a sense of caste-like hierarchy and by imposing norms restricting inter-group interaction in their everyday life. Sometimes identities imposed from outside, which carry derogatory meaning, help construct new identities by the local tribal communities. As an illustration Sarkar refers to the present day Nishings and the Adis of Arunachal Pradesh who used to be identified as the Dafla and Abor respectively by the people of the plains of Assam. The terms Dafla and Abor mean 'barbarous' and 'independent' or 'unruly'. In order to reject these terms the members of these tribes have chosen names for their distinct identity as Nishing and Adi, meaning 'hill people' (Sarkar, 1982).

Biswajit Ghosh in his paper 'What explains the salience of Ethnicity? Some Conceptual Clarifications' examines the existing theoretical paradigms, namely, (a) Primordialist Logic, (b) Instrumental Perspective, (c) Modernisation Approach and (d) Social Constructionist Theory, critiques all of them, arguing that none of the theories is comprehensive enough to address the vastness and complexity of the problem called ethnicity. Drawing from his own studies in Tripura and from the studies of contemporary scholars he makes some interesting observations which bear testimony of his insight of the problem.

Ethnicity, for Ghosh, is a social construct; common culture and cultural concerns are one of many factors, and not the only factor, which constitute the 'sufficient' condition for formation of ethnicity. He writes: '...ethnicity is not simply a product of socio-economic, cultural or ideological issues of the 'insiders' against the 'outsiders'; they meet the 'necessary' but not the sufficient conditions.' Peoples' identities, for Ghosh, cannot always be treated as free floating objects as there are limits both to plasticity of ethnicity as well as to its fixity and solidity. He argues that ethnic attachments cannot be totally imaginary without any socio-cultural base. Hence, the process of boundary and identity formation can best be viewed from both structural and discursive points of view.

Ghosh further argues that modernisation does not necessarily de-ethicise cultural communities, but may provide them solidity. Drawing from his research and the studies done by other scholars Ghosh observes that movements seeking separate identity or distinctiveness are neither parochial nor opposed to modernity. Had that been the case, concern for 'power' and 'politics' would not have remained the axial point of tribalism in Tripura (Ghosh, 2003). A study of the nature of ethnicity and insurgency in Tripura (2003) led Ghosh to argue that such processes are influenced by some *necessary* conditions and supplemented by other *sufficient* conditions. Ethnicity cannot easily be evoked if only necessary conditions prevail. The presence of sufficient conditions induces qualitative change in the nature of group mobilisation. The *necessary conditions* include several socio-economic factors like demographic compulsions, cultural deprivation, poverty, land alienation and eviction, unemployment and underdevelopment, etc. The *sufficient conditions*, on the other hand, include an acute sense of discrimination among the group members, emergence of a strong elite leadership, political competition and manipulation, state policies and actions and easy accessibility to external support.

Ghosh observes that change and mutability are endemic to ethnic identities and movements as they are essentially fluid, situationally contingent and negotiable. Also, ethnic movements are not necessarily 'threat' to the state; they may work as organs of civil society to strengthen democracy and thus help address the questions of inequality, injustice and exclusion. Hence, these movements should be viewed from a wider and historical perspective and not in a narrow and time-bound framework.

III

The section on 'Ethnicity in the East' to we have included eight papers, seven on West Bengal and one on Odisha. Arun K. Jana in his paper 'The Construction of a Kosli Identity and the Movement for a Separate State of Kosal in Western Odisha' gives an account of an otherwise little known Kosal statehood movement in Western Odisha. Taking a look into history Jana observes that the integration of 24 princely states after independence created an area which came to known as Western Odisha, a region that is for many reasons different from Eastern Odisha, which was curved out of Bengal in

1936. People in Western Odisha have been raising voice about its distinctive identity while maintaining a boundary with the mainstream Eastern Odisha. According Jana's account by early 1990s an ethnic movement started taking shape with its epicentre at Sambalpur town of Western Odisha on the claim that Sambalpurias are not Odiyas. The movement for a separate state spearheaded at different times by the organisations like Kosal Kranti Dal, Kosal Sena, Kosal Sangram Parishad, Western Orissa Liberation Front, Western Orissa People's Front, and so on, *gained* momentum in 2012-2013. The demand was the creation of a separate state of Kosal consisting of eleven districts of Western Odisha. The movement was launched on the claim that Koslis or Sambalpuris have a distinct Kosli-Sambalpuri ethnic identity. The demand is rooted in a perception of neglect of Western Odisha, a shared understanding that the coastal (or Eastern) Odisha is developed while the Western Odisha is plunged into neglect and underdevelopment. Second distinctness is that the region has a large percentage of tribal population, the poorest of the poor. For its large percentage of tribal population Western Odisha separates it from coastal Odisha; boundary is also maintained in linguistic and cultural lines. Thirdly, the feeling of separateness stems from a sense of deprivation; the districts of Western Odisha despite being the richest among the districts in terms of deposit of natural resources have remained underdeveloped or backward over the years in both relative and absolute terms. Jana observes that despite showing periodic sparks the movement has not met with much success because of a series of electoral failures and divisions in the rank and file of the movement. The lack of unity among the organisations and the occasional opportunist, electoral understanding with the mainstream political parties has left the movement directionless. The union government's decision to create a separate state of Telengana, bifurcating the neighbouring Andhara Pradesh, has enthused the supporters of a separate Koshal state in recent months.

The second paper in this section is by historian Rup Kumar Barman on 'Changing Identities of the Scheduled Castes in Colonial and Post-Colonial Bengal'. In his paper Barman tracks down the history of caste-based movements of the *Namasudras*, *Rajbanshis*, *Poundras* and *Malos* of West Bengal. According to the author, these caste groups have reacted in different ways to the neglect and humiliation they have received at the hands of the Hindu caste order in the colonial as well as post-colonial Bengal. The caste-based movements have travelled through different phases: (i) a phase of internal reforms, a phase of *kshatriyaisation,* when these caste groups have strove for elevation of their position in the caste hierarchy, (ii) took part in elections and lodged caste-based political movements, and (iii) a contemporary phase of sharing of state power with the ruling parties. These caste-based communities had developed a kind of consciousness about their caste identity in the second quarter of the twentieth century, when they started asserting themselves for a 'place' in the political map of Indian democracy. They collectively established themselves as a 'bargaining political force' in the context of political autonomy of Bengal under the colonial rule. But after the partition of Bengal in 1947, these caste communities (officially recognised as Scheduled Castes since 1936) have changed the nature of their ethnic consciousness. Barman draws our attention to the changing nature of ethnicity of caste-based social groups of Bengal. Barman highlights the fact that despite Bengal being the province that experienced early modernisation, urbanisation, and industrialisation, and spread of Marxism the caste consciousness has survived and the downtrodden had to resort to caste-based ethnicity to fight against different forms of injustices. The social movements by the caste groups, the author argues, although have brought about no revolutionary transformation, have at least restored some self-respect among their members and reinvigorated a collective consciousness, placing these communities in a place from where they can work out a better bargain with the power hierarchy.

Kanchan Mukhopadhyay, a senior anthropologist, in his paper 'Protest and Power: The Matua Sampraday of Bengal' uses Garmasian concepts of hegemony and counter-hegemony to explain the emergence of the Matuas (the Namasudra subaltern caste) as an organised caste-based ethnic group in certain pockets of Southern Bengal, particularly in Nadia, North and South 24 Parganas districts. In Mukhopadhyay's analysis, power is mediated by the 'dominant' through the organs of civil society while the 'dominated' can also take the social and cultural route to mobilisation in order to challenge the hegemony. In their long history of caste-based mobilisation the Matuas have drawn heavily from the storehouse of cultural symbols, focusing on unity, education, and empowerment and making occasional alignment with the ruling power. The coalescence of class and caste relations, backed by religious movements, has helped the rise of Matua caste consciousness and unity over the years, right from the days of colonial Bengal. The strengthening of the unity of the *sampraday* in the recent years speaks for the continuation of the relevance of the caste-based mobilisation in post-colonial politics in West Bengal. In recent years it appears that the Matuas have realised the 'electoral value' of their unity as they go for hard bargain in power sharing with the mainstream political parties. It remains uncertain if such alllignments and power sharing would empower the common Matuas enough to fight against the injustices or would end up creating a small group of neo-elite that would use the united support of the *sampraday* (community) for their selfish benefits. A worrying factor for the Matua ethnic movement, according to Mukhopadhyay, has been that neither the Matua philosophy nor the members of the Matua *sampraday* remained monolithic and static entities in their history of existence; both have been faced with various opposing forces both from within and without.

Having lost their ancestral place and the social-cultural and political space to the immigrant communities the Lepchas of Darjeeling hills face unprecedented identity crisis. The dominant immigrant Nepali speaking people makes effort to swallow them within the cover of Gorkha identity and want them to be a part of the Gorkhaland statehood movement. The Lepchas, who have a long tradition of free living, however, find it difficult to accept this move of the dominant Gorkhas that would leave them subjugated forever. In this paper, D. C. Roy, an economist by training, who has been following the course of Lepcha identity movement for some time, highlights the long unresolved problems of the Lepchas of Darjeeling hills and their recent movement for setting up the Lepcha Development Council within the state of West Bengal. The paper constructs a short history of the Lepchas and their land, narrates the long standing problems of the Lepchas and scripts a narrative of the recent movement of the Lepchas for separate Development Council.

Tagore's philosophy was to take education and development transcending all boundaries, barriers and narrowness with a view of serve the downtrodden. Tagore wanted the members of the depressed communities surrounding Visva-Bharati to be an integral part of this project. Social activist and freelance writer Dipak Piplai, who is also an anthropologist by training, argues that the construction of boundary wall encircling Visva-Bharati university campus has been a point of departure from Tagore's philosophy since its has created a spiritual break between the première institution and nearly 400 Santal families, who have been living in *Baganpara,* located on the fringe of the campus, for generations. The Santals, who had been living there even before Visva-Bharati was established, maintained a close affinity with the space where the institution has come up. Before the construction of the wall the Santals could take short-cut through the campus to reach the places of work and other places of importance like schools, market and hospital and used the campus as grazing field and for many other purposes. But the boundary has not only ceased their 'natural' rights over the campus but also has forced them to take a long route to reach those places of importance. The boundary wall has cut their physical attachment with the university space and inflicted a strong sense of alienation and anger. In fact the Santals have always been 'academically untouchable' since there has been no step to integrate them into the system of higher education and the university, which is located in their courtyard. While the university authorities have 'othered' them; they, in turn, have launched movements against the university authorities and the boundary wall reinventing their otherness and ethnic consciousness.

Rajib Nandi's 'Constructing Ethno-histories of the Rajbangsi People in North Bengal' is the second paper, after the one by Rup Kumar Barman, in this volume that deals with the evolving history of Raibanshi ethnic identity formation in North Bengal. Drawing from pre-colonial history of the movement and its post-colonial continuation Nandi points to a major shift at its core.

In his view, the Rajbangsi Kshatriyaisation movement in pre-independent Bengal in early twentieth century was essentially a reformist cultural movement which gradually gave way to a transformative political movement in the post-independent India. In the late twentieth century the caste movement took the shape of Kamatapur movement on the demand of creation of a separate Kamtapur state within the Indian union. Nandi argues that the shift of identity from 'Rajbangsi Kshatriya' to 'Koch Rajbangsi' is articulated through a more intense political action ruptured with an ambiguous historicity and a paradoxical strategic dilemma. Consequently, the Rajbangsi social movements have been faced with a strange identity crisis. The strategic essentialist nature of the movement influenced by the contextualised social, cultural and political factors strengthens and at the same time weakens the Rajbangsi social movements.

Nandini Basistha, a political scientist, also deals with 'modes of ethnic formation among the Rajbangshis' of North Bengal. The Rajbangshis, Basistha observes, are now an ethnic community bearing imprint of backwardness in the sphere of education, employment, and income and over-all development. Their shared despair and disappointment have found expression in agitations and movements for a separate state. However, it seems that the Rajbangshis are in a state of confusion on the ideological issues, mode of mobilisation and on the objectives of the movement. Thus, despite having same ethnic and historical past, being part of the same dynasty, common 'Kamtapuri' language and same culture, they seem to be a fragmented lot, participating in different streams of movements on the demand of creation of separate political entity carving out from more or less same geographical area. According to the author, the Kshatriyaisation movement in the colonial period had brought a sense of unity among the Rajbangshis and a section of them started movement for Rajbangsi homeland in form of a separate 'Kamtapur' state under 'Union of India'. Second stream of movement is mainly backed by the middle class intelligentsia in demand of the proper implementation of Merger Agreement 1949 and to regain separate entity of Cooch Behar as a Union Territory under the control of Central Government. The differences among the leaders on the ideology and objectives of the movement have left the community fragmented and the statehood movement has failed to gain any momentum.

Tracking down the course of *adivasi* ethnic movements in Dooars and Terai regions of Jalpaiguri and Darjeeling districts of North Bengal since 2008 Sanjay K. Roy in his paper 'Marginalisation, Alienation and Ethnic Identity Formation: The Case of the Adivasis in Dooars and Terai Regions of North Bengal' argues that the shared perception of land loss and a common experience of marginalisation in the economic, social and political spheres together have prepared the ground for the on-going *adivasi* ethnic movement. Roy observes that for many decades in post-colonial India, the *adivasis* had kept their faith on the state and the systemic forces, like the political parties of left and centrist ideologies for decades, yet they have progressively lost control over the productive resources, land and labour in particular, and continue to be in a process of marginalisation. The steps undertaken during the left rule, in the form of land redistribution and wage protection and empowerment through *panchayats* have only slowed down and not arrested the process of marginalisation. Loss of faith in the mainstream political parties and trade unions has created an ideological void and the *adivasis* looked inward to work out an ethnic movement for the creation of an autonomous tribal council under the Sixth Schedule. For the first two years since its beginning in 2008 the movement promised the formation of a united civil society of the otherwise voiceless *adivasis* of the region on ethnic line but thereafter factional squabbles, frustration and opportunism effected a drift from the initial promise of a united movement and the movement gradually made itself open to mediation and manipulation by the systemic political forces. The *adivasi* leaders, split in factions, have made opportunistic alliances with the Gorkha Janmukti Morcha and the ruling Trinamul Congress sacrificing the promise of *adivasi* empowerment that the movement initially had. In the process, the support of the common *adivasis* has used as a means to selfish material gain by the leaders of the movement. Bewildered at the opportunistic 'sell out' by the leaders the common *adivasis* in the region are again slowly turning towards the Left parties.

IV

In the section on 'Ethnicity in the North-East' we have two papers. Noted anthropologist N.K. Das's paper 'Indigenised Ethnicity, In-Group-Out-Group Syndrome and Governance Issue in Northeast India' unravels how the foundations of ethnic unrest in north-eastern India were laid in the colonial era, through introduction of various repulsive laws, division of hills and plains by installing an Inner-Line, and promoting and 'importing' a huge non-indigenous workforce, to protect economic interests of the colonisers. The author discusses the issues of indigenised ethnicity, growing minority syndrome and governance breakdown which, according to him, have triggered and sustained the ethnic unrest in post-colonial northeast. Das has used an ethno-historical approach to elucidate how a range of colonial 'exclusionary' strategies and continuity of outmoded 'divide and rule' policies in post-colonial era marginalised the communities and reinforced the sentiments and identities like insider-outsider/ minority-majority which, in turn, ignited the ethnic unrest, autonomy movements and armed militancy in the region. The author has also reviewed the efforts of the state and the civil society organisations in bringing peace in the region. The efforts taken in governance of the region include empowerment of the indigenous tribes through constitutional legislations, devolution of power at grassroots level and strengthening of democratic institutions. The state initiated efforts of normalisation often failed on account of rivalries within the leadership of the ethnic communities and the hegemonic style of functioning of dominant tribes.

Surajit Kumar Pal, another senior anthropologist, in his essay 'Political Aspiration and Autonomous Council Movement: A Study of the Rabha of Assam' has captured the genesis of the ethnic movement of the Rabhas in lower Assam. The Rabhas have been in a movement for setting up an autonomous council, challenging the hegemony of the Assamese over the regions and communities in post-colonial Assam. The author discusses how a social reform movement under the spell of modernism turned into a political movement and succeeded in establishing the Rabha Hasong Council. The long-standing social reform movements turned into a movement for introduction of Rabha language as the medium of instruction at the primary level in the areas where the Rabhas were numerically dominant in the 1980s. The movement took the shape of a united mass movement and forced the state government to introduce Rabha as a medium of instruction in primary schools. Because of the persuasion of the Rabha ethnic organisations the Government of Assam agreed to introduce the Rabha language as medium of instruction in the primarily level in 70 schools in 1988.

The paper narrates the course of marginalisation of the Rabhas in their own land. He observes that the factors like inflow of Muslim migrants from across the border, the systematic destruction of forest resources by the migrants and the state, eviction of the tribal peasants from forest land, land alienation, and usury have contributed to marginalisation of the Rabha and other tribal groups and prepared the ground for an ethnic mobilisation for a political demand.

Encouraged by the success of the language movement the Rabha Hasong Demand Committee (RHDC), formed in 1992, took the movement to a new height turning it to a movement for setting up an autonomous council, Rabha Hasong Autonomous Council, under the Sixth Schedule. Despite being largely democratic the movement under the aggressive young leadership turned violent at times, provoking the state to resort to coercion in order to 'discipline' the movement. The intensity of the movement forced the state government to first sign an accord, namely, 'Memorandum of Settlement (Rabha Accord)' in March 1995 and then pass an Act called Rabha Hasong Autonomous Council Act 1995. In its 18 years of existence the Rabha-Hasong autonomous council has not been an effective organ to meet the aspirations of the Rabhas. The leaders of the Council allege that the state government is reluctant to hand over the necessary power and money to the council as was agreed upon in the accord and then in the Act. The future of the council hangs in balance as it has moved the High Court against the state government charging that the latter is not sincere in implementing the provisions of the accord.

V

The final section of the book 'Ethnicity in Gujarat' has only one paper 'Towards a Specialised Understanding of Ethnicity: Making of Everyday Borders and Identities in the Walled City of Ahmedabad' by a geographer Aparajita De. The paper is outside the scope of the area used in the title of the book, because it talks about different kind of ethnicity, based on religion. The uniqueness of the paper like in De's argument that 'space' as a category of analysis is usually overlooked. Set against the backdrop of Gujarat riots in 2002 the paper explores how 'space' is created and recreated in the light of the changing dynamics of intercommunity relationship and gives an account of a specialised understanding of the processes of construction of ethnic identities. The paper draws out attention to the processes how the ethnic identities of Hindus and Muslims are constructed in everyday lives in the walled city of Ahmedabad. The territorialised 'politics of belonging', according to the author, is central to the construction of ethnic identities.

From her visits to the walled city of Ahmedabad in the aftermath of 2002 riots the author observes that a sense of belonging to different spaces and cultural locales creates a sense of difference along the line of religion. The processes of bordering create distinct idea/s of home, of self and others, of ethnic identities and vice-versa. These constructions of self and other are not simplistically derived from religious ideologies but from a more complex understanding of the different values and ways of life that symbolise self and the other. De observes that borders and border-making processes are an inherent part of our everyday life-worlds

De observes, in the context of the walled city of Ahmedabad, that the border narratives tell a story of how self and their homes are different and unique in sharp contrast to the others' areas and how 'safe' they feel here in their own homes. Predictably, the *kot*, the walled city, is a highly bordered and divided places of Hindu/Muslim self vis-à-vis Muslim/Hindu others. Yet this may not necessarily indicate the construction of Hindus and Muslims as antagonistic binary opposites. Border narratives, De argues, infuse the spirit of the people, their feelings, shared values and belongingness in the borders. Thus, borders enclose 'inside' notions of self and their particular cultures – their ways of living, of seeing and understanding the world. The existence of borders of 'my place/places' ensures the survival of these particular cultures at one hand. On the other, the demarcation of borders of 'their place/places' suggests not the intolerance of the other but recognition of the other and its culture, albeit on the outside. Thus, a border emerges as an act of strategy that not only creates a distinct self from the other but ensures the survival of the self and the other.

VI

The papers included in this volume would give the readers a squire view of the sophisticated theorisation of the process called ethnicity in social sciences and give a representative view of 'politics of culture', both in theory and praxis, in the eastern and north-eastern regions of India. From the papers, dealing with individual ethnic movements, one would understand that there are forces in the liberal democratic order, both in its morphology and praxis that essentially exploit, marginalise and alienate the downtrodden, who, having minimal control over productive resources, constitute the categories like lower castes, minorities and the subaltern classes. The sense of deprivation and exclusion are often articulated in caste, community or ethnic movements. However, such movements soon falter in the absence of solid ideology and leadership and under the pressure of the systemic forces. The movements suffer from sustainability problem and end up making 'chauvinistic' political compromises with the mainstream political parties. The 'liberation aspiration of the ethnic communities' lose way in the nitty-gritty of liberal-democratic politics. In the process, the leaders, the ethnic neo-elite draw some material and 'power' benefits while the real-life issues of the ordinary members of the ethnic communities and their sufferings remain unaddressed. The papers raise a serious doubt the efficacy of the ethnic movements in arresting systemic intrusion and in meeting the aspirations of the ethnic communities in the region.

References

Appadurai, A., 2006. *Fear of Small Numbers: An Essay of the Geography of Anger*. London: Duke University Press.

Ghosh, Biswajit, 2012. 'Introduction', in Ghosh Biswajit (ed.) *Interrogating Development: Discourses on Development in India*. New Delhi: Rawat Publications: 1-14.

Ghosh, Biswajit, 2003. 'Ethnicity and Insurgency in Tripura', *Sociological Bulletin*, Vol. 52, No. 2, pp. 221-243.

Phadnis, U., 1989. *Ethnicity and Nation Building in South Asia.* New Delhi: Sage Publications.

Rattansi, A., 1994. 'Western' racisms, Ethnicities and identities in Post-Modern Frame', in A. Rattansi and S. Westwood (eds.), *Racism, Modernity, and Identity on the Western Front*. Cambridge: Polity Press.

Roy, Sanjay K., 2005. 'Conflicting Nations in North East India', *Economic and Political Weekly,* Vol. XL, No. 21, May 21, 2005, pp. 2176-2182.

Roy, Sanjay K., 2013. 'The Levels of Cultural Praxis and Contesting Identities' in Danda, A.K., Nadeem Hasnain and Dipali G. Danda (eds.) *Contested Identities in the Globalised World*, Jhargram: INCAA, pp. 1-27.

Sarkar, Jayanta, 1982. 'Development of Identity Formation among the People of Arunachal Pradesh', in K.S. Singh (ed.) *Tribal Movements in India*. New Delhi: Monohar Publications, pp. 201-209.

Sen, Amartya, 2005. *Argumentative Indian*. London: Allen Lane.

SECTION–I

PERSPECTIVES ON ETHNICITY

SECTION I

PERSPECTIVES ON ETHNICITY

1. Modes of Ethnic Identity Construction

   [illegible]

2. Modes of Ethnic Identity Construction in India: Some Observations

   [illegible]

3. What Explains the Salience of Ethnicity? Some Conceptual Clarification

   [illegible] Ghosh

1

Modes of Ethnic Identity Construction

Rajat Kanti Das

Broadly speaking, ethnicity refers to a group identity displaying certain common characteristics and on the basis of which one may arrive at some kind of common substantive core which may function as an ethnic group. Again, each ethnic group displays an identity on the basis of some common characteristics arranged in a particular order, which may not find favour with some others who will come out with alternative lists. So what we actually have is not one complete list but lists of features defining ethnic identity, each overlapping with others at certain points in time. Listing of characteristics for defining ethnicity or, more specifically, ethnic group identity is more a subjective construct and therefore a certain degree of arbitrariness is unavoidable. Still, some characteristics at the ethnic group level may find a common place in all the lists, which may include socio-cultural experiences, geographical proximity of territorial integrity and physical affinity. Even if identity is a construct, it presupposes a level of consciousness on the part of the members of an ethnic group. There may be differences of opinion about the characteristics of identity, but on one point there is no difference, i.e., all the members are deeply involved with the question of identity. Ethnic identity is therefore a high level of 'consciousness of a kind' amongst its members. The consciousness may be based on caste, tribe, community living, territoriality, religion, sect, language, race, nation, common cultural traditions, all of which may not be equally effective at one particular point of time but may be inducted depending on the need of the concerned peoples and strategies adopted by them.

The use of the term 'ethnic group' suggests contact and interrelationship between different groups in a particularistic situation marked by cultural heterogeneity. The same, however, cannot be said about ethnic identity, which is a problem for the state to tackle. The position that ethnic group manifestation of tribes is not the direct contribution of culture or cultural particularities has many takers. Barth (1969b), Cohen (1974a), Despres (1975b), Nash (1988), Vermeulen and Govers (1994), Rex (1996) and other, have suggested that culture and cultural variations are irrelevant in the study of ethnicity dealing with ethnic identities. Contemporary political developments have greater impact on ethnicity formation. As Cohen contends, ethnicity does not require a cultural or historical explanation; contemporary politics and 'structural conditions' are the key to understand the phenomenon. Of course, Cohen's stand is not above criticism and Peel (1989), in particular, has raised serious objection to his attempt to undermine history. According to Peel, historical accounts not only provide 'source of documenting actual events more or less accurately', these also signify how the 'narratives' view their past. He is also critical of those studies of ethnicity which ignore cultural history and cultural factors for serious consideration. Culture, to Peel, can offer an interpretation of tribal ethnicity when seen from a broad historical perspective. This does not mean cultural history as it is presented but to reproduce the history that happened, which could be brought to light through genuine contact with people's experience. But it should also be noted that not all tribals bear a deep sense of history and particularly those, who have long lost their ancestral connections and have settled in a different territory marked by a different geo-political surroundings, have for strategic reasons aligned themselves with the new situation by eking out a space for themselves by virtue of their performance of crucially important economic activities and also because of their strategically important placement. Even when they are deprived, the deprivations run through the group making them organisationally stronger. Cultural history takes a back seat in such a case. Urban migration and urban contact also weaken the cultural base to a considerable extent. The need for remembering and reenacting ancestral culture is never so strongly felt as in a situation when the people are faced with the prospect of pauperisation of culture.

African scholars like Chazan et al (1992) would like to see ethnicity as the 'interest-oriented social action' which ensures participation by ethnic group, each manifesting an identity of its own in social, political and economic processes in a post-colonial situation. The question may be asked about the advantages of ethnic group participation. The advantages are derived ones and that's why, have to be judged from the 'we' and 'they' perceptions of one another and more importantly, their differential access to resources. Ethnic group formation helps the concerned group of people gain a voice of assertion to increase their bargaining power. Another aspect of the post-colonial phase deserves mention. It is well known that the concept of nation-state as a central building of the world order had gained currency during this phase. Importantly, it had strong ethnicity roots. As a post-colonial development many countries, after throwing off the shackles of colonialism, had adopted the nation-state as the ideal vehicle in which to undertake the journey towards progress and modernisation. But in the early 1990s it became apparent that nation state could not be the sole integrating force in the face of diverse groups or communities and state's own contradictions as well as functional deficiencies. The rise of ethnicity could be the logical outcome of the decline of the nation state. It is actually the citizens who have started challenging the capacity of the nation state to deliver the goods; academics and intelligentsia have even gone to the extent of singing its swan song. That phase is probably not yet over.

The forces of globalisation have added a new dimension to ethnicity issues at the national political level. Be it 'capitalist globalisation' or 'socialist globalisation', the result may be the same. Both will create 'transnational politics'. But there is a difference. Sassan (2006) is of the view that under socialist globalisation 'transnational political practices will be democratic coalitions of self-governing and co-operative communities', while capitalist globalisation tends to promote 'unaccountable, un-elected and individualistic transnational capitalist classes. And such a class produces a 'cultural-ideology of consumerism'. But this may be too reductionist a proposition. Market socialism in China might have followed capitalist practices, just as social democracy in Europe is guided more by socialist principles posing a challenge to capitalist globalisation. The Indian situation may not clearly belong to any one of the two forms of globalisation. But in all these situations there has been a significant rise of ethnicity related issues pertaining to formation, display and assertion of ethnic identity. Recently, the Chinese government had to come down heavily on the Uighur Muslim rebels demanding autonomy of their own. What is of particular importance is the gradual loss of nationalistic values or cohesive power of national forces in the context of globalisation. Unchecked globalisation sets in a process of 'denationalisation' (at the tribal level one may call it 'deterritorialisation'). It may be in the form of articulation of locally conditioned practices with global dynamics. What is considered 'national' now is in fact different from what had historically been considered and constituted as national sphere. It means global forces can directly target these sub-national sites, sometimes bypassing the national sites. Global-national interaction is expected to take its usual course or direction, which envisages as something fixed. Clearly national is far from a compact unit today. It now accommodates multiple sites – local, regional, institutional, sub-national – each trying to express itself and setting its own term for acceptance or recognition. Identity question is also related to it.

Ethnicity in the form of ethnic differences has to be considered in the light of specific socio-political situation. From another consideration, ethnic differences seem to be directly associated with variations in power and material wealth. But what happens if the groups have almost equal importance in the power structure? The observation of Giddens (1989) in this context seems to be relevant. He observes: 'Groups of equal power may mutually enforce principles of closure, their members keep separate from each other, but neither group dominates the other.'

Even if neither group dominates the other, they may be engaged in a bitter struggle for supremacy, consolidating their position and never allowing any erosion into their power base. The Naga-Kuki relationship may be a pointer. By now, it is well known how the decision of the government of Manipur to create a new district by curving out some Kuki-dominated areas and incorporating them into the proposed district predominantly inhabited by the Nagas to counter the Kuki protest movement. A blockade of the National Highway was imposed by the Kukis stopping the movement of all commodities including the essential items. There was a double blockade as the Nagas also joined the fray. It had an adverse impact on the economy of the state as the National Highway was the lifeline to Manipur. A scarcity-like situation was created and prices of all essential commodities soared abnormally. On getting assurance from the Union Home Minister P. Chidambaram that their interests would be safeguarded, the Nagas ended the blockade after sixty days. The Kukis, however, remained adamant and refused to lift the blockade. Ultimately, the state government was forced to stop implementing the administrative decision at least for the time being. Probably the relationship between the Nagas and Kukis has reached a point of closure. The Nagas in Manipur are not in a position to dominate over the Kukis as the latter are making their presence increasingly felt in the power structure. The Kukis are now in a position to take up roles which have so long been monopolised by the Nagas. Following the example of the Nagas, the militants of Kuki National Army (KNA) started operating from their Myanmar base. As an underground outfit, it is now a force to reckon with. Since the eruption of Naga-Kuki clashes they have become active. In 1996 in an encounter some Kuki rebels even killed two Assam Rifles men. The State Government's decision to create a separate Sadar Hills District including the Sadar Hill sub-division of the present Senapati district saw the beginning of a phase of ethnic clashes between the two groups. Incidentally, in the Sadar Hills sub-division the Kukis far outnumber the Nagas. The Naga-Kuki relationship was never cordial and there was always an undercurrent of mistrust, if not enmity. The State Government's decision added fuel to fire. Makui, a Liangmai Naga village about 100 kms. from the capital town of Imphal, and surrounding areas became the source of continuing tension ever since the Government took the decision to create a separate Sadar Hills district. Makui is situated inside the Khanglatombi forest reserve in Senapati district's trouble-torn Sadar Hills sub-division. Its strategic location was a source of concern for the Kukis and they considered it an encroachment into their territory.

They blamed the state government for showing leniency towards the Nagas. Violent clashes between the Nagas and Kukis erupted here and the government had to deploy armed forces to control violence. The whole question of Naga-Kuki conflict has to be seen from a historical perspective. The level of social consciousness and cultural specificity displayed by the Nagas or Kukis are at variance with strategic action for group solidarity to be used for mastering power in the political field. Both the groups have been trying for creating and reproducing a political identity bearing the stamp of cultural specificity and territorial integrity and it is this convergence of interest that has probably brought them in a conflicting situation. Taking recourse to conflict the two groups is, in fact, trying to maintain ethnic distinctiveness. 'Self-consciousness' and 'self-conception' are at the root of ethnic identity, where 'self' is identified with the group to which one belongs. 'Self-location' involves the whole life process and the experience of life as it is lived. At the group or community level, the experiences are bound to be different because their cultural and territorial roots are different. Of course, any construction of the 'self' has to be seen in a person's 'relatedness' with other members of the society, which is of cultural value. Culture has a leveling effect instigating members of a society to think and behave in the same way. It remains ingrained in the individual consciousness. Taking a cue from Leach (1967), Epstein (1978) analyses the process of self-conception in the context of the group to which one belongs. The process emphasises more on projecting the self and, through it, one's own group. It is paraphrased in the following way:

If I am I, simply because I am I, and thou art thou simply because thou art thou, then I am I and thou art thou. But if I am I because thou art thou, and thou art thou because I am I, then I am not I and thou art not thou.

Self-projection of the individual is not entirely an individual phenomenon. An individual is determined not only by culture and society, but also by environment or territory, psychology, or a combination of all these. Ethnic consciousness as a manifestation of self-consciousness amounts to self-projection where in-group characters are displayed and sometimes overplayed to the extent that they strengthen in-group solidarity at the cost of out-group alienation.

References

Barth, Fredrick, 1969. *Ethnic Groups and Boundaries: The Social Organisation of Culture Differences*. London: Allen and Unwin.

Charan *et. al.,* 1992. *Politics and Society in Contemporary Africa*. Colorado: Lynne Rienner Publishers.

Cohen, Abner, 1974. *Two-dimensional Man*. London: Tavistock.

Das, Rajat Kanti, 2001. 'The Problem of Ethnicity', *Journal of Anthropological Survey of India*, 50, pp. 37-47.

Despnes, Leo (ed.), 1975. *Ethnicity and Resource Competition in Plural Societies*. Mouton..

Epstein, A.L., 1978. *Ethos and Identity: Three Studies in Ethnicity*. London: Tavistock.

Giddens, Anthony, 1989. *Sociology*. Cambridge: Polity Press.

Nash, Manning, 1988. *The Cauldron of Ethnicity in the Modern World*. Chicago: University of Chicago Press.

Okely, Judith and Helen Callaway, 1991. *Anthropology and Autobiography*. ASA Monograph 29. London: Routledge.

Peel, J.D.Y., 1989. 'The Cultural Work of Yoruba Ethnogenesis', in E. Tonkin and M.M.M. McDonald and M Chapman (eds.) *History and Ethnicity*. London: Routledge.

Rex, J., 1996. *Ethnic Minorities in the Modern Nation State*. Working Paper in the Theory of Multiculturalism and Political Integration. London: Macmillan.

Sassen, Saskia, 2006. 'The State and Globalisation: Denationalised Participation' in *Territory, Authority, Rights: From Medieval to Global Assemblages*. Princeton: Princeton University Press.

Tonah, Steve (ed.), 2007. *Ethnicity, Conflict and Consensus in Ghana*. Accra: Woeli Publishing Services.

Vermunelen, Hans and Govers Lora, 1994. *The Anthropology of Ethnicity: Beyond Ethnic Groups and Boundaries*. Amsterdam.

2

Modes of Ethnic Identity Construction in India: Some Observations

Jayanta Sarkar

Each and every community has some distinct cultural or physical traits which are considered as markers of their separateness from other group of people. In order to maintain cultural separateness the communities adopt certain mechanisms in their way of life and try to draw a boundary while imposing norms, considered to be unique of them. The norms may be related to social, cultural, religious and political and such other spheres. Identity may be associated with many apparent factors like the geographical area of habitation, occupation, religion, mode of living, mythical origin and so on.

In the caste-based Hindu society, specific identity of each caste has been ascribed by the traditional scriptures. Specific names have been given to each caste/community by the scriptures. Traditionally each caste has some identifiable characteristics which are believed to have socio-religious sanction. Therefore, discontent of any type amounts to showing disregard to the sacrament and to the tradition and norms. The other two major religious groups, namely, the Muslim and the Christians of various denominations also have their separate identifiable characteristics. Those who lived outside the caste-fold also were given specific names like Yabana, Kirata, Nishada, and so on.

Beyond these three major religious groups, there lives a sizable population of scheduled tribes, almost all of whom until recent past were animist. They constitute about eight per cent of total population of India. Majority of them lived in comparatively inaccessible geographical areas beyond the interactional level with the populations of the three major religious groups. However, a few of these tribes had some marginal socio-economic interaction with the population living in the plain land. Such tribes who had long contacts with the caste Hindus were also placed in a distant position with a specific separate identity. Like the caste Hindus, each tribe believes to have originated from either a mythical or legendary ancestor and, therefore, their identity is also ascribed by birth.

As against such automatically inherited ascribed identity, there are also instances in which a caste or a tribe makes conscious efforts to construct a new identity keeping aside their inherited identity. Identity through such conscious efforts is usually achieved through a number of social processes. To what extent a tribe would get involved in the processes of construction of an identity depends primarily on the nature and extent of their exposures to the neighbouring communities and also to the outside world.

Modes of construction of identity, based on the social processes, at certain stage may get politicised to achieve a targeted goal of the concerned community. Such politicisation of social processes usually gets accelerated with the involvement of elite section of the community. The present exercise, however, will focus only on the social processes which are apparent in many areas of India.

The identity, we know, varies according to the context. An ethnic group may have one kind of identity at the social level and may have a different kind of identity in political level. Therefore, the contact situation and the contexts are most important factors that need proper examination to ascertain mode of construction of identity by a group of people.

In Indian context it has been observed by many scholars that when a tribe experiences exposures through generations, the members of that society usually get involved in the process of social mobility in order to achieve a desired position in the local social hierarchy that may attribute a different identity to them.

Social Mobility

In a country like-India where many ethnic groups inhabit in close association with the caste Hindu population for centuries together, such groups accept each other's separateness primarily within the frame of *Varna/jati* system.

The population who lived in close association with the caste Hindus inhabiting the fringe areas, because of the tolerance, slowly got assimilated within caste system and many of such scheduled tribes achieved a separate identity within the *Varna/jati* system. Thus, the Bhumij (Sinha, 1962), Gonds of central India and sections of the Bhil tribe of western India (Sarkar, 1986) achieved the identity of Rajput.

Elsewhere, while discussing the emergence of a number of small endogamous groups, each having a separate identity, among the Bhil tribe of western Madhya Pradesh I mentioned the processes and mechanism that have been adopted by these small endogamous groups (Sarkar, 1992).

The western part of Madhya Pradesh and the adjoining part of Rajasthan and Gujarat is the home land of a number of tribal groups like the Bhil, Bhilala, Barela, Patelia, Rathia, Mankar and many others who are referred to as the Bhil sub-groups by the Census of India. These sub-groups are again divided into a number of groups either on the basis of their place of habitation or on the basis of superiority or inferiority concept. Thus, among the Bhils we find the Ujala and Kala, Langotia, and Dhotia, and Durbar, Urpe and Rathia among the Bhilala and Nihal Chowkhar among the Mankar and several such groups. Each of these groups has been constantly claiming a separate identity declining any relation with others. All these groups are involved in the process of social mobility in different degrees, keeping the Rajputs as their reference model.

During their involvement in such mobility process they first try to accept some cultural traits to identify themselves as somewhat 'superior' to the others. Then to establish this 'superiority' firmly and also to maintain a distance and separate identity, constant and conscious efforts are made by imposing certain restrictions towards acceptance of cooked foods, etc. This is usually followed by the cessation of marriage relations with the group considered as 'low' which in turn results in the formation of endogamous small populations. Besides such biological separation, such endogamous small populations always try to maintain certain differences at the level of some rituals related to their life cycle and thus construct a separate identity (Sarkar 1992).

Limited Exposure and Reinterpretation of Identity

Conscious efforts to construct and establish a specific identity are usually made by a group of people inhabiting in a geographical area relatively secluded from other communities. Such a group of people when come in contact with the outside population on many occasions realise that they are being identified by these outsiders by a name that actually carries some derogatory connotations. Under this situation they make conscious efforts to reinterpret their ascribed identity. The present day Nishings and the Adis of Arunachal Pradesh used to be identified as the Dafla and Abor respectively by the people of the plains of Assam. The terms Dafla and Abor mean 'barbarous' and 'independent' or 'unruly'. In order to reject these terms, the members of these tribes have chosen names for their distinct identity as the Nishing and the Adis, meaning 'hill people' (Sarkar, 1982). In this process of construction of identity, more than one ethnic groups, originally having separate identity of their own, for some reasons highlight certain common characteristics of each such group and establish their commonness and manipulate a single identity for all such otherwise separate groups to achieve a desired goal.

During the colonial rules, though administration at different levels was introduced even in the remote areas of Arunachal Pradesh inhabited by the tribal populations, there was, in general, no conscious efforts by such groups to emphasise on the separate identity primarily as the British preferred to allow the tribes to live largely in accordance to their own cultural norms without much interference, unless the same was against the administrative interest. After the Independence of India, increase in communication facilities in this heather to inaccessible geographical area of Arunachal Pradesh resulted in large-scale migration of people to this region in search of livelihood. This disturbed the ecological balance of the hilly regions. Introduction of formal education in many areas ultimately caused resentment as in most of the cases medium of instruction happened to be a language which is alien to the local tribes. Interaction of a section of the tribes with the outsiders at many stages disturbed the balance of their socio-economic condition. Some kind of inequality found roots in an otherwise egalitarian society. The elite section of such societies exploited this situation to fulfill their aspiration and raised the issue that their culture is in danger because of imposition of several factors by the groups of people who are alien to their homeland. Imposition of alien language on them and adoption of cultural traits of outsiders remained two major issues that were highlighted by the elite section. In order to retain the characteristics of separate identity they initiated several actions to regenerate an identity consciousness of belonging to a separate ethnic group.

The Case of Adi Identity

The tribes living in the foot hills of Arunachal Pradesh by and large were very much concerned about the possibilities of losing their identities because of their constant interaction with the people of plains. The elite of the foot hills tribes took steps for bringing the ethnic groups categorised by the Census of India as sub-tribes, initiated conscious efforts in taking precautions by establishing various organisations and associations to safeguard their tribal heritage. This they did through incorporating a negative attitude among their own groups against the plains people.

The Adis comprise a number of groups who originally have a distinct identity of their own. As a normal practice when two persons of a tribe come in contact, they identify each other suffixing their clan or village names. The Padam, Miniyong, Gallong, Bori, Pasi, Pangi and a few other sub-tribes of the Adis identify themselves as separate group so far as their social/cultural arena is concerned. Each of these sub tribes has specific cultural traits known to them, though all of them believe to have originated from a common mythical ancestor. A Pasi will identify himself/herself as Pasi when interacts with a Padam or any other groups at social level. But the same Pasi, Padam, Miniyong and others will project themselves as the Adi at the level of Politics or when they come in contact with the non-tribal populations. Sometimes even at a different context they would identify as the Arunachalese (Sarkar, 1982).

Apprehension of Cultural Decadence and Revival of Identity

In the process of construction of Adi identity the apprehension of some Adi scholars regarding possible 'moral degradation' and 'cultural decadence' of the people of this area on account of the uncontrolled adverse impact of the people of plains worked to a significant extent.

Many subscribers of such views realised that involvement in the process of modernisation is almost inevitable for the development of the people of the region though, they also realise that such involvement in modernisation processes may lead to the disintegration of the society. Therefore, in order to have a compromise, this section, especially the erudite students, took initiatives in reviving some of their traditional customs and norms along with the modern ways of life. In this venture a number of organisations were set up. One of the important objectives of such organisations remains—'to take steps for revival of traditional culture, a marker of their ethnic identity'.

Immediately after Independence in 1947, a union called Adi Mishing Students Union was established at Pasighat. In 1971, the Adis established District Social Welfare and Cultural Society of Siang District at the district headquarters. Along with the objective of taking steps towards protecting their glorious cultural identity from the adverse effects on the Adi culture (Sarkar, 1982:234-235). Subsequently NEFA Student's Union was established which was renamed as All Arunachal Pradesh Students Union (AAPSU) in 1972. The Union has similar objectives. The preamble of the constitution of this Association declares that 'The objective of the AAPSU is to promote unity and fraternity among the students in particular and the people of the state in general, to preserve and promote the tradition and culture of the people of Arunachal Pradesh.'

Construction of Identity in Exceptional Demographic Condition

A fourth process of construction of identity may operate when a number of ethnic groups of different identities live together in an incompatible socio-demographic situation, that leave no other alternatives to them but to project all of them as one ethnic group having a single identity.

Many of us might be acquainted with the ethno history of Andaman and Nicobar Islands situated in the south east of the mainland India in the Bay of Bengal. The ethno-history of the six original inhabitants of the archipelago is full of struggle for survival. Let me mention of a community having a population of 45 heads, known as the Great Andamanese. This small tribe who now have been resettled in a tiny island called 'Strait Island' at a distance of about 40 nautical miles from Port Blair in reality one comprised of individuals of 10 territorial groups who had distinct identity of their own.

When Radcliffe Brown under took anthropological investigation in 1922 he could locate as many as ten territorial groups who had distinct identity like the Aka, Bea, Aka Jeru, Aka Chari. Aka Kora, Aka Bo, Aka Kede, Aka Kol, Oko-Juwoi, A-Pu-Ikwar and Aka Bele. However, Brown put all these groups under a single identity the 'Great Andamanese' (Radcliffe-Brown, 1948).

These ten groups together with another Negrito tribe then called as the Jarawa, were the sole inhabitants of the Great Andaman Islands. However, when the penal settlement at Port Blair was established by the British Colonial rulers in 1858, these tribes had to face many encounters and counter encounters with the newly arrived populations. Ultimately, the British rulers could establish their dominance over the ten territorial groups. The situation became worse when the Japanese initiated indiscriminate bombing on the islands in 1943-1945. How such dominance of powerful immigrants from outside the islands severely affected in the biological sphere of these groups and at one stage the combined strength of these ten territorial groups reduced to only 19 heads in 1961, is now known to the world.

The separate identities that these ten groups nurtured for centuries together were in stake. In 1974, these 19 individuals and a few half breed of these people, totaling 28 heads, spread over many parts of the Great Andaman Islands were brought together by the Andaman administration at the Strait Island and gave them an opportunity to survive as a single community.

The identity of the Great Andamanese imposed by Radcliffe Brown on these ten distinct territorial groups was accepted as the official identity of these 28 individuals for the convenience of administering these endangered people.

Conclusion

The processes described here are of different nature. In case of the Bhils and its sub groups the process aims at establishing a new identity through involvement in the social mobility making conscious efforts of establishing differences in some of the cultural traits from their inherited Bhil identity.

In contrast to construction of identity through such social mobility process, where small groups emerge out of projection of each of the group's specific differences from others, another process of construction of identity could be observed among the tribes of India. In this process of formation of identity more than one ethnic group, originally having separate ascribed identity for some reasons highlights some of the common cultural characteristics of each such group and establish their commonness and construct a single identity for all such otherwise separate groups as could be observed among the tribes of Arunachal Pradesh who had least interaction beyond their own people because of the inaccessible geographical area. The elites of the Adis made direct efforts to bring all the sub groups with distinct identity under a broad common umbrella of new identity emphasising upon the prevalence of many common cultural traits of the constituent sub groups. In order to construct such identity and establish the same firmly, a number of groups, categorised as sub tribes, make conscious efforts to politicise the whole process of achieving a desired identity through formation of various organisations that take conscious efforts to politicise the initial social and cultural processes.

Like the Adis, the identity of Great Andamanese of Andaman Islands is applicable to a number of territorial groups having separate distinct identity. However, the processes differ. While the Adi identity has been constructed through constant conscious efforts made by the members of the component groups, in case of the Great Andamanse the actual process of formation of their identity was imposed on them by the outsiders.

References

Radcliffe-Brown, A.R., 1948. *The Andaman Islanders*. Glencoe, III: The free Press.

Sarkar, Jayanta, 1982. 'Development of Identity Formation among the People of Arunachal Pradesh', in K.S. Singh (ed.) *Tribal Movements in India*. New Delhi: Monohar Publications, pp. 201-209.

Sarkar, Jayanta, 1986. *Social Mobility in Tribal Madhya Pradesh*. Delhi: B.R. Publishing Corporation.

Sarkar, Jayanta, 1992. 'Formation of Small Populations: Its Nature and Cultural Characteristics', *Journal of the Indian Anthropological Society,* 27(2), pp. 116-122.

Sinha, S.C., 1962. 'State Formation and Rajput Myth in Tribal Central India', *Man in India*, Vol. 42, No. 1, pp. 35-80.

3

What Explains the Salience of Ethnicity? Some Conceptual Clarification

Biswajit Ghosh

Introduction

Today, we are witnessing a series of explosive ethnic revivals across the globe. In Africa and Asia, ethnic movements have been gaining force since the 1950s. Initially, it was believed that ethnicity is found mostly in developing world because of cracks and strains in the secular sphere (Phadnis, 1989). But a few years later Rattansi (1994:1) wrote, 'The spectre that haunts the societies of the "West" is no longer communism, but both within and outside their frontiers, a series of racisms and ethnocentrisms'. In Europe and America, ethnic movements unexpectedly surfaced from the 1960s. The downfall of Soviet Union has only encouraged the move. Many new nations based upon dominant ethnic affiliation have been recognised since 1990. The rise of such nations led Hutchinson and Smith to comment that, "end of history, it seems, turns out to have ushered in the era of ethnicity" (1996: 'Preface'). Ethnicity is one of the fastest growing contemporary phenomena and there are also very strong connections between globalisation and ethnicity. Like globalisation, ethnicity is both 'local' in its claim and 'universal' in its applications. Its fact growth on the contemporary world scene articulates the process whereby 'subjectivity' can be demonstrated to be an instance of the objective consequences of globalisation (Poppi, 1997: 289). It is not the unexpected survival of ethnic particularism. Rather, it is the emergence of new forms of ethnic expressions despite the actual decline of ethnic solidarities in the sociological sense of kinship and community and despite the narrowing of cultural difference (Fenton,1999: 230).

What then explains such a rise and how would one explain the process of formation of ethnic identities in the 'modern' world? There appears to be confusion and debate among social scientists about the nature and modalities of unfolding of ethnic identities. This paper, based on a review of relevant literature and supplemented by field experience, seeks to explain the conditions that seem to promote conflictual ethnic mobilisation in the world today.

What is Ethnicity?

We all know that the term ethnicity is of American provenance and popularly used in the US from the early 1960s. The word comes from the ancient Greek *ethnos*, which seems to have referred to a range of situations in which a collectivity of humans lived and acted together. In Sociology and Anthropology, an ethnic group is frequently seen as culturally rather than physically distinctive. According to Giddens (2006: 487), 'Ethnicity refers to cultural practices and outlook of a given community of people that set them apart from others'. But, while defining ethnicity, we often confuse between the two seemingly identical terms: 'ethnic group' and 'ethnicity'. Even though ethnicity cannot be evoked unless there is an ethnic group, the presence of an ethnic group itself does not guarantee the rise of ethnic sentiments. This means that ethnic groups and ethnicity are not the same phenomena. As Paul Brass (1991: 19) argues, 'ethnicity is a sense of ethnic identity and hence ethnicity is to ethnic category what class consciousness is to class.' In other words, ethnicity refers to the expressive aspects of ethnic identities. We all know that ethnic groups are based on three predominant attributes, namely, (i) biological attributes like descent, kinship, (ii) cultural attributes like language, religion and (iii) territorial attributes like region, locality. But the transformation of a group/category into a 'subjectively self-conscious community' having psychological unity of a kind takes place through a complex process and here we have to offer explanations for the rise of ethnicity. Moreover, owing to subdivisions within members of a community/group and consequent accommodation of a group with other groups, formation of ethnicity may take a flexible route. It, therefore, appears that ethnicity is not a normal outcome of ethnic group identities having its own logic. Had it been the case, there would hardly been any rationale in discussing the issue altogether.

The debate, however, does not end here as social scientists have attempted to explain ethnicity from different points of view. Thus, from the Marxian point of view, ethnic differences seem to be directly associated with variations in power and material wealth. More particularly, differential allocation of resources in a class divided society gives shape to ethnic antagonism

(Cox, 1959). But, for Jenkins (1997:13), ethnicity is centrally concerned with culture—shared meaning and it is also rooted in, and to a considerable extent the outcome of, social interaction. In this sense, ethnicity is not fixed as it is produced and reproduced in social situations. Normally speaking, boundaries are often matter of cultural proximity. The more one becomes aware of the existence of 'alien' culture, the larger the scope for the formation of native group. But usually, such formation gets momentum only when the majority tries to assimilate and integrate the minority into the mainstream. Rajani Kothari (1988) has, therefore, argued that ethnic upsurges are a consequence of the homogenising trend of modern states and of their technological/educational imperatives. He links the ethnic movements with the movements of marginalised people and of those seeking indigenous authenticity. It is interesting here to read Gupta (1996, 2003) who has shown that as against ascriptive movements like communalism, ethnic movements clearly thematise the nation state. In other words, ethnicity is basically a political process. The 'others' in ethnic uprisings are enemies of the nation state, and are, therefore, portrayed as communities that owe allegiance to hostile powers outside the national boundaries. In communal movements, the 'others' are legitimate members of the nation-state, but are seen as too greedy, demanding and grasping. Thus, ethnic movements turn insiders into outsiders.

Interestingly, a host of social scientists have suggested that while culture and cultural variation are irrelevant in the study of ethnicity, political processes have greater impact on such formation. For Cohen (1974), for instance, ethnicity does not require a cultural or historical explanation; contemporary politics and 'structural conditions' are the key to understand the phenomenon. This argument is, however, criticised on the ground that historical accounts of any ethnic movement including cultural factors provide significant inputs for any study of ethnicity (Peel, 1989).

Given such varied explanations, ethnicity can be defined as the process of formation and reformation of consciousness of identity (real or supposed) in terms of one or more social-cultural-political symbols of domination/subjugation of a group(s) or community by another that emerge out of the processes of assimilation, acculturation, interaction, competition and conflict. It should be noted that cultural contents of ethnicity makes it different from other related notions: class, caste, community, race and nationality. Ethnicity is primarily used in contexts of socio-cultural differences, whereas, for instance, race is used to refer to physical of visible differences.

Explanation of Ethnicity

There are four major theories explaining ethnicity from different standpoints. While considering such theories, it should be kept in mind that each of the theories does contain different shades or versions within itself. Hence, in order to develop a comparative assessment, their internal differences are not taken into consideration. Let me now critically explain each of them.

(A) Primordialist Logic

This conservative model recognises ethnicity to be essential aspects of human nature. It had a deep historical root in the reactions to enlightenment rationalism. This ideology of primordialism naturalises ethnic groups and justifies ethnic sentiments. The primordial approach was first proposed by the Shils in 1957 (Haralambos and Holborn, 2000: 232). Shils claimed that people often had a primordial attachment to the territory in which they lived, or from which they originated, to their religion and to their kin. This attachment involves strong feelings of loyalty and a state of comprehensive solidarity. Barth (1969) had identified four theoretical features of this 'taken-for-granted' model of ethnicity:

(i) Ethnic groups are biologically self-perpetuating;

(ii) Members of this group share basic cultural values manifest in overt cultural forms;

(iii) The group is a bounded social field of communication and interaction; and

(iv) Its members identify themselves and are identified by others as belonging to that group.

Barth, thus writes, '...we are led to imagine that ...a world of separate people, each with their culture and each organised in a society which can legitimately be isolated for description as an island to itself' (1969: 11). This theory is strengthened by the earliest anthropological notions of 'ethnic group' as the Western colonial interest in the uncivilised people of the colonies or ex-colonies. The 'orient', for example, was constructed as the 'other' or the contrast of western culture. The belief that tradition has a complete sway over the minds of most people, particularly in the less developed societies, is taken to be an absolute truth. Within anthropology, the name that is most often identified with a primordial model of ethnicity is Clifford Geertz (1973). Drawing upon the works of Edward Shils, Geertz was concerned to understand the obstacles that 'primordial attachments', deriving mainly from kinship, locality and culture, enforce. He defined ethnicity as the 'world of personal identity collectively ratified and publicly expressed' and 'socially ratified personal identity' (*Ibid.*, 268, 309).

Criticisms

(i) McKay (1982) suggests that though this approach can account for the emotional strength of ethnic bonds, it tends to be deterministic and static. It assumes that members of ethnic groups have little choice about their sense of attachment.

(ii) Criticisms of this approach have mainly come from the Instrumentalists who argue that 'ethnicity in heart' or 'hot ethnicity' may go hand in hand with 'cold ethnicity' or 'ethnicity in head'. In other words, primordial attachments are not sufficient for explaining its rise particularly in the contemporary context.

(iii) Too many ethnographic evidences suggest that ethnic identification is not given, static or trans-historical. They are rather fluid and in a state of flux.

(iv) Cultural tradition has very little to do with ethnic movements. Neither Shiv Sena in Maharashtra or Sikh extremism in Punjab drew on tradition in any significant sense. There was no history of Maharashtrian and South Indian antagonism, neither in Mumbai, nor elsewhere in India. Likewise, the Sikhs were considered for the past three centuries to be the sword arm of Hinduism. Suddenly, in a few short years they were transformed into killers of Hindus and wreckers of the Indian state (Gupta 2003). In case of Tripura, the rise of ethnic classes typically undermines the processes of *sanskritisation* undertaken by the tribal kings of the princely state and the resultant acculturation of the tribals with the Bengali Hindu tradition (Ghosh, 2003).

(v) Brass (1991) has pointed out the following problems with this model:

(a) Some primordial attachments are variable (language, kinship, caste);

(b) Migration may create new attachments with land;

(c) Ethnic attachments do not necessarily belong to non-rational part of human personality;

(d) Ethnic attachments may not be based on 'old' culture, it may create new symbols and cultural objects;

(e) Even where there is a persisting core culture, knowledge of its substance may not be in much use in predicting the form of ethnic movement or its development.

So, we may conclude that mere membership of a group does not transform a social category into a 'subjectively self-conscious community'. Primordialism, therefore, fails to explain ethnicity properly.

(B) Instrumental Perspective

The opposition to primordial model was offered by the 'instrumentalists' or 'mobilisationists' who suggest that ethnic identities are actively created, maintained and reinforced by individuals and groups in order to obtain access to social, political and material resources. This approach had derived inspiration from the work of Barth (1969). Barth was however influenced by Weber's writing, who as early as in 1922, had argued that 'ethnic membership does not constitute a group; it only facilitates group formation of any kind, particularly in the political sphere. On the other hand, it is primarily the political community, no matter how artificially organised that inspires the belief in common ethnicity' (Weber, 1978: 389). For Weber, therefore, ethnicity is a *consequence* of collective political action rather than its *cause*. Even though an ethnic group appears to be a particular form of *status group* for Weber, he did argue that the possibilities for collective action rooted in ethnicity are 'indefinite'.

Barth, in his *Ethnic Groups and Boundaries* (1969) has emphasised that ethnic identity is generated, confirmed or transformed in the course of interaction. Ethnicity is a relational concept as it takes at least two to be ethnic. Ethnicity is also a matter of politics, decision making and goal-orientation. Hobsbawm and Ranger (1983) believed that through ethnicity cultural tradition as boundary markers are 'invented' and put into place according to selective agendas whose rationale is entirely determined by contingent circumstances. The shift from a static to an interactional approach was carried on further to argue that people can and do shift as well as alter their ethnic ascriptions in the light of circumstances and environment. The pursuit of political advantage and/or material self-interest is the calculus which typically influences such behaviour. Certainly, explaining ethnicity as instrumental and opportunistic is comparable with an action framework. The individual actor is viewed as making a calculation 'will it reward me to identify as an A in this situation'? Similarly, the idea that people identify ways in different contexts implies a measure of choice and openness in social life quite contrary to the idea of social identities as ascriptive.

Following the same logic, Brass (1991) has argued that ethnicity arises out of specific types of interactions and competition among elites. Ethnic identity formation is seen by him as a process in the dynamics of elite competition and manipulation.

Criticism

(i) This approach has been able to identify the flexible and situational nature of ethnic identity formation. Yet, it is criticised on several grounds. Thus, to begin with, the equation of 'instrumental' view of ethnicity with 'choice' need not be complete (Fenton, 1999: 106). Many of categories like Bengali, Tamil, Hindu, Muslim, Scheduled Caste or North-Indian are very often than not coercive in many respects. A person might not emotionally 'feel' about his/her group/community; but due to the process of 'othering', he/she might be forced to align with members of the group/community.

(ii) McKay (1982) argues that the instrumentalists tend to underestimate the emotional bonds and assume that ethnicity is always related to common interests being pursued by the group. The fact that some ethnic groups pursue political and economic interests does not mean that all ethnic groups have identical interests.

(iii) Moreover, in real life situation, a person may be least calculative in xpressing solidarity with the members of his community/group. Calculations do not always work and even a 'calculative' person may turn out to be 'emotional' at the last resort. What is more interesting is that an identity group often becomes a reality due to labeling. It is, therefore, possible for ethnic identities to be both coercive and situational.

(iv) Again, this approach, by putting stress on the factor of 'elite competition' for evocation of ethnicity, has ignored spontaneous voices of the common man at large. Can political 'bosses' always fool men in the street and dictate terms to them. On the contrary, popular voices may limit or shape political actions. Ethnicity cannot be evoked unless there is certain objective social reality to allow the elites to enter into the fray. In other words, along with some 'situational' factors, there must be certain structural reasons leading to the rise of ethnicity. The role of the state and other agencies also become significant in such mobilisation.

(v) Furthermore, ethnic movements may themselves become a rallying point for some to become elite. The case of Bimal Gurung may be cited here to explain the way he has ascended to leadership of the Gorkhaland movement, riding the crest of anti-Subhas Ghising sentiment, with no political experience in the hills of Darjeeling (Bagchi, 2012: 146). There are plenty of such instances from different parts of India which would prove that ethnicity may produce 'mass' leaders instead of elites making use of ethnicity. Looking into experiences of varied ethnic movements in India and elsewhere, it would be safe here to argue that evocation of ethnicity very often than not involves complex processes that would deny credibility to any particular attribute or line of argument.

(C) Modernisation Approach

According to the theorists of this school, ethnicity is an aspect associated with pre-modern 'archaic' societies. In the evolutionary scheme of Marx, Durkheim, Tonnies and Weber, social, economic and cultural changes in the modern society were argued to be associated with the decline of attachment to primordial loyalties including ethnicity. This theory assumes that identity groups are temporary phenomenon and these will be assimilated into modern nation state with growing passage of structural changes from a 'traditional' to 'modern' society. The three elements of modernisation, namely, industrialisation, nationalism and capitalism are believed to be forces that would undermine ethnicity. The modernists believe that the emergence of 'universal homogeneous' state would exert a leveling effect and sideline cultural differences gradually.

The theorists of modernisation approach also put forward certain logic to account for the failure of this project to homogenise differences:

(a) The resurgence of ethnicity is a proximate and not an ultimate consequence of modernity;

(b) It is due to inadequate modernisation in the developing countries that ethnicity is gaining salience;

(c) It is the distorted form of modernisation that accounts for the revival of ethnicity.

Criticism

1. The basic problem with this approach is its failure to explain the rise and proliferation of ethnic groups in the advanced Western countries. The 'bourgeois revolution' and the 'proletarian revolution' could not do away with the so-called socio-cultural differences of its population. The 'new' nations, the USA, Canada, Australia, for instance, have different layers of population who are racially and culturally different. Cultural groups, minorities and nationalities of Europe and America often clash with each other on the question of ethnic identity. The post-11 September developments in America, recent riots in London or intermittent ethnic clashes in Australia have challenged the claim that these advanced societies are 'multi-cultural' in true spirit and form. Similarly, the disintegration of former USSR, Yugoslavia and Czechoslovakia on ethnic lines disappointed the Marxist expectation that the growth of class solidarity and the emergence of a socialist state would do away with ethnic loyalties. From the Marxists point of view, ethnicity (an element of Superstructure) is nothing but expressions of economic/class (related to 'base') differences within people.

2. It has further been argued that ethnic movements tend to rise as a reaction to the dehumanising face of modernity. According to Kothari (1990), ethnicity is a response including reactions to both homogenisation and 'majoritarianism'. Revivalism is often a corrective response to the homogenising and commercialising force of modernisation and development. In this sense, ethnicity is 'a call for celebrating diversity' (*Ibid.*, 224). We may, therefore, argue that modernisation may not de-ethicise cultural communities, but may crystallise them. In fact, my research (and many others) proves that movements seeking separate identity or distinctiveness are neither parochial nor opposed to modernity. Had that been the case, concern for 'power' and 'politics' would not have remained the axial point of tribalism in Tripura (Ghosh, 2003). In case of *Adivasi* movements in Jalpaiguri and Darjeeling districts of North Bengal, the shared perception of losing their land and a common experience of marginalisation in the economic, social and political spheres together have prepared the ground for the formation of the ethnic movement. The movement promises the formation of a civil society of the otherwise voiceless *adivasis* of the region on ethnic line although maintaining the solidarity and achieving its political goal prove to be very difficult in the midst of the integrationist efforts and strategies of the systemic forces. Roy (2012: 81-103) has highlighted the negative role of integrationist forces for the rise of ethnicity among members of a class. This research proves that one can explain ethnicity from a positive

point of view. Like many civil society organisations, Akhil Bharatiya Adivasi Vikash Parishad (ABAVP) today argues for expansion of democratic rights including right to life and self-determination of the people of Dooars and Terai regions and is ready to utilise its ethnic identity and strength for secular gains. In this sense, ethnicity becomes a means to the end of what is commonly termed as 'development'. It appears that in the heterogeneous and hierarchical societies such as India, organised groups and communities should also be recognised as legitimate inhabitants of civil society.

3. The process of modernisation marked by objectivity, universalism, achievement and individuality may simultaneously generate a craze for particular, local or social things. For instance, economic globalisation has led to the rise of demand for ethnic food, dress or cultural items in India (Ghosh, 2011: 156). Similarly, in multi-ethnic societies, issues of economic security and class contradictions are very conveniently transformed by the elites into ethnic, caste and religious issues. In other words, rise of new inequalities in the modern societies contribute to either opposite tendencies among the opponents of 'modern project' or 'secular' distortion and exploitation of ethnic identities by elites. We may argue that the quest for 'community' is likely to crystallise more easily among the deprived (a sense of relative deprivation in a global economy) and such deprivation is perceived not only in economic terms, but also in terms of denial of one's cultural identity.

4. The emphasis of unity and universality of culture by the nation state has often led to undermining of local identities. For instance, the tribes of India are constantly relegated to the receiving end by forcing them to assimilate with the mainstream. No one would claim today that tribes are 'backward Hindus'. It has been observed that the state does not even take the justified demands of ethnic minorities seriously unless the movement takes an anti-India or ethno-national character. Its approach is one of tension management preferably with force (Oommen, 1997: 158). Gupta's (1996) research also exemplifies that the Punjab agitation, which began with some secular demands like Chandigarh as capital of Punjab, water sharing between Punjab and Haryana and territorial tribunal to settle the dispute was ethicised by the Central and the Congress party for political gains. Yet, when the *Akalis* came to power in 1977, it did precious little on these demands even though it was a significant member of the national level Janata Party government in new Delhi. There was also clear involvement of the government machinery in Delhi and Gujarat in riots during 1984 and 2002 respectively. My own research (2003) also corroborate the fact the ethno-nationalism is encouraged and sustained by the lack of developmental initiative on the part of corrupt state administration as well as untimely or delayed state response. It may fairly be concluded that the nation state remains at the central focus of the entire episode of ethnicity and hence ethnic movements often thematise the nation state as against any communal movements.

(D) Social Constructionist Theory

The idea of 'ethnicity as a social construction' is an extension and revision of the arguments of the instrumental perspective on ethnicity as it tries to offer a comprehensive view on the matter. An early sociological disposition of this model can be located in the writings of Weber and Hughes. The Chicago sociologist Hughes wrote a short paper in 1948 where he, like Weber, rejected the commonsensical notion of ethnicity based on cultural traits (Hughes, 1994: 91-6). From this point of view, ethnic groups are what people believe or think them to be; cultural differences mark groupness, they do not cause it; ethnic identification arises out of and within interaction between groups. Touraine (1977) has gone a step further to argue that in modern societies, marked by *historicity*, knowledge of social processes is used to reshape our identities. In other words, objectives of a social movement (including ethnic movement) are shaped by encounter with others who hold divergent views and vice-versa. Touraine has therefore suggested that social movements should be studied in the context of what he calls *field of action*. From a different position, Castells (1996) has stressed on the fact in the 'network society', personal identity becomes a much more open matter. This is because, we now do not take our identities from the past; rather we actively make them in interacting with others. Such 'social reflexivity' (Giddens, 2006: 123) and construction of our identities in daily life discourages the intrusion of biologically based conceptions of 'race' into social analysis.

The social constructionist approach tries to distinguish between 'group identification' and 'social categorisation'. The *first* occurs inside the ethnic boundary and the *second* outside and across it. The processes of social categorisation are situationally variable and contextually negotiable. Social groups are not 'things' in any positivist sense. They are contingent and immanently changeable. From this point of view, ethnic identity is probably ubiquitous, race is not. While outlining the basic social constructionist model of ethnicity, Jenkins (1997: 40) has identified four elements of this model:

1. Ethnicity emphasises cultural differences;
2. Ethnicity is cultural;
3. Ethnicity is to some extent variable and manipulable; and
4. Ethnicity as a social identity is collective and individual, externalised and internalised.

Thus, ethnic meanings and collective identities change in form and content as circumstances change. Hence, for Jenkins, ethnic identity is likely to be segmentary and hierarchical. In other words, two groups differentiated from each other as A and B in certain context may combine as C to oppose D. For instance, the two competing caste groups, namely, Harijans and Yadavs did form a collectivity to challenge the Brahmin domination in Bihar. Cultural traditions as boundary markers are, therefore, 'invented' and put into place according to selective agendas whose rationale is entirely determined by contingent circumstances (Hobsbawm and Ranger, 1983).

The social-constructionist view comes closer to the post-modernists view of ethnicity which argues that identities are relatively 'free-floating', detached from the bases of social structure. Stuart Hall (1990), for instance, has argued that cultural identities are not fixed but always evolving. Hall has emphasised the role of discourses about ethnicity in creating *new* identities. The idea of *new ethnicity* here implies that internal differentiation within ethnic groups provide the foundation for a plurality of ethnic identities. Hall also did not deny the possibility of 'hybridisation' and 'cut and mix' in the formation of new ethnicity. In this sense, ethnic movements differ from *old social movements* based solely on class, caste, community or tribal identity and thereby constitute *new social movements*. Hall writes: 'We should think of identities as a production which is never complete, always in process, and always constituted within, not outside, representation' (1990: 222). Allen (1994) has also stressed that awareness of ethnicity is not constant throughout an individual's life; it emerges only in specific contexts. In short, the post-modern, post-structuralist view of ethnicity stresses on the following features: (a) stress on differences and diversity, (b) attack on essentialism, (c) stress on the role, of discourses, and (d) formation of fractured identities.

It is worth noting here that fragmentation of identities may result due to: (a) internal split, (b) external fragmentation, (c) fragmentation as a result of general process of social change, and (d) fragmentation as a synonym for individuation. As a combination of such factors, the process of identity formation in the contemporary world is marked by contextuality, fluidity, hybridity and plurality.

Evaluation and Conclusion

The process of formation of ethnicity appears to be very complex and often contradictory. Hence doubts are expressed about the theoretical potentiality of the concept. It might also appear to a reader that many of the approaches on ethnicity, I have discussed in brief, contain assorted arguments. The problem probably lies in the nature of ethnicity itself. Weber (1978) had reminded us that since the possibilities of collective action in ethnicity are 'indefinite', the ethnic group, and its close relative the nation, cannot easily be precisely defined for sociological purposes. Phadnis also, therefore, considered the concept 'methodologically unsound' (1989: 241). But, McKay (1982) argues that we may combine these approaches to explain the process. In doing so, McKay is able to distinguish five types of ethnicity, namely, (a) ethnic traditionalist, (b) ethnic militants, (c) symbolic ethnics, (d) ethnic manipulators, and (e) pseudo-ethnics. These types running from 'high' to 'low' merits, however, do not subsume the mixed types, and they also do not explain why ethnicity takes one form or another. Yet, this model can be used to examine how ethnic groups change over time and move from one type to the other.

The argument here, however, goes beyond the simple *melting pot* model of ethnicity which stressed on blending of identities as an outcome of ethnic diversities. Research has proved that there are *sequences* (Smelser, 1963) in the development of social movement, including change from one phase to the other depending on the context (Oommen, 1997). One may cite countless instances of internal differences among the 'insiders' that are responsible for changes in the nature and character of their mobilisation. For instance, the *Shiv Shainiks* who initially attacked the South Indians later made friends with them and turned them against the Muslims and Communists. Similarly, the social base of Jharkhand movement later got broadened to include the non-tribals so as to transform it from an ethnic to a regional movement. The fission and fusion of boundaries, hence, make it impulsive for us to treat it as a discursive process with different levels or phases of integration.

Herein, we may accept the Post-modernists argument that human beings themselves function as active agents in the construction of their identities. This approach also rightly stresses on plurality and heterogeneity of our identities. Identities are variable and they are situationally constructed. But, it must also be recognised that identities are not completely and all the time free floating objects. There are 'limits to plasticity of ethnicity as well as to its fixity and solidity' (Jenkins 1997: 169). One may go with the old dialectical tenets that 'people make history as much as history makes people' (Poppi 1997: 304). Steve Fenton (1999: 21) similarly argues that there is 'double contextualisation' in ethnicity. Ethnicity as a social phenomenon is embedded in social, political and economic structures which form an important element of both the way ethnicity is expressed and the social importance it assumes. At the same time, ethnicity, as an element of individual consciousness and action, varies in intensity and import on the context of action. Ethnic attachments cannot, therefore, be totally 'imaginary' without any social-cultural base. The social structure in which each of us is located put constraints and limits the possible range of identification. It is due to these limits that ethnicity is not totally 'instrumental in the hands of elites' always.

Therefore, to conclude, the process of boundary formation is based on both structural and discursive conditions. An analysis of the nature of ethnicity and insurgency in Tripura (2003) led me to argue that such processes are influenced by some *necessary* conditions and supplemented by other *sufficient* conditions. Ethnicity cannot easily be evoked if only necessary conditions prevail. The presence of sufficient conditions induces qualitative change in the nature of group mobilisation. The *necessary conditions* include several socio-economic factors like demographic compulsions, cultural deprivation, poverty, land alienation and eviction, unemployment and underdevelopment, etc. The *sufficient conditions*, on the other hand, include an acute sense of discrimination among the group members, emergence of a strong elite leadership, political competition and manipulation, state policies and actions and easy accessibility to external support. Interestingly, ethnic movements themselves pass through different phases of transformations and I have identified five different phases of the ethnic movement in Tripura.

As change and mutability are endemic to ethnic identities, they seem to be fluid, situationally contingent, perpetual and negotiable. Hence, it would be untenable to view ethnic movements as necessarily constituting a threat to the state. Ethnic movements may work as organs of civil society to strengthen democracy. Hence, these movements should be viewed from a wider and historical perspective rather than a narrow and time bound framework. It may be argued that the attempt to produce fixed categories like 'tribal' or 'Bengali' represents a strategy of power, one that is often involved in preserving a hegemonic representation of the category. In reality, however, the boundary of a particular category is both constructed through and challenged by other social identities. This makes occasional intersection of both social categories and identities possible. As a result, contested boundaries and multiple identities are dominating the passage of time and space in the contemporary world and they would continue to do so in years to come.

References

Allen, S., 1994. 'Race, Ethnicity and Nationalism: Some Questions of Identity', in H. Afshar and M. Maynard (eds.), *The Dynamics of 'Race' and Gender* (85-105). London: Taylor and Francis.

Bagchi, Romit, 2012. *Gorkhaland—Crisis of Statehood*. New Delhi: Sage Publications.

Barth, Fredrik, 1969. 'Introduction', in Fredrik Barth (ed.), *Ethnic Groups and Boundaries: The Social Organisation of Cultural differences*. London: George Allen and Unwin.

Brass, Paul, 1991. *Ethnicity and Nationalism: Theory and Comparison*. New Delhi: Sage Publications.

Castells, M., 1996. *The Rise of Network Society*. Oxford: Blackwell.

Cohen, Abner, 1974. *Two-dimensional Man*. London: Tavistock.

Cox, Oliver C., 1959. *Class, Caste and Race: A Study in Social Dynamics*. New York: Monthly Review Press.

Fenton, Steve, 1999. *Ethnicity: Modernity, Racism, Class and Culture*. London: MacMillan Press.

Geertz, Clifford, 1973. *The Interpretation of Cultures*. New York: Basic Books.

Ghosh, Biswajit. 2003. 'Ethnicity and insurgency in Tripura', *Sociological Bulletin*, Vol. 52, No. 2, pp. 221-43.

——, 2011. 'Cultural Changes and Challenges in the Era of Globalisation - The Case of India', *Journal of Developing Societies*, 27(2), pp. 153–175.

Giddens, Anthony, 2006. *Sociology* (Fifth edition). Cambridge: Polity Press.

Gupta, Dipankar, 1996. *The Context of Ethnicity: Sikh Identity in a Comparative Perspective*, Delhi: OUP.

——, 2003. 'Between Ethnicity and Communalism: The Significance of Nation State', *Edinburgh paper in South Asian Studies*, No. 18.

Hall, Stuart, 1990. 'Cultural Identity and Diaspora', in J. Rutherford (ed.), *Identity: Community, Culture, Difference*. London: Lawrence and Wishart.

Hobsbawm, E. and T. Ranger (eds.), 1983. *The Invention of Tradition*. Cambridge: Cambridge University Press.

Haralambos, Michael and Martin Holborn, 2000. *Sociology—Themes and* Perspectives (5th Edition). London: Collins.

Hughes, E.C., 1994. *On Work, Race and the Sociological Imagination* (edited with an Introduction by L.A. Coser). Chicago: University of Chicago Press.

Hutchinson, J. and A.D. Smith. 1996. *Ethnicity*. Oxford: OUP.

Jenkins, Richard, 1997. *Rethinking Ethnicity—Arguments and Explorations*. London: Sage.

Kothari, Rajni, 1988. *State against Democracy: In Search of Humane Governance*. Delhi: Ajanta.

——, 1990. *Rethinking Development—In Search of Humane Alternative*. Delhi: Ajanta Publications.

McKay, James, 1982. 'An exploratory synthesis of primordial and mobilisationist approaches to ethnic phenomena, *Ethnic and Racial Studies*, 5 (4), pp. 395-420.

Oommen, T.K., 1997. 'Social movements and the State response: The Indian Situation', in A.M. Shah, B.S. Baviskar and E.R. Ramaswamy (eds.), *Social Structure and Change* (Vol. 4, pp. 134-162). New Delhi: Sage publications.

Peel, J.D.Y., 1989. 'The Cultural Work of Yoruba Ethnogenesis', in E. Tonkin and M.M.M. McDonald and M. Chapman (eds.), *History and Ethnicity*. London: Routledge.

Phadnis, U., 1989. *Ethnicity and Nation Building in South Asia*. New Delhi: Sage Publications.

Poppi, Cesare, 1997. 'Wider Horizons with Larger Details—subjectivity, ethnicity and globalisation', in Alan Scott (ed.), *The Limits of Globalisation – Cases and Arguments* (284-305). London: Routledge.

Rattansi, A., 1994. 'Western' racisms, Ethnicities and identities in Post-Modern Frame', in A. Rattansi and S. Westwood (eds.), *Racism, Modernity, and Identity on the Western Front*. Cambridge: Polity Press.

Roy, Sanjay K., 2012. 'The Adivasis in a Liberal Democratic Order and their Struggle for a Self', in Biswajit Ghosh (ed.), *Interrogating Development – Discourses on Development in India today* (81-103). Jaipur: Rawat Publication.

Smelser, Neil J., 1963. *Theory of Collective Behaviour*. New York: Free Press.

Touraine, Alan, 1977. *The Self-production of Society*. Chicago: University of Chicago Press.

Weber, Max, 1978. *Economy and Society*. New York: Bedminster Press.

SECTION–II

ETHNICITY IN EASTERN INDIA

4

The Construction of a Kosli Identity and the Movement for a Separate State of Kosal in Western Odisha

Arun K. Jana

Introduction

On 1 April, every year, when the whole of Odisha celebrates Utkal Diwas or Odisha Day, in some prominent towns of western Odisha 'Kala Diwas' or 'Black Day' is organised and this is being done since 1990. In 1990, on 1 April, for the first time there was a massive boycott of Odisha Day or Utkal Diwas celebration by people of Sambalpur an old town located on the banks of the river Mahanadi and a *bandh* was observed in the town from dawn to dusk on the demand for a separate state consisting of several districts of Western Odisha. It was also reported that a parallel meeting was organised in support of separate state of western Odisha on the day or on the previous day, i.e., on March 31, 1989 (Das, 1993).

Twenty two years later, on 1 April, 2012 in Sambalpur, this author found that a small group of protesters belonging to the Kosal Kranti Dal (hereafter KOKD) shouting slogans like 'Aame Nuhe Odiya Aame Sambalpuria' (we are not Odiyas we are Sambalpurias), 'Kosal Raj amar dabi' (our demand is a Kosal state), Kosal Raj Amuku Diya (give us Kosal state), 'Kosal Sarkar Amuku Darkar' (we need Kosal sarkar), and so on. The activists of the KOKD who assembled and demonstrated near the Gole market area when interviewed were found to be mainly from the professional background. Almost one year later, similar incidents were reported by the Bhubaneswar edition of prominent English daily. On 2 April, 2013 The New Indian Express reported that the 'Utkal Diwas celebrations in many parts of Western Odisha were marred by black flag demonstrations by people demanding separate Kosal state. Some of the demonstrators were arrested' (*New Indian Express*, 2 April, 2013). The daily also reported that on 1st April, 2013 the protesters of the Kosal Sena raised slogans and staged demonstrations outside the district auditorium in Sambalpur where Utkal Diwas celebration was underway alleging apathy of the state government towards the region. Hence in Sambalpur town there were two black flag demonstrations one by the KOKD and the other by the Kosal Sena independently on the same day for the same cause. Another daily reported that in Balangir 'Even as the official celebration of the day was observed at a meeting in the Town Hall, KKD members led by its President Pramod Mishra opposed the celebration and carried the 'dead body' of the Odisha Government throughout the town. Earlier in the evening, Panchanan Pattnaik of the KKD hoisted a black flag before the District Collectorate and Gorekhnath Sahu of the party tore up and burnt the Odisha map at the Bhagirathi Chowk' (*The Pioneer*, 3rd April, 2013).

All these incidents that occurred on 1st April every year since 1990 indicate that in Sambalpur town there are some people who claim that they are Sambalpuris and not Odiyas. In some other towns of western Odisha, like in Balangir and further south west, the members and activists of the KOKD and some other organisations argue that their language is Kosli and not Odiya. Thus what one notes is that in Western Odisha there is an attempt being made in order to construct a Kosli or a Sambalpuri or Kosli-Sambalpuri ethnic identity, rejecting the Odiya identity. They argue vociferously that Odiya language and culture is an alien imposition on them. They demand the formation of a separate State of Kosal claiming that they have a separate language and culture, and their region and people are neglected. In this paper, I would examine this construction of an ethnic identity in Western Odisha, where the ethnic organisations often collaborate yet differ on issues and the mode of the movement for the formation of a separate state of Kosal consisting of 11 districts of western Odisha.

Western Odisha

The state of Odisha as it exists today was formed in two successive stages. Firstly, when Odisha was carved out of Bengal province on the 1st of April 1936 much before independence and an Odisha province was formed and, secondly, when after independence out of 26 princely states (located mainly in Western Odisha) that acceded to India, 24 finally merged with Odisha. Thus, modern Odisha emerged or took its shape after the accession of the Princely states to India slightly after independence and the merger of these states with Odisha on 1st January, 1948 except the princely state of Mayurbhanj which acceded to India and became a part of the state a little later. How distinct is western Odisha from the rest of Odisha? How far has the distinctness, geographic, linguistic, social-cultural, and economic, contributed to the growth of organisations that mobilise people along ethnic lines? How far does the distinctness make it convenient for the ethnic leaders to construct ethnic identity or mobilise on ethnic lines in the region? Let us turn first to the distinctness and then see whether the distinct features contribute to or make it convenient for the ethnic organisations to construct ethnic identities and mobilise on ethnic lines in the region.

We note that there are three distinct features of western Odisha which are easily discernible. Firstly, as we have noted earlier, the western Odisha in modern times was never a single entity but a large part of the region was not directly under British rule unlike that of coastal Odisha. There were 26 princely states located in western and north western parts of Odisha of different geographical size and population, all acceded to India and 24 merged to form Odisha, two princely states merged with the state of Bihar. Hence a large part of the state what has been referred to as the highlands of the state by Bailey (1960) and others was never a direct part of British India.

This distinct feature was at least partly responsible for the distinctness in the voting pattern in Western Odisha for more than two decades after independence. The people in the region voted for parties other than the Indian National Congress. This was in sharp contrast to the pattern witnessed in the coastal region of the state where the Congress was the dominant party. The relative absence or weakness of the Congress in the region is not startling since the 'Congress System' was known to be weak in the former princely states throughout the country. Since the chunk of western Odisha was under princely rule the Congress had no or very little organisational strength in the region. The national movement which had affected coastal districts had no or very little impact in the princely states. As a consequence, for long after independence it was the All India *Ganatantra Parishad* later renamed as Ganatantra Parishad a party of and led by feudal chiefs of the former princely states enjoyed electoral dominance in the region. The Congress and later the Janata Party (after 1977) that had a base in the coastal belt entered western Odisha later. The Ganatantra Parishad was local in character and hence was concerned with local issues. It was primarily concerned with the question of regional imbalance within Odisha and for the regional imbalance it held the Odisha government responsible. Later, in 1962, the Ganatantra Parishad merged with the Swatantra Party and formed a formidable force in the state. Although the Congress had made serious attempts to make dents into the stronghold of the Ganatantra Parishad since 1952 (Ray, 1974) but it was only from 1977 onwards that All India political parties, the Congress and the Janata Party, entered into the region strongly.

The second distinct feature of Western Odisha is that it is home to a large proportion of tribal population. The tribals, who constitute 23 per cent of the state's population, mainly inhabit the western region and are concentrated predominantly in the north-western and south-western districts of the state. As per the 1991 census the north-western undivided districts (Sundargarh, Keonjhar, and Mayurbhanj account for 35.3 per cent of Odisha's tribal population and the south-western undivided districts (Koraput, Kalahandi, Phulbani, and Balangir) accounted for another 39.4 per cent (Government of Orissa, Planning and Coordination Department, 2004: 5). In the post-1992 period, after the bifurcation of the districts, the districts in which the tribals are heavily concentrated are Koraput, Mayurbhanj, Kendujhar, Phulbani Kalahandi, Sambalpur, Sundargarh, Gajapati, Rayagada, Malkangiri, Navarangpur, Kandhamal, Deogarh, Jharsuguda, Balangir and Nawapara.

As elsewhere in the country the tribals are the poorest of the poor in state population. We note that even official reports found that the 'tribal population in Orissa is among the poorest, most vulnerable and exploited groups in the State' (*State Development Report,* 2001: 435). It has been estimated that around 90 per cent of the tribals in the state live below the poverty line of which a sizable section suffers from the problem of chronic poverty. The condition of the tribals as per Orissa Human Development Report had deteriorated in the period of liberalisation since Odisha as a state had opened up to large scale construction and mining works. The number of poor seems to have declined marginally in recent years. The presence of a large percentage of tribal population in western Odisha separates it from coastal Odisha also in linguistic and cultural terms. The tribals or tribal groups speak languages which are different from those of coastal plains and are culturally distinct since many of the tribal groups in the region cannot be classified as Hindu. This linguistic and cultural distinctness of the tribals and others (migrants to the region) who inhabit the region (around 2.5 crore people) is being used, as we shall see later, to construct a Kosli or Sambalpuri identity as opposed to the Odiya identity. Interestingly this attempt is being made not by the tribals but by others, mainly by the Utkal Brahmins, who had migrated to the region several centuries ago. The tribal population is also being mobilised on the issue of 'Greater Jharkhand' by Jharkhand Mukti Morcha (JMM) and other *Jharkhandis* in some of the districts of the state located mainly in the North-western part of the state.

Thirdly, the districts of Western Odisha despite being the richest among the districts in terms of deposit of natural resources have remained underdeveloped or backward over the years in both relative and absolute terms. The districts are the most backward districts of the poor state in terms of several indicators. Why have the districts remained backward, is a question which we need not address here in details but what must be noted is that the backwardness or underdevelopment of the districts has led ethnic organisations in the region to use the argument of backwardness/underdevelopment or even internal colonialism for constructing ethnic identities. Though it is difficult to establish that backwardness or underdevelopment is directly responsible for the growth of organisations that demand separate state what we note is that parties and organisations demanding Kosal state use the argument to criticise the Odisha government and mobilise support for its objective. We will note later that the ethnic organisations in the region allege that western Odisha has remained underdeveloped, backward or poor because successive governments in Odisha have neglected the entire region while extending a preferential treatment to the coastal region. They argue further that the resources of western Odisha is siphoned off to coastal Odisha and is utilised for the purpose of development of coastal Odisha. Hence western Odisha is exploited for the development of the coastal part of Odisha. The argument is extended further in the claim that western Odisha is being treated as a colony of coastal Odisha. Hence, what we note is that the backwardness of the region both in absolute and relative terms have given ethnic organisations the scope to use backwardness/underdevelopment/internal colonialism as an alibi for the mobilisation of ethnic groups or for the construction of a separate ethnic identity.

The Construction of Kosli Identity

The distinctness of western Odisha from that of the coastal region was first highlighted by the former princely rulers more particularly by the most active of the former princely rulers R.N. Singhdeo, the former ruler of Patna. After independence but before the accession of the Princely states with India R.N. Singhdeo actively propounded the theory that the 'feudatory states of Odisha and Sambalpur did not form a part of Odisha; they represented the erstwhile Kosala kingdom of the Chauhans of the medieval period.' In a pamphlet which was published sometime around 1946 he mooted the idea of Eastern States Federation. Justifying the formation of Eastern States Federation he argued that such formation would be beneficial to the member-states as it will be able to overcome the handicaps of small units and develop the natural resources through central planning and provide such services as are beyond the capacity of individual states. He argued that economically and financially the Eastern States Federation will be very stable and sound and will, therefore, raise the standard of living of the people of the state's higher than many other units. The expenditure on social services will also be higher than many units. The federation will provide benefits of centralisation, without destroying the individuality of the states, which will enable local patriotism to have scope for incentive and control over local affairs...there will no danger of exploitation, subordination of interests or of encroachment on rights of one unit by another. The number of units of more or less similar size will make it a well-balanced combination (Anonymous, 'Wither Koshal? 1946). Samablpur was envisioned as the capital of the proposed Eastern States Federation with a population of eighty lakhs and an area of 95,000 sq. kms. (Mishra 2004: 274). Singhdeo argued that Sambalpur had inherited the glorious legacy of the Kosala Kingdom of the Indomitable Chauhans and linguistically and politically was a distinctly separate entity having no links with Odisha (*ibid.*).

With the above agenda the Raja fuelled the anti-Hirakud agitation. He had secretly organised meetings with Anti-Dam agitators at Bolangir and provided moral and material support to the agitators and sought the moral support of the agitators for the cause of separation of Sambalpur from Odisha so that the proposed Kosala province becomes a reality. After the administration of the former princely states except that of Mayurbhanj became an integral part of Odisha on 1 January, 1948 R.N. Singhdeo formed Kosala-Utkala Praja Parishad on 7th October, 1948 with its headquarters at Sambalpur. The organisation protested against the misrule of the Congress government in Odisha and its main demand was the right to self-determination. The Kosala-Utkal Praja Parishad was renamed as the Ganatantra Parishad in 1950. With the formation of the Ganatantra Parishad, Odisha entered almost into a period of bipolarisation to which we have referred earlier. The final outcome of the activities of the Parishad and later on the Swatantra party created a deep wedge between the people of the hills and the coastal region.

A later attempt to reconstruct or re-invent the Kosal identity dates back to the early 1970s. Several other developments took place which attempted to construct a different identity for the western Odisha region and its people. In 1973 Paschim Orissa Gana Samkhya was formed consisting of all the non-Congress parties of Western Orissa region to redress the grievances of that region. Similarly in 1977, a separate political conference of leaders of western Odisha was held at Baragarh to give a united fight against the coastal Odisha leaders (Das, 1993). The development of the late 1980s and early 1990s, however, was of greater significance. In February 1989 the students from Western Odisha in Delhi formed the Western Orissa Liberation Front (WOLF) under the leadership of Chitrasena Pashayat with the sole objective of focusing on development of the western part of Odisha and for putting pressure on central leaders for a fair deal for the western region. On 16th February, 1989 Balagopal Mishra of Loisinga raised his voice against the discrimination made out to Bolangir. In the same year on 29th September Western Orissa People's Front (WOPF), under the leadership of P.R. Dubey, was formed. The WOPF was a party which registered itself with the Election Commission and contested elections in some select constituencies of western Odisha as a registered and un-recognised political party in 1990. Dubey claimed that it was a political party of the people of western Orissa, a claim almost identical to the claim of the leaders of Ganatantra Parishad (Das, 1993). A little later, on the Republic Day in 1992, Kalahandi Liberation Front (KLF) was formed by a group of unemployed educated youth. Madhu Mohanty a mechanical engineering graduate led this organisation. He gave a call for the formation of a separate Kalahandi state through violent means (Das, 1993). The formation of organisations and political parties in the 1970s and 1980s with the nomenclature of WOLF and the WOPF suggest that the leaders of the region were attempting to construct a distinct identity for the western Odihsa region. The Kosal identity which was invented and propagated in the second half of the 1940s, 1950s and early 1960s mainly by the former princely rulers was not used in the 1970s and the early 1980s. The name Kosal was revived slightly later.

The formation of the WOPF by P.R. Dubey was significant but the electoral performance of the organisation indicates that it had a very limited impact in the politics of the region. During the Assembly elections neither the West Orissa People's Front (nor the Kosal party that was formed later) was able to secure much electoral support. They did not succeed in winning seats in the constituencies or even securing a sizable chunk of the votes in the constituencies which they contested. The percentage of votes which the candidates secured was very low. The WOPF contested seven seats in 1990 but secured only 2521 votes in all which was only 0.02 per cent of the total valid votes polled in the state and 0.46 per cent of the valid votes polled in the seats contested (www.eci.gov.in). The WOPF fielded candidates in Pallahara, Padampur, Melchhamunda, Bargarh, Sambalpur, Jharsuguda and Rairakhol (SC) constituencies. The founder leader of the party P.R. Dubey, who was considered as a mass leader, contested elections from the Samabalpur constituency but secured only 591 votes which was only 0.67 per cent of the votes in the constituency.

The re-construction of a Kosal or Kosli identity began in the early 1990s. In the early 1990s the western Odisha identity is dropped and the Kosli identity is adopted once again. In the early 1990s, a Kosal Sammelan was held and the Kosal Sangram Parishad was formed and later P.R. Dubey formed the Kosal Party. Prayag Dutt Joshi, a Sanskrit scholar of Khariar, a small town (now in Nuapada district), who for the first time called the language of western Odisha as Kosli, had some influence in forming the Kosal Party. Joshi for the first time tried to establish that Kosli is a separate language and not a dialect of Odiya. He spearheaded the Kosli language movement by contributing significantly to the language by authoring books and articles and also as an activist of the Kosli language. Most of his writings appeared in the 1980s. Since then vehement attempt is being made to establish that the people of Western Odisha speak a distinct language called Kosli or Sambalpuri and are culturally distinct from that of the people of coastal Odisha. To them, Kosli is closer to the language spoken in Chattisgarh but it is not a dialect of Odiya.

Das (1993) reports after an interview with P.R. Dubey, the President of Kosal Sangram Parishad, that the demand for a separate Kosal state was put forward for the first time on 4th November, 1991 in the name of Kosal movement. The movement was, however, restricted to a few urban elite. Later, a Kosal Sammelan was convened in Goyal Bhawan of Bolangir on 29th January, 1992 under the chairmanship of P.R. Dubey, a senior advocate of the region from Sambalpur. In this Sammelan, Dubey criticised the state government for observing 1st of April every year as *Utkal Diwas* since the merger of the princely states that were located in western Odisha was reached only on 24th December, 1947. Dubey declared to observe Pausa Purnima as the Kosal Day. The Sammelan adopted two crucial resolutions. The first resolution demanded the formation of a separate state in western Odisha on the basis of language. The other resolution demanded the inclusion of Kosli language in the eighthth Schedule of the Indian constitution. After the Sammelan a Kosal Rath Yatra was launched on 15th February, 1992 in an open jeep by P.R. Dubey, the President of Kosal Sammelani (*Ibid*).

In a closed door meeting the Sammelan also expressed grave concern over the demand of the JMM for the inclusion of Sambalpur and Sundargarh districts in the proposed Jharkhand state and the subsequent Report of the Committee on Jharkhand issue. P.R. Dubey, the President of the Sammelan, wrote to the Home Minister on 7 April, 1993 opposing the demand of the Jharkhand Mukti Morcha (JMM) and their allies. He argued that the Kosli speaking tract of Odisha has long remained neglected and socio-economically exploited by the Government of Odisha. The Government of Odisha since independence is systematically destroying the linguistic and cultural heritage of the Kosali ethnic groups hence there is no option for the Kosli people but to demand a separate homeland for their survival. In this context, any move to transfer Sambalpur and Sundargarh districts, which are inhabited by Kosli ethnic groups who constitute 78 per cent of the total population of these districts, was unjust. Hence he demanded that the Government should grant them a fair opportunity to meet and discuss before taking a final decision on the Jharkhand issue (Das, 1993, Annexure II).

Other organisations like the Kosal Sangram Parishad (KSP), the Kosal Party and Kosal Liberation Front (KLF) also emerged during this period. Apart from the formation of a separate state, the other demands of the Kosal movement were: setting up another secretariat at Sonepur, because Sonepur is located in a advantageous position, railway line connection between Talcher and Sambalpur, and between Khurda and Bolangir, establishment of an Aluminium plant in Langigarh of Kalahandi district, setting up of a Regional Development Council, establishment of proposed coal company at Sambalpur, separate Doordarshan studio at Sambalpur and the demand for a white paper from the Odisha government on the total revenue collected and spent on western Odisha for development since independence (Das, 1993: 128).

The Kosal Party was a party registered with the Election Commission and remained active in the 1990s. In pursuit of the demands in the early 1990s it submitted two memorandums. In November 1991, it submitted a memorandum to Ajit Panja the then Hon'ble Minister of Information and Broadcasting, Government of India, for setting up another Doordarshan station at Sambalpur on the ground that the peasants of western Odisha do not follow language spoken in coastal Odisha. On 1st June, 1992, the Kosal Party submitted a memorandum to the President of India for recognition of Kosli Language as an official language of Odisha (Das, 1993).

Like its predecessor the WOPF, the Kosal Party (KSP) contested elections. Some of the WOPF candidates who contested in 1990 including P. R. Dubey contested the legislative assembly elections of 1995. It is, however, not known whether they contested as Kosal Party candidates. There is also no evidence that KSP contested the 2000 assembly elections. The Election Commission report points to the fact that the Kosal Party (KSP) which contested four seats in the Assembly elections in 2004 could not win any seat and polled only 11,062 votes which was 0.07 per cent of the total votes polled in the state and 2.50 per cent votes polled in the seats contested. The number of votes which the parties could win clearly indicates that these parties despite having some following among the urban voters were not in a position to translate the support into electoral success. From the electoral performance of the WOPF and the Kosal Party it can be said that the voters in the region decided to vote for the established parties rather than the ethnic parties that had been established by P.R. Dubey and others to support the cause of Western Odisha or Kosal. Out of the four seats in which the KSP had contested three had gone to the BJP-BJD alliance which emerged as the ruling alliance and one had gone to the Congress. The BJD candidates won from Rairakhol (SC) and Titlagarh constituencies, the BJP from Talcher and the INC candidate from Brajrajnagar constituency.

Thus, it is evident that the scholars and political activists of the Kosal movement in western Odisha had not only tried to establish that the language of the people inhabiting the region is Kosli which is very different from that of Odiya but also argued that culturally the people of the region are distinct from that of the rest of Odiya speaking people of the state. Odiya culture to one of the cultural activist-scholar has been very much influenced by Bengali culture. To him Odiya culture is closer to the Bengali culture. The distinction between the two cultures, Odiya and Kosli, lies in the fact that they have been influenced by two different geographical conditions. Odiya culture has been influenced by the sea culture since it lies near the sea whereas Kosli culture has been and is influenced by the hills. To him Odiya culture is 'sea' culture whereas Kosli culture is 'hi' culture.

The Kosli Identity, the Kosal Kranti Dal and the Demand for Separate State

The organised demand for separate state of Kosal erupted in the late 1980s on linguistic and cultural grounds to which we have already referred to. However, the demand appeared to have subsided in the late 1990s or remained a low key affair with the decline of the Kosal Party notwithstanding its efforts to remain afloat by contesting the Assembly elections of 2004. The demand for a separate state surfaced once again after the three states of Chattisgarh, Uttaranchal and Jharkhand were carved out in 2000 by the BJP-led National Democratic Alliance (NDA) government that came to power at the centre in 1999. A report in the Frontline in one of the issues in 2001 reads: '...demand for a separate Kosala Raj state, which remained low key for over 15 years, has gained momentum with the formation of the Kosala Party (KP) and the Kosala Ekta Mancha (KEM)' (Kalyan Chaudhuri, *Frontline*, Vol. 18, Issue-15, July 21-August 03, 2001). It was reported that several organisations such as the Western Orissa Janajagaran Parishad (WOJP), Orissa Sanskriti Samaj (OSS) and the Western Orissa Liberation Front (WOLF), joined the Kosal Party and the KEM to intensify the movement in the beginning of the century (*Ibid.*). The movement then took a militant turn. Utkal Divas was boycotted. In May 2001, a conference was held in Sambalpur where a deadline of 15th October 2005 was set for the formation of the new state (*ibid.*)

It was reported in the *Frontline* that P.R. Dubey, the chairman of the KSP criticised the Odisha government and alleged that the main concern of the Odisha government was the development of the coastal region. He alleged that the western region has been neglected. People of this backward region are victims of acute poverty and deprivation. Sale of children, a high rate of infant mortality, and deaths due to malnutrition are major features of life in western Orissa to him (*Ibid.*). P.R. Dubey an influential leader of the movement but the key figure in this renewed movement in western Orissa was the independent and later Bharatiya Janata Party legislator Balagopal Mishra. The BJP's central and state leaderships, however, did not support Mishra or his demand. But Mishra had the indirect support of legislators from western Orissa belonging to all parties (*Ibid.*).

Mishra the state legislator from Loisingha constituency was, to a large extent, responsible for the renewed agitation for a separate state of Kosal. It has been reported that in March 2001 in the Legislative Assembly of the state Mishra blamed the state government for turning a blind eye to the demand for a separate state which to him would cover 11 districts of the state. These districts to him were Bolangir, Sambalpur, Jharsuguda, Deograh, Bargarh, Sonepur, Boudh, Koraput, Sundargarh, Nuapara and Kalahandi (*ibid.*). Mishra was also responsible for the formation of a Kosal State Action Committee which took a key role in the movement. The action committee, in its meeting at Sambalpur either in December 2003 or early January 2004, passed a resolution to intensify its struggle for a separate Kosal state in a democratic and peaceful manner. It was reported that more than 500 delegates from all the concerned districts attended the meeting of the action committee (*Deccan Herald*, Sunday, 4th January, 2004).

Just before the 2004 Lok Sabha and Assembly election, Mishra carried on his campaign demanding such a state and travelled throughout the region in his 'Koshal Mukti Rath' to generate public opinion in favour of his demand. The yatra was to culminate in a public meeting on 13th March, 2004 at Sonepur (The Hindu, 7th March, 2004). It has also been reported that in late 2003 or in early January 2004 Mishra also launched a *Rath Yatra* in the region starting from Samaleswari temple in Sambalpur that ended in Bolangir covering all the eleven districts of the region. The objective of the tour to Mishra was 'sensitising the people of western Orissa on the need for a separate state'. During the *yatra* he is said to have stated: 'We have been in chains for several decades. The Orissa government generates most of its revenue from here and spends it on the development of coastal areas. It is time we free ourselves by carving out a separate Kosal state' (*Deccan Herald*, 4th January, 2004). Mishra was supported by some of the activists who formed the KOKD later but they withdrew support after a while. The supporters of Balagopal Mishra from Sambalpur allege that some of them including Pramod Mishra betrayed the movement led by Balagopal Mishra.

The KOKD which has been spearheading the movement in recent years was formed in the mid-2007 in Rourkela. Pramod Mishra one of the founders and former President of the Party in an interview to the author narrated the developments leading to the formation of the KOKD in the following manner. In 1992 to him a Maha Sammelan was organised in which 72 socio-cultural and semi political organisations participated. Four resolutions were passed in this Mahasammelan out of which the most important were: (a) constitutional status for Kosli language and (b) the development of the region. But he asserts that at this point of time there was no demand for the formation of a separate state. To him on February 22nd, 1998, Kosal Ekta Manch (hereafter KEM) was formed at Bolangir in which a Presidium was constituted of which he was the Secretary General. Some of the important members of the Presidium were; Ram Prasad Mishra, P.R. Dubey of Sambalpur, Gopal Krishna Mishra from Baragarh and Kishore Mahapatra. The Presidium to him was a democratic body. A Secretariat was also constituted with Pramod Mishra as the Secretary General. To him with the formation of the KEM, the Kosal movement actually took a proper shape. In 2000 a Vichaar Manthan Sammelan was held consisting of literary, political and cultural activists. The movement to him was divided into three parts; cultural, political and literary. The political forum which came up was the Kosal *Gana Parishad* (hereafter KGP). KGP was a part of the larger organisation, KEM led by Pramod Mishra. The important leaders of this Parishad were; Balagopal Mishra, Irfan Mohammed of Khariar and Sikhar Mishra of Bolangir. The Parishad could not do much work because two important leaders, Balagopal Mishra joined the BJP and Sikhar Mishra joined the Congress. To Pramod Mishra these two leaders betrayed the movement.

To Pramod Mishra the historical turning point to the Kosal movement is the Maha Sammelan which he organised on 12-13 April, 2000. The Maha Sammelan was attended by 700 delegates including some MLAs and MPs of the region. In this Maha Sammelan a resolution was adopted demanding a separate state. This resolution to him was a historic resolution and it is from then onwards the Kosal movement took a vigorous turn and a large number of demonstrations took place thereafter. The leaders tried to force the MLAs and the MPs of the region to take up the issue of a separate state and went for a large number of demonstrations like Rail roko, Road blockades etc. Some of the leaders also travelled to Delhi to submit memorandums to several important people.

The KEM therefore to him could spread its wings and from 2005 onwards the idea of forming a political party to attain the central objective was mooted. The final outcome of all these efforts was the formation of the Kosal Dal soon renamed as Kosal Kranti Dal in 2007 in Rourkela in hotel Radhika which was called the Birsa Munda Bhawan. After its formation Baidyanath Mishra, the party secretary announced that the party would fight for a separate state comprising ten districts of western Odisha and Athamalik sub-division of Angul district. The formation of a separate state is necessary to him because the areas have remained 'neglected' by successive Odisha governments during the past 60 years. He claimed that the party has been recognised by the Election Commission and it will contest the next assembly and Lok Sabha elections. The party he said would organise its next convention at Bolangir on December 2, to mobilise public opinion. It became more active from late 2009. The immediate context of the activism from late 2009 was the announcement of the Centre of its decision to grant statehood to the Telangana region of Andhra Pradesh in response to the movement led by Telangana Rashtriya Samiti (TRS). This had a great impact on the activities of the KOKD and the Kosal movement.

The leaders of the KOKD and the other leaders of the Kosal movement harp on the twin themes of economic underdevelopment due to neglect and distinct language and culture of the region. The central argument which they put forward is neglect and consequent underdevelopment of the region. They argue that their region is the poorest in India despite having a huge mineral and forest wealth. They further argue that in Odisha the process of economic growth has been regionally lopsided during the last 60 years. While the coastal region has benefited mostly from the economic policies pursued by the state, the Kosal region remains largely neglected, marginalised, and deprived. The leaders are armed with the report of the Ghadei Commission which was appointed by the State Planning Board to study regional disparity in the state and which submitted its report on 27 September, 1994. The Ghadei Commission found out that out of 314 C.D. Blocks in the state 75 developed ones were mostly located in the coastal region. In the western region of the state there was not even a single developed block. The finding of the Commission is used as an argument in order to justify the movement.

The other argument which they put forward is the ethnic or identity argument and that is to them Kosli is a separate language and people of Kosal have a separate culture and have separate traditions to which we have also referred earlier in the paper. Thus to them they have nothing in common with the Odiya people. Jayakrishna Sahu for example an advocate from Bolangir justifying the demand for separate state writes, 'Even demand for a Separate Koshal state is not irrational or baseless. No honest student of history can deny the fact that Utkal and Kosal are historically, culturally, linguistically and ethnically two separate entities, since time immemorial, till British occupation… Linguistically also both are different entities. Oriya language has its root in Magadhi group, while Kosli originated from Eastern Hindi Group. Claiming Kosli a Sambalpuri or sublanguage of Oriya is akin to claiming, as it was done in the past; that Oriya is a branch of Bengali' (Jayakrishna Sahu in *Jai Kosal*, the Mouthpiece of Kosli Ekta Manch, 2004).

Baidyanath Mishra, Secretary General of the KOKD in a small essay 'Smaller State: Better Governance' commenting on the reasons behind the demand for smaller state argues that small 'states demands are mostly due to economic and political negligence. In places like kosalanchala, poverty, hunger, death, farmer's suicide, labour exodus, lack of infrastructural facilities, low per capita income are the reasons which have surfaced due to years of negligence by successive governments. These regions are rich in natural resources but economically less developed and are therefore among the backward regions.' While justifying the formation of smaller states he further argues 'small is always beautiful. If America could have 50 states why India cannot? It is time for constitution of the second state reorganisation committee and consider the genuine demands of different areas under Articles 2 and 3 of the Indian Constitution' (Baidyanath Mishra, *Jai Kosal*, Organ of Kosal Kranti Dal, 2010).

Hence the proponents of separate Kosal state justify it on the basis of underdevelopment and separate language and culture. There are several periodicals which are published almost regularly like, *Kosal Sikha*, *Kosal Horizon* (an English weekly), *Kosal Katha*, and so on by different organisations supporting the cause of Kosli language and a separate state. They play an active part in the construction of the Kosal identity. The Kosal Discussion and Development Forum (KDDF) which claims itself to be a non-political and non-separatist organisation focuses on the development of the Koshal or Western Odisha region submitted a memorandum to the Prime Minister of the country and others on 20th September, 2011 for inclusion of Kosli Language in the Eighth Schedule of the Indian Constitution on the grounds that Kosli language spoken in western Odisha is a separate language and is the mother tongue of 40 to 50 per cent of the population of Odisha (*The Hindu*, 22nd September, 2011).

In pursuit of their objective, the KOKD has resorted to a series of demonstrations throughout western Odisha including road blocks, rail stoppages, collection of signatures in the region, submission of memorandums in favour of their demand, and so on. Pramod Mishra in an interview admitted that with the intensification of the movement for a separate state of Telangana and the announcement by the central government that it will pave the way for the formation of Telangana state, KOKD threatened to launch a series of agitations throughout the region. In the mid-December 2009 Pramod Mishra announced that the party would begin a series of protests with demonstrations in all the district headquarters across the region on December 17 which was to be followed by mass protests in front of Raj Bhawan in the capital, Bhubaneswar on December 23. The leaders also threatened a rail roko at Sambalpur, Bolangir, Rourkela, Jharsuguda and Baragarh in the first week of January of next year. Mishra also said that a call would be given for western Odisha Bandh in the same month and then in February, 2010, the party would organise a series of road blockades in the National highways in western Odisha (*The New Indian Express*, 15th December 2009). In the second half of December, the party also prepared and published a map of the proposed state which was to consist of 11 districts of western Odisha and the maps were distributed in Bolangir and later in other towns of western Odisha. The districts which the map showed were; Bargarh, Bolangir, Boudh, Deogarh, Jharsuguda, Kalahandi, Koraput, Nuapada, Sambalpur, Subarnapur and Sundargarh (The New Indian Express, 19th December, 2009). Later in the same month, the Kalahandi unit of KOKD submitted a memorandum to the Union Home Minister through the Kalahandi Collectorate demanding the formation of a separate Kosal state in the western part of Odisha consisting of those districts which come under the jurisdiction of the Western Odisha Development Council (WODC)[http://www.dailypioneer.com/223861/K'handi-Kosal-Dal-demands-separate State.html].

The party intensified its campaign in early 2010 when it staged rail rokos in Bolangir, Sambalpur, Jharsugada, Bargarh, Kesinga and Boinda railway stations and around 500 activists were arrested (*The New Indian Express*, 11th January, 2010). In the mid of February, the KOKD launched an economic blockade in Bolangir and blocked NH-210 and 224 and burnt the effigy of the State government (*The New Indian Express*, 15th February, 2010). In Ainthapali the activists of the party blocked NH-6 demanding the creation of a separate state which to them was the only solution for removing the regional imbalance in the state. The police arrested around 20 activists including women and removed the road blockade (*The New Indian Express*, 16th February, 2010).

KOKD as a political party was most active in 2010 when it organised a large number of demonstrations and rallies. The party demanded referendum on the question of separate state. The leaders of the party felt that public involvement is necessary to achieve the goal and urged the people of western Odisha to boycott Odiya cinema, Odiya opera, Odiya albums etc. It urged the people to register their mother tongue as Sambalpuri or Kosli and not Odiya. In mid March 2010 the party resolved to hold Kosal Chad Samabesh (Quit Kosal mega convention) on 1 April, at Sambalpur town (*The New Indian Express*, 16th March, 2010). The party demanded greater allocation of resources for the completion of the Khurda–Balangir rail project connecting eastern with western Odisha directly since this will bring socio-economic development of the region.

It also pressurised the MLAs and the MPs of the region to raise the issue of Kosal state and threatened that the representatives who do not raise the issue would be socially boycotted by the year 2014. The party also demanded that the headquarters of WODC must be shifted from Bhubaneswar to the western Odisha districts. In 2010 when election to three vacant seats to the Rajya Sabha (RS) was due it demanded that candidates from western Odisha should be nominated to the RS by political parties. It also alleged that the BJD has functioned as a political party representing the interests of the coastal districts. The BJD government to it had not addressed the issue of distress selling of paddy, suicide of farmers, distress selling of girl child, etc., in the region. To Pramod Mishra those who live in Kosalanchal but do not support the movement for a separate Kosal would be asked to leave the region. To the party the Odisha government should leave the region permanently and entrust the administration to the natives.

In the second half of July 2011, it launched a mass contact programme in western Odisha to mobilise opinion for a separate Kosal state. In this mass contact programme members of Bar Associations, civil society members, ethnic groups and caste based organisations were approached for their support to the cause of a separate state. In the second phase, the Dal members were to meet the politicians of the region to assess their attitude towards the formation of separate state and pressurise them to work for the independence of the region from the bondage of colonial rule of coastal Odisha (*The New Indian Express*, 20th July, 2011). On July 8, 2012, the KOKD held a one day national conference on the issue of smaller states at Sambalpur. The conference as stated by Baidyanath Mishra had twin objectives; to unite new states activists in one platform and to pressurise the government to form the second State Re-organisation Commission (SRC). On 22nd March, 2013, protesters of the KOKD sat in a Dharna in front of the state assembly demanding separate state. The protesters submitted a memorandum to the Chief Minister Naveen Patnaik explaining the reasons behind such a demand. Copies of the memorandum were also handed over to the representatives of the Kosal region and they were urged to take up the demand of a separate state in the Assembly within two months and a ultimatum was served on them if they failed to do so they will be gheroed in their respective constituencies (*The New Indian Express*, 2nd March, 2013).

On April 1, 2013, the activists of the KOKD observed 'Black Day' in several prominent towns of the region to which we have referred earlier. The protest was the strongest in Bolangir where the activists of the KOKD after staging a dharna putting on black badges, raised slogans against the government of Odisha and cut the map of Odisha state besides burning a symbolic effigy of the Odisha administration (The Pioneer, 3rd April, 2013). On 10 May, the KOKD took out a rally in the evening with the purpose of spreading awareness among the masses about the creation of a separate Kosal state under article 2 and 3 of the Constitution (The Pioneer, 12th May, 2013). In the foundation day Maha Sammelan in June 2013 certain amendments to the Constitution were made and Bunde Dhurua a tribal and a former leader of the BJP who joined the KOKD a couple of years back has been made the new President. Dhurua is a tribal leader and the KOKD expects that he would be able to mobilise the tribal population of the region on the issue of separate state. The party had recently rejected the demand of the Biju Janata Dal for special category status to Odisha on the grounds that if Odisha is granted special category status and there is an increase in central assistance then the lion's share of the grant will be spent for the development of the coastal districts which ultimately will widen the gap between the coastal and western districts. To Pramod Mishra the only alternative for the development of the region is to grant statehood (*The Pioneer*, 10th June 2013).

Following the WOPF and the KSP, the KOKD had registered itself with the election commission and contested both the Assembly as well as Parliamentary elections in the region in 2009 as a registered (unrecognised) party. It fielded 18 candidates in the Legislative Assembly elections and three in the Lok Sabha elections. For the Patnagarh assembly constituency it fielded Baidyanath Mishra, the General Secretary of the party. Although Pramod Mishra had announced that it will field Baidyanath Mishra as the MP candidate from Bolangir Lok Sabha constituency to end dynastic rule prevailing in Bolangir since the last 50 years, the party finally fielded three candidates in the Lok Sabha constituencies. The KOKD brought out its election manifesto in which the demand for a separate Kosal state topped the list. The other issues which the party raised in its manifesto were inclusion of Kosli language in the eighth schedule of the constitution, social and economic alleviation of the tribals and dalits of the region, land for the landless and irrigation facilities in the region. While releasing its manifesto Pramod Mishra had stated that the formation of a separate state of Kosal was the only solution to put to an end to the growing regional imbalance in the state and the consequent resentment among the people of the region against imbalance and neglect (*The New Indian Express*, 12th April, 2009). To him it was unfortunate that the representatives of the region had never raised their voice against the issue of regional imbalance.

Out of the 18 assembly constituencies, which the party contested, it won none but secured 26575 votes which was 0.15 per cent of the valid votes polled in the state and 1.24 per cent of the votes in the seats contested. Even though it did not win any seat what is however interesting to note is that in some of the constituencies the party candidates could secure more than 2,000 votes. Baidyanath Mishra, the Secretary General of the party contesting from Patnagarh constituency secured 2284 votes. The Lok Sabha seats which the KOKD contested were Sambalpur, Sundargarh and Bargarh. In the Sundargarh parliamentary constituency, the KOKD candidate Sagar Singh Manakee secured 12,934 votes, from the Sambalpur constituency, Ashok Kumar Naik secured 10,374 votes and from the Bargarh constituency, the KOKD candidate Niladri Behari Panda secured 19436 votes. In all the three constituencies the candidates of the INC won. The number of assembly seats and the Lok Sabha seats which the KOKD contested and the fact that in some of the assembly seats, the KOKD candidates could secure more than 2,000 votes, and in the parliamentary seats each and every candidate of the party could secure more than 10000 votes indicate that the KOKD as a political party has some base in western Odisha particularly in the urban areas and this base seems to be much wider than what the WOPF and the KSP had enjoyed in the region earlier.

Although the social base of the movement and the Dal had remained confined to the intellectual, business and professional classes including retired government employees but during the protest demonstrations in late 2009 and throughout 2010 it was reported that many of the students union of the colleges supported the demand for a separate state. In the mid of December, Pramod Mishra had claimed that the students union of Sambalpur University led by its president Padmanav Mishra have extended support to the Kosal movement and students would boycott classes demanding formation of separate state (*The New Indian Express*, 15th December, 2009). The All Kosal Students Union had been one of the important wings of the party. In January 2010, the AKSU participated in the *Rail Roko* movement launched by the KOKD. On January 2, 2010, the AKSU members had burnt Planning and Co-ordination Minister A. U. Singhdeo's and WODC chairman Niranjan Panda's effigy for reportedly speaking against Kosal state demand (*The New Indian Express*, 11th January, 2010). Along with students, the lawyers had also supported the demand for a separate state. For example, during the peak of the movement in the mid of December 2009, the Sambalpur Bar Association (SBA) President Pradeep Bohidar welcomed all the organisations demanding creation of separate state comprising districts of Western Odisha and assured all support in the stir (*The New Indian Express*, 17th December, 2009).

Conclusion

What we note is that since the late 1980s or early 1990s in Western Odisha there is an attempt being made in order to construct a Kosli or a Sambalpuri or Kosli-Sambalpuri ethnic identity. Organisations that attempt to construct it arguethattheyare Koslisor Sambalpuris and have a distinct culture.

Odiya language and culture is an alien imposition on them. On this basis, they demand the formation of a separate state of Kosal consisting of eleven districts of the state lying in western Odisha. But the Kosal movement as it stands today has not received support from all the sections of the society in Western Odisha. The movement has the support of the urban educated elite which includes the professional classes like lawyers, businessmen, ex-servicemen, and so on. The movement is urban based and the organisations that mainly spearhead the movement, the KOKD like the WOPF and the KSP—are all urban-based political outfits. Others who support the Kosal movement but are not members or activists of any organisation are advocates, teachers, businessmen and the government employees, both retired and working. The educated in the region feel a sense of injustice done to the region by the state government in all sectors from jobs, infrastructure and irrigation and so on and this has led to the development of grievances which find expression in the movement for a distinct identity and a state.

The support base of the movement seems to have broadened when compared to the movement of the 1990s and this can be inferred from the 2009 Assembly election results where the KOKD fared much better than the WOPF and the KSP in terms of vote share. The KOKD was contested 18 Assembly seats as compared to the four the KSP had contested in the 2004 elections. The KOKD was also able to contest three Parliamentary seats and secure good number of votes. There is a likelihood that the KOKD will grow as an organisation and the movement for a separate state of Kosal will intensify in future particularly if Andhra Pradesh, a bordering state of Odisha, is bifurcated and the state of Telangana is created by the Congress led UPA government at the Centre. There are reports of greater political activity in the form of road blocks, *rail roko*, signature campaigns and so on in western Odisha by the KOKD and other Kosal demanding organisations after the Congress Working Committee and also the United Progressive Alliance (UPA) recommend to the central government creation of a separate state of Telangana on 30th July, 2013. An analysis of the core argument extended by the KOKD in support of its demand suggests that the organisation harps more on the theme of economic backwardness, neglect, and internal colonialism and less on the question of distinct culture and identity. On the issue of identity, the KOKD and other Kosal supporting organisations differ if not radically but to a great extent on the nomenclature of the language spoken in the region. There lies a division between the Sambalpuris and others. The leaders from Sambalpur claim that the language spoken in the region is Sambalpuri whereas the leaders of other parts of the region claim that the language is Kosli and not Sambalpuri or Sambalpuri-Kosli. This difference has come into the surface time and again. For example, in early May 2013, some of the prominent educationists in the Sambalpur region protested the attempt by people in other parts of western Odisha to call the language of the region as Kosli and not Sambalpuri.

According to them, the language of the people of Western Odisha was Sambalpuri and not Kosli and any effort to call the language as Kosli would be protested (*The Pioneer*, 9th May, 2013). The KOKD and other organisations also suffer from the problem of funds and part-time activity by the leaders. The problem of fund was admitted to by Pramod Mishra the president of KOKD in an interview. To him the organisation is a small and finds it difficult to mobilise sufficient funds to run its political activities. Political activity thus gets hampered by fund constraint. More importantly, the leaders of the movement are not full time activists but only part timers. They engage in politics only on a temporary basis after meeting the demands of their professional career.

Notes

1. On the 1st of April 2010 the KOKD had given a bandh call throughout western Odisha to protest against the 'injustice' and 'apathy' towards the people in the region (http://www.merinews.com/article/kosal-kranti-dal-kkd-observed-black-day-on-april-1/158).
2. Some were lawyers, some were retired government servants and some were students.
3. Balangir is also spelt as Bolangir.
4. Similarly in Sonepur, the Central Committee of the Kosal Ekta Manch (KEM) along with the KOKD staged demonstration and submitted a memorandum addressed to the President of India through the Collector. In this memorandum the leaders of the organisations citing from the 2011 census said about 2.5 crore people of the state of Odisha speak Kosali/Kosli and hence it should be included in the 8th schedule of the Indian Constitution. It also raised its main demand of formation of separate state of Kosal consisting of 13 districts from Nabarangpur to Sundargrh (*The New India Express*, 2nd April, 2013). This is how the various splinter organisations protest on the first day of April when the state government celebrates Odisha day or Utkal Diwas throughout the state.
5. As per some recent reports the movement leaders demand the Kosal state to consist of 10 districts and the Athamallik subdivision of Anugul district (*The New India Express*, 10th August 2013).
6. In the first General Assembly elections of 1951 the All India Gantantra Parishad secured 31 seats with 20.50 per cent of votes in the state. Most of the seats came from the North Western and Western part of Odisha. In 1957 the party improved its position and won 51 seats with 28.74 per cent of votes. In 1961, the party could however secure only 37 seats with 22.34 per cent of votes. In 1971, much after it had merged with the Swatantra party it secured 36 seats with 17.44 per cent votes. In the Lok Sabha elections also the Ganatantra Parishad later on the Swatantra

party had done well till the 1977 elections (Report on Legislative Assembly Elections from the website of the Election Commission of India). Thus in the state and more particularly in the western part of the state there was no Congress System, the opposition which was rooted in the tribal dominated region of the state had a very strong presence.

7. As per the Economic Survey 2012-2013, 'as per recent estimates made by the Planning Commission poverty in Odisha has declined by 20.2 percentage points from 57.2 per cent in 2004-05 (61st round of NSS) to 37 per cent in 2009-10 (66th round of NSS). This is the highest poverty reduction by any state in India in 2009-10. Poverty declined in all NSS regions and all social classes of Odisha including Scheduled Tribes, (STs) Scheduled Castes (SCs), Other Backward Classes (OBC) and others. This implies inclusive growth in Odisha. The extent of poverty in southern and northern regions as well as among ST and SC communities is still high and remains a matter of concern' (Government of Odisha, Planning and Coordination Department, Directorate of Economics and Statistics, February 2013).
8. The pamphlet is entitled 'Whither Koshal?' The pamphlet does not carry the name of the author and is widely accepted that it was written sometime around 1946 by R.N. Singh Deo. The stated objective of this pamphlet was to examine the possibilities of reunion of Koshal.
9. In all the constituencies where the WOPF contested except in Sambalpur the seats were won by the candidates of the Janata Dal, the party which eventually secured 123 seats in the state out of 147 and formed the government.
10. Some of the books and articles which he authored were: Khadial Anchalara Lokabhasa, Saptarshi, June, 1981; Upabhasa Nuhen, Dainik Koshal, Sambalpur, 17/10/1981; Kosali Bhasa, Dainik Kosal, Sambalpur, 26/01/1982; Abahelita Bhasa, Dainik Koshal, Sambalpur, 15/12/1984; Swatantra Kosli Bhasa, Dainik Hirakhand, September 15, 17, 19, 20, 1983, Basant Milan Souveneir, 18/02/1983; Kosli Bhasa ra Ghara Samparkiya Sabdabali, Girijhar, Bhawanipatana, November 1984; Paschim Odisha ra Bhasa Kosli, Hirakhand Basant Milan Souvenir, January 1985; Swatantra Kosli Bhasa, Dhuan Aru Dhuka, Saptarishi, July, 1986; Swatantra Kosli Bhasa, Bidwatbimoha, Saptarishi, July, 1987; Swatantra Kosli Bhasa ra Parichay, Saptarishi, March, 1988 (*Kosal Horizon*, A Weekly Newspaper, Rourkela, 03.03.2013-09.03.2013).
11. The exact date of the Sammelan is not known. Das gives two different dates in his dissertation. In one of his chapters he states it was held on 29th of March 1992 whereas in the annexure he states that it was held on 29th of January 1992 (Das, 1993). But what is sure is that it was held in the beginning of 1992.

12. P.R. Dubey published the first newspaper for the Kosal state 'Kosal Khabar'. He also constituted the Kosal Sena. For the first time he prepared a map of the proposed Kosal state in 1990. He authored a book Hame Kosli Hamar Bhasa Kosli and Why Kosal State? He wrote an article 'The Politics of Language', in which he argued that Odiya language was planted as a spoken language of Sambalpur and Kalahandi districts in the Records of British Government. Subsequently, Sambalpuri speaking regions were claimed as Oriya speaking regions.
13. Binod Kumar Das (1993) informs us that on February 23, 1992 newly formed Kosala Sangram Parishad (KSP) threatened to launch an agitation for a separate Kosal State.
14. Some of the demands were also the demands of the Samajwadi Janata Party which was active in some parts of western Odisha.
15. The Kosal Party was a political party registered under representation of People's Act by the Election Commission of India.
16. The second memorandum to which we have referred was submitted by the Kosal Party under the signature of its President P.R. Dubey (Das, 1993).
17. The Kosal Party candidates in 2004 were Balaram Sah from Titilagarh (SC) assembly constituency, Pramod Chandra Behera from Talcher (SC) constituency, Sitaram Rungta from Brajarajnagar constituency and Lal Bahadur Bag from Rairakhol (SC) constituency.
18. Interview with Ghasiram Mishra on 16/03/2013 at Balangir.
19. This was also argued by Pramod Mishra, the President of the KOKD during an interview at Bolangir on 15/03/2013.
20. The party contested only four seats and the fact that that the party could contest only four seats in 2004 indicate that there was a decline in the support for Kosal party and the movement by the late 20th century. There is no evidence that the Kosal Party candidates had contested the 2000 assembly elections.
21. Balagopal Mishra contested and won as an independent candidate in 1995 but joined the BJP later and won from the same constituency in 2000. He had contested the Bolangir Lok Sabha constituency in 1989 as a Janata Dal candidate and won but lost the seat in 1991 as Janata Party candidate.
22. Mishra's *yatra,* however, faced opposition from his own party and the leadership of the BJP denounced openly any move to bifurcate the state. He was also criticised by the Chief Minister and the President of the BJD Naveen Pattanaik for his actions (*Deccan Herald*, 4th January, 2004). There was a BJP-BJD alliance government at the state level.

23. Sapan Mishra, an important leader and activists of the Kosal Sena, a newly formed outfit informed the author that Balagopal Mishra withdrew from the movement after 2004 (interview on 19/03/2013 in his Sambalpur office).
24. The state unit of the BJP did not support the activities of Balagopal Mishra. But it did not take any action against the leader. It was, however, reported that the BJP legislators of the region had offered tacit support to Mishra (*Deccan Herald*, 4th January, 2004).
25. This is what the researcher came to learn from Sapan Mishra, an important leader and activists of the Kosal Sena, a newly formed outfit whom he interviewed on 19/03/2013 in his Sambalpur office.
26. Interview with Pramod Mishra at his residence in Balangir on 15/03/2013.
27. It is from him it was learnt that Balagopal Mishra and Sonatan Mishra attended the Mahasammelan.
28. Balagopal Mishra had formed the Kosal Rajya Kriya Anusthan Samiti but to Pramod Mishra he betrayed the movement when he decided to join the BJP (htpp://articles.timesofindia.indiatimes.com/2009-04 12/Bhubaneswar/28057795_I-bjd-Is-e).
29. Some activities were also reported at the end of December 2008 as well. In late December 2008 it was reported that the legal cell of the KOKD in Bhawanipatana, Kalahandi urged the advocates of the western part of Odisha to demand for the establishment of a separate state and hence for a separate high court. To the President of the KOKD instead of demanding for a high court in any part of western Odisha the advocates must demand for a separate state. If a separate state comes into existence, then automatically a high court will be established htpp:/welcomeorissa. com/Orissanews.php?opt= view&Id =17970&Chosen Day=30&ChosenMonth=12&ChosenYear=2008).
30. The Kosal Discussion and Development Forum citing from some source claimed that there are five registered newspapers and seventy magazines available in Kosli language.
31. This is what was also admitted by Pramod Mishra during an interview with the researcher on 18/03/2013 at Balangir.
32. It was reported in *The New Indian Express,* 8th March, 2009.
33. The KOKD contested the elections from the Bijepur, Bhatli, Brajarajnagar, Jharsuguda, Talsara (ST), Sundergarh (ST), Biramitrapur (ST), Raghunathpalli (SC), Rourkela, Rajgangapur (ST), Kuchinda (ST), Rengali (SC), Rairakhol, Sambalpur, Deogarh, Patnagarh, Balangir and Kantabanji assembly constituencies.

34. The assembly election was dominated by the BJD which eventually won 103 seats out of the 129 that it contested in the state. Before the elections the BJD had decided not to enter into any seat adjustment with that of the BJP in the state. The BJD secured 44.16 per cent of the votes in the seats that it contested and 38.86 per cent of the valid votes polled in the state (Election Commission of India website).
35. In the Bargarh constituency the KOKD focussed on critiquing Dr Hamid Hussain the BJD candidate from the constituency who joined the BJD just before the 2009 elections. Dr Hamid Hussain is a native of Jharsuguda and a retired civil servant was active in the Kosal movement. He was the All India Convener of the Kosal Ekta Manch (KEM) and visited several places in Western Odisha to spread the message of separate statehood. He was also one of the leading members of the delegation who went to Delhi to submit a memorandum to the President demanding separate western Odisha state. The KOKD criticised him by saying that he had deceived the people of entire western Odisha. Hussain secured 298,931 votes from the constituency in the 2009 elections (htpp://articles.timesofindia.indiatimes.com/2009-04-12/Bhubaneswar/28057795_I-bjd-Is-e).
36. B.K. Das a young researcher in 1993 during his field trip found that in the rural areas only 2.24 per cent of the people supported the movement whereas in the urban areas 26.92 per cent of the people supported the movement. On the basis of this he argued that the movement for a separate state of Kosal 'is purely confined to the urban educated elites and it has yet to get the support of village illiterates masses' (Das 1993).

References

Primary Sources

Election Commission of India, Key Highlights of General Election to the Legislative Assembly of Orissa (for various years).

Government of Orissa, 2004. Human Development Report 2004. Planning and Coordination Department.

Government of Odisha, 2013. Economic Survey 2012-2013. Planning and Coordination Department, Directorate of Economics and Statistics.

Sahu, Jayakrishna, 2004. 'The Means to End Regional Disparity Development or Disintegration', *Jai Kosal* (Mouthpiece of Kosli Ekta Manch), Kosli Ekta Manch, Bolangir.

Mishra, Pramod Kumar, 2004. You Can't Befool us Anymore', *Jai Kosal* (Mouthpiece of Kosli Ekta Manch), Kosli Ekta Manch, Bolangir.

Mishra, Baidyanath, 2010. 'Smaller State: Better Governance', Jai Kosal (Organof Kosal Kranti Dal), Special Issue published on the occasion of 4th Foundation day, Kosal Kranti Dal, Rourkela.

Kosal Discussion and Development Forum, 2011. 'Memorandum for Inclusion of Kosli Language in the 8th Schedule of the Indian Constitution submitted to Dr.Manmohan Singh, the Prime Minister of India, and others' on 20th September, 2011.

Secondary Sources

Anonymous, 'Wither Koshal?', n. p., n. d.

Bailey, F.G., 1960. *Tribes, Caste and Nation*. Manchester: Manchester University Press.

Chaudhuri, Kalyan, 2001. 'Ferment in Orissa', *Frontline*, Vol. 18, Issue 15-July, 21 – 3 August.

Das, Binod Kumar, 1993. *Politics of Sub-Regional Assertion in Orissa: A Case Study of Kosal Sangram Parishad* (KSP), Unpublished M. Phil. dissertation submitted to Jawaharlal Nehru University, New Delhi.

Mishra, P.K., 1992. 'Shaping Identity: History of the Emergence of the New Socio-political Entity of Western Orissa', in Madhusudan Pati (ed.), *West Orissa: A Study in Ethos*. Sambalpur: Sambalpur University, pp. 260 – 283.

Pati, Biswamoy, 2001. 'Identity, Hegemony, Resistance, Conversations in Orissa, 1800-2000', *Economic and Political Weekly*, Vol. 36, No. 44, pp. 4204-4212.

Pati, Biswamoy, 2006. 'Tata's and the Orissa "Model" of Capitalist Development', *Social Scientist*, Vol. 34, Nos. 3-4: 37-42.

Pradhan, Jaya Prakash, *et. al.* 2004. Interpreting the Demand for Koshala State in Orissa: Development versus Underdevelopment, KDF working Paper No. 1, New Delhi: Kosala Development Forum.

Richter, William L., 1971. 'Princes in Indian Politics', *Economic and Political Weekly*, Vol. 6, No. 9.

—, 1972. 'Return of the Congress', *Economic and Political Weekly*, Vol. 7. No. 27.

Ray, Amal, 1974. 'Sub-Regional Politics and Elections in Orissa', *Economic and Political Weekly*, Vol. 9. No. 49.

Panda, Ghanashyam, 1992. 'Placing Western-Orissan Society on the Post Industrial Trajectory: A Theoretical Discourse on a Scheme of Transition', in Madhusudan Pati (ed.), *West Orissa: A Study in Ethos*. Sambalpur: Sambalpur University, pp. 31-45.

News Paper Reports

The Hindu, 7th March, 2004. 'BJP Legislator Spearheads Koshal Slogan'.

The Hindu, 24th December, 2009. 'Demonstration Held for Separate Koshal State'.

The Hindu, 22nd September, 2011. 'Plea to Include Kosli in 8th Schedule of the Constitution'.

The Hindu, 23rd March, 2013. 'Separate Koshal State Demanded'.

Kosal Horizon (A Weekly Newspaper), Rourkela, 3rd March, 2013. 'Pandit Prayagdutta Joshi'.

The New Indian Express, 16th February, 2010. 'Balangir Lawyers to Block Government Vehicles'. *The New Indian Express*, 2nd April, 2013. 'Black Flag Demos Mark Utkal Diwas'.

The New Indian Express, 11th January, 2010. 'Campaign for Koshal State Intensifies'.

The New Indian Express, 31st July, 2010. 'HC Bench Demand: Rourkela Joins the Race'.

The New Indian Express, 1st September, 2009. 'HC Bench in W. Orissa: Lawyers Paralyze Courts'.

The New Indian Express, 20th July, 2011. 'KKD Launches Mass Contact Programme'.

The New Indian Express, 15th December, 2009. 'KKD to Launch Stir for Separate Koshal State'.

The New Indian Express, 7th July, 2011. 'KKD Ups the Ante for Separate Koshal State'.

The New Indian Express, 8th March, 2009. 'Koshal Dal Takes the Poll Plunge'.

The New Indian Express, 12th April, 2009. 'Koshal Kranti Dal Releases Manifesto of Promises'.

The New Indian Express, 9th June, 2012. 'Koshal State Need of the Hour: KKD'.

The New Indian Express, 24th February, 2010. 'Koshal State: KKD Seeks Referendum'.

The New Indian Express, 17th December, 2009. 'Koshal State: Lawyers up the Ante'.

The New Indian Express, 27th February, 2009. 'Lawyers Intensify Stir for HC Bench'.

The New Indian Express, 2nd February, 2010. 'Lawyers Issue Ultimatum to Government Over HC Bench'.

The New Indian Express, 21st May, 2011. 'Lawyers Paralyze Court Work'.

The New Indian Express, 19th December, 2009. 'Maps of Separate Kosala Distributed in Orissa'.

The New Indian Express, 21st April, 2011. 'Politicos Slug it Out for Rly. Wagon Factory'.

The New Indian Express, 16th March, 2010. 'Quit Koshal Convention from April 1.

The New Indian Express, 28th May, 2010. 'Nominate W Orissa Candidates for RS'.

The New Indian Express, 8th February, 2010. 'Sambalpur Bandh on Feb 10'.

The New Indian Express, 11th February, 2010. 'Sambalpur Bandh Paralyses Life'.

The New Indian Express, 13th December, 2009. 'Sambalpur Bar Threatens to Intensify Stir'.

The New Indian Express, 16th February, 2010. 'Separate Koshal State: KKD Blocks NH'.

The New Indian Express, 24th August, 2010.'Stir to Continue till HC Bench is Set Up'.

The New Indian Express, 24th December, 2009. 'Students Join Lawyer's Stir'.

The New Indian Express, 9th February, 2010. 'W Orissa Students Stage Agitation'.

The New Indian Express, 25th February, 2011. 'Will Khurda-Balangir Project Get Allocation?'

The Pioneer, 21th April, 2013. 'B'ngir BJD Protests Centre's 'Neglect' Towards KBK'.

The Pioneer, 13th June, 2013. 'Kosal Dal Rejects Special Category Claim'.

The Pioneer, 19th March, 2013. 'Kosal Demo before Assembly on March 22'.

The Pioneer, 31th March, 2013. 'Kosal Kranti Dal to Observe Utkal Diwas as Black Day'.

The Pioneer, 15th February, 2010. 'Koshal Activists Begin Economic Blockade'.

The Pioneer, 27 April, 2013. 'Mostly Peaceful in Western Odisha'.

The Pioneer, 9th May, 2013. 'Move to Call Sambalpuri Dialect as Koshali Opposed'.

The Pioneer, 3th April, 2013. 'Odisha Map Torn, Burnt on Utkal Divas in B'ngir'.

The Pioneer, 10th June, 2013. 'Seek Statehood for Kosalanchal: Kosal Dal to Naveen'.

The Pioneer, 12th May, 2013. 'Torch Rally Held in B'ngir for Kosal State'.

5

Changing Identities of the Scheduled Castes in Colonial and Post-Colonial Bengal

Rup Kumar Barman

Introduction

Etymological source of the term 'ethnicity' is Greek *ethnos* which originally means heathen or pagan (William, 1976: 119). But in common sense understanding it means 'nation' or people of the same race with a 'distinctive culture'. Ethnicity is a kind of 'consciousness' about the status and problem of an 'ethnic group' (Brass, 1991: 1-9). This 'consciousness' is based on certain characteristics such as language, religion, beliefs, race, caste and certainly a common cultural tradition (Shills, 1968: 167). According to Fredrik Barth, 'difference' (whether real or imaginary) is a basic feature of ethnicity (Barth, 1969). This 'difference' leads to the formation of a kind of a feeling of 'otherness'. A sense of 'otherness' and a positive desire of identification as 'other' mobilise the ethnic groups to the formation of a social identity. This sense also drives ethnic groups to assert for their share in economic resources and 'power'. Again, ethnicity is 'situational' and 'contextual' where it is multidimensional and can be used for a collective action (Phadnish, 1995: 14-15; Azam, 2001: 15). On the basis of these features we do notice the existence of a large number of ethnic groups in the broader context of Indian society.

Certain caste-based ethnic groups of Eastern India have drawn wide attention of social scientists for the changing nature of their ethnic identities in the 20th and early 21st Centuries. Among such caste communities, the Rajbanshis of Northern Bengal, the Namasudras of Eastern Bengal, the Poundras of coastal Bengal, the Malos of Eastern Bengal deserve special mention. These caste-based communities had developed a kind of consciousness about their caste identity in the second quarter of the twentieth century, when they started asserting themselves for a political 'place'. They collectively established themselves as a 'bargaining political force' in the context of political autonomy of Bengal under the colonial rule. But after the partition of Bengal in 1947, these caste communities (known as Scheduled Castes, SCs, since 1936) have changed the characters of their ethnic consciousness. In this paper I will highlight all these aspects of changing nature of ethnicity of caste-based social groups of Bengal.

Caste Communities of Present Study

In the present paper, we are concerned about such low caste communities of Bengal which had been into a kind of social movement for the formation of a standard 'caste identity' in the colonial period and transformed their movements into politico-cultural/regional or class movements in post-colonial West Bengal. Among such communities we will discuss about the Malos, Namasudras, Poundras and Rajbanshis, who were classified as Depressed Castes (Scheduled Castes since 1936) in the colonial administrative records. These caste communities had established their settlements in Bengal Delta and Sub-Himalayan Bengal in distant past. Pre-colonial literary and archeological evidences and colonial records give us an idea about their distribution and occupations. The Malos (the Jhalo Malos) were fishermen of Bengal. In the early nineteenth century, Buchanan Hamilton (a British ethnographer), had found that the Malos were engaged in fishing throughout Bengal although majority of them were concentrated in Eastern Bengal (Martin, 1976: 531) particularly in Maymensingh, Coomilla, Pabna, Jessore, Nadia and Murshidabad districts. Fishing was their primary occupation although some of them were engaged in agricultural works. They had developed their own techniques and technologies of fishing. Namasudras, on the other hand, were the members of largest Schedule Caste community of Bengal (except Cooch Behar State). In the pre-colonial period and even in the nineteenth century they used to be called *Chandal*. However, since the latter half of the nineteenth century, the Chandals of Bengal began to identify themselves as Namasudras. Risley (a British civil servant-cum-ethnographer) had recorded in 1891 that 'the Chandals of Bengal invariably call themselves as Namasudra, and with characteristic jealousy higher division of the caste apply the name Chandal to the lower, who in their turn pass it to the Dom' (Risley, 1981: 184). The Namasudras had significant concentration in Dacca, Maymensingh, Faridpur, Bakharganj, Tippera, Jessore, Nadia, Khulna, Noakhali, Rangpur, Pabna, and Rajshahi districts of Eastern Bengal. They had little concentration in Midnapur, Burdwan,

24 Parganas and Murshidabad. From the occupational point of view, the Namasudras were mainly engaged in the primary sector of economy and this can be understood from their sub-groups, such as, Halwah (cultivators), Ghashi (Grass-cutters), Kandho (palanquin-bearers), Karral (the fishermen), Bari (carpenters), Berua (fishermen), Baqqal (trader and hucksters), and so on. Like the Namasudras, the Poundras of Bengal were engaged in different occupations of primary sector, including agriculture, fishing and trading. They had large scale distribution in Midnapur, 24 Parganas, Khulna and Nadia. The Poundras were also called Pod, Punro, Padmaraj and Baleya in colonial Bengal.

Fourth caste community of our study is the Rajbanshi. The Rajbanshis were second largest (except Cooch Behar) in terms of population figure among the SC communities. They had significant concentration in the districts of northern Bengal like Rangpur, Jalpaiguri, Dinajpur, Maldah and Darjeeling. They had highest concentration in Cooch Behar State. The Rajbanshis were also distributed in Lower Assam. The Rajbanshis of Southern Bengal, however, were different than their brethrens of North Bengal in terms of occupation and social affiliation. From occupational point of view, the Rajbanshis of undivided Bengal were dependent on the agricultural works. The Southern Rajbanshis particularly of Nadia, Murshidabad, 24 Parganas and Midnapur were engaged in fishing along with agricultural works.

Table 1: Population Figures of the Scheduled Castes of Present Study (excluding Cooch Behar and Tripura States) and Traditional Occupation

From	*1931 Population*	*Traditional Occupation(s)/Status*
Jhalo Malo	197789	Fishing, selling fish and making fishing implements
Namasudra	2086213	Agricultural works, Fishing, Manual jobs, Artisans, Carpenters
Pod	667731	Agricultural works, Trade, Artisans
Rajbangsi	1487469	Agricultural works, Fishing

Source: Census, 1931 and compiled by self from Risley (1981); Government of West Bengal (2005) and field data.

From the occupational classification it appears that the caste communities of present study were underprivileged and belonged to the lower class. A few persons of the Namasudra, Poundra and Rajbangsi communities had placed themselves as landlords, *zotedars* or as *talukdars*. Majority of them were very poor and had a measurable class status. Regarding the Poundras, Risley had recorded in 1891 that 'the great majority of the caste are engaged in agriculture as tenure holder, and occupancy and non-occupancy *ryats*. A few have risen to be *zamindars* and some at the other end of the scale work as nomadic cultivators on freshly cleared land in the Sundarbans, changing their location every two or three years according to the fortune of their crops' (Risley, 1981: 176).

Condition of the fishermen section of these communities was more deplorable as majority of them were 'captured fisheries' without capital goods. Very often they had to meet the extra demands of the *zamindars* and their officials (Risley, 1981: 66; Hunter, 1876: 367). The fishermen were often charged with extra levies called *Pani Charai* by the government officials, too (Hunter, 1876: 29). The fishermen, however, had customary rights of fishing in the big rivers without charge.

There were three categories of fishermen in Bengal in terms of their possession of capital goods. Fishermen having boats, nets and other implements belonged to first category. They could enjoy major share of profits of fishing as the owner of capital goods. The *aratdars* (commission agent) and the *nikaris* (fish mongers) were also the fishermen of first category.

The primary fishers who did not have nets and boats of their own and bulk of the 'share-fishers' constituted the second category of fishermen. We can designate them as 'water labourer'. They were exploited both by the fishermen of the first category and the owners of the fisheries. Third category comprised of the fish retailers generally called *paikar*. The *paikars* were also very poor. About their condition, Hamilton wrote (1807):

> ...none of these have a capital of above 100 Rs and many are so poor that they purchase the fish on trust and after having sold their fish in the market, go next morning to the actual fishermen, pay him for what fish they received, and take a fresh load on credit (quoted in Martin, 1976: 593).

Bulk of the traditional fishermen, on the whole, was very poor in terms of their class position in the society. For fishing they had to depend on the whims of the nature. They were thus floaters having no assured mode of living.

Social status of the Scheduled Caste communities of present study was very much disgraceful. Ancient law books (*shastras* and *smritis*) had treated them as *sudra* or as *antaja* (people of inferior rank) and often almost as *asprishya* (untouchables). *Brihaddharma Purana* had treated them as *madhyam sankara* (mixed caste of average social rank) and *antaja*. Similarly, the *Brahmabaibartya Purana* had classified them as *satsudra* (Sudra caste of respectable rank), *asatsudra* (inferior Sudra) and as *antaja* (Tarkaratna, 1314: *339*-40). So it appears they had inferior social rank in the traditional caste society. The *mangala* literature and the *charitas* (biographies) of the Vaishnava saints written in the late medieval period have also recorded their disgraceful social status.[1] The colonial literatures have recorded miserable social condition of these caste communities with elaborate description.

Although agriculture was the backbone of Bengal economy, the agriculturists, composed of the Namasudras, Poundras and Rajbanshis did not enjoy social respect like other upper caste agriculturists. The Namasudras in the nineteenth century were not allowed to enter even into the outer circles of the 'Aryan system' (Risley, 1981: 183).The Rajbanshis had to bear social injustice because of their origin (Barman, 1985: 43-46). The Poundras also had similar experiences. In this context, observation of Risley regarding the Poundras is noteworthy. He wrote (in 1891): 'social status of the Pods is decidedly low. They will eat sweetmeats, drink and smoke with the fishing sub-castes of Bagdis, and these are ordinarily deemed to be nearly their equals in ranks. Brahmins and the members of the Nava Shakha groups will not take water from them' (Risley, 1981: 176).

The Brahmins and other upper castes (such as the Kayasthas and Baidyas) did not accept water and food from the people of these castes as they were considered polluted and *ajalchal* (Sanyal, 1981: 38) social groups, although most of them were the followers of Hinduism. They had no right to dine with the upper castes in public ceremonies. So, they were 'almost untouchables'.

Assertion for Self-identities: Caste Movement for Social Justice and Dignity

The introduction of the decennial census in 1871-72 gave an opportunity to the low caste communities of Bengal to correct their status in the given caste order. Method of social stratification of the colonial government on the basis of caste, race and religion instigated Indian caste communities (both lower caste and twice-born) to determine their caste status in the official records (Dirks, 2001: 198-227). The caste communities of our study claimed 'Kshatriya' (such as the Rajbangsi, Malo, Poundra, etc.) and a respectable Sudra (Namasudra) caste status in order to correct the injustice done to them. These demands were raised by the emerging middle class of these communities for attaining respect in the society by discarding traditional interpretation of the Hindu scriptures. This phenomenon can be interpreted as an attempt for establishing social rights of the marginal people.

***Kshatriyaisation* Movement in Bengal**

Most significant case of *kshatriyaisation* in colonial Bengal was the Rajbanshi caste movement which had started in 1891 when Mr F.A. Skyne, District Magistrate of Rangpur, issued an order to classify the Rajbanshis as 'Koch', in the census report.[2] The 'educated' and 'landed' middle class of the Rajbanshis were not prepared to accept this order considering the later as inferior. For a change of place in caste-roder they began to organise under the banner of their caste organisation called Rangpur Bratya Kshatriya Unnati Bidhayani Sabha (Singha, 1940: 8). Their social movement became stronger with the foundation of the Rajbanshi Kshatriya Samiti in 1910 in Rangpur under the leadership of Panchanan Barma (Sarkar), a lawyer by profession.[3] In order to popularise their Kshatriya identity, educated section of this community had popularised the view that Rajbanshis are the descendents of a Kshatriya ruler called Bardhan. *Rajbanshi Kulapradip* (1315 B.S. or 1908) of Hara Kishor Adhikary, *Rajbanshi Kula Kaumudi* of Jagamohan Singha (1913) and a few other writings published by the Rajbanshi scholars in the early twentieth century had constructed an imaginary Kshatriya lineage of the Rajbanshis of North Bengal and Lower Assam (Barman, 2004: 286). Their demand for Kshatriya caste identity status was eventually recognised by the colonial government in 1911. In 1913, the supporters of the movement gathered at Deviganj of Jalpaiguri district and declared themselves as *Kshatriya* in the public.

Like the *kshatriyaisation* of the Rajbanshis, the Malos and Poundras had also attempted to construct their Kshatriya identity by composing self-history. The Pods began to identify themselves as Pundarika, Padmaraja, Punro, Poundra or as Pundari. *Jati Chandrika* (1893) and *Bratya Kshatriya Parichay* (1893) of Srimanta Naskar (Naskar, 2012: 39-111), *Jatibibek* (1893) of Beni Madhab Halder (Naskar, 2012: 117-227) and so on had constructed an imaginary Kshatriya identity of the Poundras. Their caste organisations like Poundra Conference (1891), Bratya Kshatriya Samiti (1909) and so on were eventually transformed into the Sarba Banga Poundra Kshatriya Samiti in 1917 under the leadership of Raicharan Sardar, Anukul Chandra Naskar, Jay Krishna Mandal, Mahendra Nath Karan and a few other enlightened persons of this community. Anukul Chandra Naskar, being the secretary of the organisation, had placed a demand to W.H. Thomson, the Superintendent of Census, to declare the Poundras as a Kshatriya caste. Thomson wrote (on 17th January, 1921) that 'I have no objection to the use of the word Poundra in place of Pod.'

Similarly the caste organisation of the Malos called 'Jhal Mal Bandhav' or Bratya Kshatriya Samiti was founded under the leadership of its landed and educated Middle Class. Brajanath Das, Ananta Chandra Das, Kripanath Das, Uddhav Chandra Malla Barman (Pabna), Jatindra Mohun Das (Maimansingh), Sashi Bhusan Das Ray, Suresh Chandra Barman and Dinanath Talukdar had contributed significantly to the *kshatriyaisation* movement of the Malos. This organisation had attempted to prove that the Malos are the descendents of the Kshatriyas of north-western India who lost their Kshatriya identity after their migration to Bengal. This fictious Kshatriya identity was strengthened among the Malos through the composition and circulation of their self-history such as *Dwitiya Varna Kshatriya* (Maimansingh, 1923) and *Sanschipta Kshatriya Tatta* (Dacca, 1923) of Mahendra Nath Malla Barman, *Jalla Malla Kshatriya Itihas* of Brajanath Das (Bagura), *Jyoti* of Shashi Bhusan Das Ray (Dacca) and *Sanschipta Jalla Malla Kshatriya Tatta* (Dacca) of Dharma Chand Malla Barman, (Barman, 2012: 77-78) and so on.

These Kshatriya aspirants of Bengal had acquired prescriptions of the Brahmins by paying suitable honouriam (Ray, 1389) to achieve their goal of respectable social status within the caste structure. With these prescriptions they held sacred thread (*paita*) what was considered as a symbol of standardisation of their caste status. The Rajbanshis, Poundras and Malos along with *paita* had also adopted Kshatriya like surnames such as Barman, Singha Das Barman, and Barma. Instead of observation of thirty days *ashouch* (ritual pollution after death) they introduced the customs of thirteen days (Barman, 2006: 35-36). However, they had given maximum emphasis on the spread of education among their people in order to share the available opportunities in government jobs and other respectable white colour professions.

From Chandals to Namasudras

Social movement of the Chandals had started in 1872 when the Kayasthyas (an upper caste Hindu community) refused to dine in a house of the Chandal headman of Faridpur who invited them in a *sraddha* (after death purification) ceremony. Even they instigated other upper castes of the locality for refusing that invitation (Bandyopadhaya, 1997:34). This humiliation had instigated the Chandals to take some immediate steps. In a meeting held in 1872, they took a few resolutions, like, (i) women must in future not visit *haats*, (ii) service of no kind whatsoever be taken from other castes, (iii) food prepared by all other Hindu castes (other than the Brahmins) was not to be partaken of (Bandyopadhaya, 1997: 34). They refused to work in the fields of upper castes or to serve the upper caste Hindus. It eventually transformed into an organised strike as a protest against the inhuman social injustice in Faridpur-Bakharganj region of Eastern Bengal. It was a movement for human dignity. It shows the structural integrity of the Chandals which was reinforced by the charismatic leadership of Harichand Thakur (1812-1878), the founder of the Matua sect.

Mukhe naam hate kaam (work and worship) was the motto of the Matuas. Harichand, rather than enforcing any formal religious culture had stressed on hard work, earning wealth and government jobs, formation of organisations and social unity. After Harichand's death, his son Guruchand Thakur took over the leadership of the Matua sect. The Matua was gradually developed as a popular sect guided by Guruchand and later by his successors.

Most significant feature of social reforms of Guruchand was the spread of education among the Chandals. He stated: 'I will not be worried whether you eat or fast, but I want your children to be educated first.' He was in firm belief that 'without education the lower castes cannot be a part of administration'. He was so passionate that he founded around 1800 schools (Roy, 2007: 41). Growth of education among the followers of Matua was proved positive in the later years in securing a greater share jobs and political power under the colonial rule.

In the meantime, the Chandals had declared themselves as Namasudra. In 1891 Risley wrote: 'in the Pirozpur thana of Bhakharganj the Chandals have recently started a combined movement to call themselves Namas, to wear shoes and not to take rice from Kayasthas or Sudras' (Risley, 1981: 176).

The mouthpiece of the Chandals called *Namasudra Surhid* and the organisation called Namasudra Samiti (1905) had spread the messages of caste feelings. Ultimately, the Chandals were recognised by the British Government as Namasudras in 1911. The Namasudras further claimed the Brahmin status called *Namabrahman* (Mitra, 1953:31).

Caste Consciousness and Politics of Late Colonial Bengal

Caste consciousness for the construction of standard of caste identity for attaining social justice was not confined within the limit of caste hierarchy. The Namasudras, Rajbanshis, Poundras and Malos along with other Depressed Caste communities of Bengal had directed their caste consciousness to share political power by participating in electoral politics under the colonial rule particularly after the adoption of the *Government of India Act (1919)*. On the basis of the *Government of India Act 1919* the first provincial election was held in 1921. The caste organisations of the Namasudras, Rajbanshis and Poundras had encouraged their leaders to contest the election in the non-Muhamedan constituencies (i.e., general seats). Here we may mention the name of Panchanan Barma and Jogesh Chandra Sarkar (from Rangpur, Rajbangsi Kshatriya Samiti), Jogendra Krishma Roy (from Faridpur South, Namasudra), and Hem Chandra Naskar (Poundra, from 24 Parganas Rural Central) who got elected to the Bengal Legislative Council. Bishmadev Das, a Namasudra lawyer, was nominated to the Council as a 'Depressed Caste nominated member' (Banerjee, 1990: 588-89). In the election of the second (1924-26), third (1926-29) and fourth (1929-36) council, the Depressed Caste leaders had maintained their victory.

In the meantime, appointment of Simon Commission (1927), Round Table Conferences (1930-32) and Poona Pact (1932) had prepared the background of the adoption of the *Government of India Act (1935)*. Under this Act, the first election was held in 1937, where the Depressed Castes (who now began to be called as Scheduled Castes) had participated under the banner of their respective caste organisations. Result of this election was very much significant. The Congress appeared as largest political unit having 54 members in the assembly while the KPP (Krishak Praja Party) and the Muslim League (ML) own 38 and 40 seats respectively (Banerjee 1990: 532; Chattopadhyaya, 1984: 145). Besides 30 reserved seats, the Scheduled Caste candidates had won two general seats (one Congress and one Independent). In such a situation, Fazlul Huq of KPP together with the ML and a number of independent (including Scheduled Caste) members had formed the coalition ministry in Bengal with 11 members. Here two ministers were chosen from amongst the Scheduled Caste members.[4]

The Independent Scheduled Caste MLAs, however, were united under the banner of the newly formed the Independent Scheduled Caste Party (ISCP, 1938) with Hem Chandra Nasker (of Poundra Caste) as its President and

Jogendra Nath Mandal (of Namasudra Caste) as secretary. Upendra Nath Barman (of Rajbangsi Caste) was the leader of ISCP in the Assembly (Barman, 2008: 80).

The Government headed by Fazlul Huq had to go through a critical period because of ideological differences, individual ambition, shifting loyalties and interplay of British imperial interests. Conflicts of interest between the KPP and the ML had compelled Fazlul Haque to resign from the ministry in 1941. Huq, however, had managed to form the Progressive Coalition Ministry in 1941 with the support of the Forward Block-led Congress (28), Nationalists (14), KPP-Shamsuddin (19), ISCP (12), KPP-Huq (42), Anglo-Indians (3) and Labour (1) (Chattopadhyaya 1984: 172). In this ministry, the Scheduled Caste members had occupied an important position. Upendra Nath Barman was entrusted the charge of the Department of Forest and Excise which was earlier held by Mr Prasanna Dev Raikat (Banerjee, 1990: 566). Khwaja Nazimmuddin with 43 Muslim League members became the opposition leader in the Assembly.

The Progressive Coalition Ministry did not last long. Resignation of S.P. Mookherjee (20th November, 1942) (Banerjee, 1990:566) from the cabinet, failure of the Cripps Mission (1942), Quit India movement (1942), formation of the *Jatiya Sarkar* (national government) in Tamluk (Midnapur district), outbreak of famine in 1943, shortage of food and irregularity in food supply and so on had worsen the political situation of Bengal. In such a situation, Fazlul Huq resigned from the post (28th March, 1943) (Banerjee, 1990: 566). Khwaja Nazimuddin of Muslim League (as Chief Minister) now formed the ministry of 13 members with the support of Bengal Swarajya Party, ISCP, Europeans, Anglo-Indians, Indian Christians, Labour Party and the independents (Banerjee, 1990: 566). Progressive Party, KPP, Nationalists, Congress (Official and Bose Group) one Indian Christian and eight SC members totaling 108 constituted the opposition in the Assembly. In this ministry the Scheduled Castes held three ministries which were highest in terms of presence of the SCs in the Government in pre-partition Bengal (Banerjee, 1990: 566). But the Ministry of Nazimuddin fell on 28 March 1945 (Chattopadhyaya, 1984: 196).

In the general election of 1946 the Muslim League got an overwhelming victory in Bengal. Out of 117 Mohammedan seats, the League won 114 seats and got the support of two independent Muslim members. Congress won 86 seats. KPP won only four seats while the Communists entered into the Legislative Assembly winning three seats. Result of the Scheduled Caste organisations like the All India Scheduled Caste Federation (AISCF), the Rajbangsi Kshatriya Samiti and Poundra Kshatriya Samiti was deplorable, although Jogendra Nath Mondal from AISCF and Nagendra Nath Ray from the Rajbangsi Kshatriya Samiti had own (Banerjee, 1990: 568-569). Most of the Scheduled Caste candidates contested under the banner of their caste organisations were defeated. Congress alone got 26 out of 30 reserved seats. It indicates that the Scheduled Caste on the eve of the partition of Bengal began to be controlled by the nationalist organisation like the Congress. This trend may be interpreted as 'a shift of attitudes of the Scheduled Castes of Bengal from caste-based politics to the nationalist politics.'

On 23rd April, 1946, the Muslim League Ministry was formed in Bengal with very minor Hindu support. Initially (23rd April to 15th October) Suhrawardy appointed seven ministers in his Government including one member from the Scheduled Caste community (Chattopadhyaya, 1984: 196). Suhrawardy, as the premier, had to work in a very critical situation when demand for Pakistan, communal tension, violence, *tebhaga* movement (1946), and other political developments had engulfed entire Bengal. The only way for the Government to turn down the violence was to get the League in the Interim Government where the Congress had already entered. On 13th October, 1946, M.A. Jinnah, the supremo of the ML, had decided to enter into the interim government. Jogendra Nath Mondal had joined the Interim Government as Muslim League representative (Singh, 1987: 195).

In such a background, the British Prime Minster Clemet Attlee (1945-47) had announced on 20th February, 1947 that His Majesty's Government's definite intention is to take the necessary steps to effect the transfer of power into responsible Indian hands by a date not later than June 1948. It clearly hinted at the possibility of partition (Singh, 1987: 214-215). The Congress Working Committee had welcomed Attlee's announcement, i.e., transfer of power to the Indians even at the cost of division of India. Later the Congress and the League, Hindu Mahasabha, and the Communists had accepted the 3rd June, 1947 Plan of Mountbatten (or Mountbatten Plan) for partition of India into India and Pakistan.

In such a situation, a few prominent Scheduled Caste leaders of Bengal realised that the Scheduled Castes as a whole would be in a great danger in the divided Bengal. The Working Committee of the Bengal Scheduled Caste Federation under the leadership of Jogendra Nath Mondal had resolved on 14th May, 1947 that 'the division of the province into Hindu and Muslim Bengal ... (was) no solution of the communal problems. It would halt the growing political consciousness and ruthlessly crush the solidarity of the Scheduled Castes of Bengal... While the Scheduled Caste of Eastern Bengal would be at the mercy of the majority community, the Scheduled Caste of Western Bengal would be subject of perpetual slavery of the caste Hindus' (Bondyopadhaya, 1998). Jogendra Nath Mondal, together with some Scheduled Caste leaders of the Rajbanshis, had come forward with a proposal for the formation of a separate homeland (called Rajasthan) for the Scheduled Caste of Bengal as an alternative (Pakrasi, 1971: 9). But the Scheduled Castes of Bengal were neither homogeneous nor politically a unified social group where Jogendra Nath and his supporters had supreme control. It has already been mentioned that most of Scheduled Caste MLAs were elected as nominees of the Congress which strongly supported the idea of partition of Bengal. Thus, the Scheduled Caste Congress

MLAs of Bengal had no hesitation to accept the partition. But the non-Congress Scheduled Caste MLAs had reservation about the partition. They always remained by the side of the Muslim League. One communist SC MLA, Rup Narayan Roy, did not vote (Pakrasi, 1971: 9). Finally, the *Indian Independence Act* was ratified on 18th July 1947 in the British Parliament and Bengal and Punjab were partitioned on 15th August 1947 to form independent India and Pakistan.

Post-Colonial Experience

With the partition of India, ethnic consciousness of the Scheduled Castes of Bengal took a new turn. Huge migration of the Malos, Namasudras and Rajbanshis, (along with other minorities) from East Bengal to West Bengal and other provinces of India had contributed to change the nature of ethnicity of these castes in Post-colonial context. 'Ethnic consciousnesses' of these castes found expression in four distinct ethnic movements, which I will discuss in the following section.

Rajbanshi Linguistic Identity and the Demand for Separate State: Partition of Bengal in 1947 appeared as a challenge for caste-based identity politics of the Rajbanshis because of their scattered distribution in East Pakistan, West Bengal, Bihar and Assam. The *Rajbanshi Kshatriya Samiti* with its head office at Rangpur (East Pakistan) lost its social influence over the Rajbanshi population of India. Local committees (*mandals*) of this Samiti began to react locally to face the new political situation. A new branch of the Kshatriya Samiti was opened on 8 November, 1962 at Dinhata called Rajbanshi Kshatriya Samiti, which emerged as a central organisation of the Rajbanshis of North Bengal (Barman, 1985: 47). It had deep sympathy for the socioeconomic and cultural development of the Rajbanshis including the formation of a linguistic state for them.[5] But the Bangiya Rajbanshi Kshatriya Samiti, cantered in Calcutta, was thinking about the development of the Rajbanshis in terms of class and political achievements.[6] Condition of the Rajbanshis of Assam was more critical since they did not accept SC status in 1936. They were declared as OBC (Other Backward Classes) in 1953. The Rajbanshis of Goalpara again were given a new name called More Other Backward Class (MOBC) (Datta, 1978: 31). So, there is no common status of the Rajbanshis in postcolonial India.

However, the postcolonial concept of 'Rajbanshi' (Koch-Rajbanshi/ Kamtapuri) has a larger connotation than that of 'Rajbanshi caste'. In its present connotation, the term Rajbanshi includes all indigenous people who have adopted Rajbanshi/Kamtapuri dialect/language as their *lingua franca* including the Rajbanshis, Koches, Paliyas, local Muslims (Nashya Shaikhs) and other tribal and non-tribal people of North Bengal and Northeast India. So the socio-political organisations founded by the Rajbanshis of North Bengal and Assam have categorically classified the Rajbanshis as a composition of 'all Rajbanshis, Koch, Mech, etc., listed as Scheduled Castes and Tribes in the

Constitution (SC and ST) Order of 1950; local Muslims and bonafide refugees entering the region' (*Maynaguri Declaration* of the *Bharatiya Kamata Rajya Parishad, Circular No.KRP/ dated 8th August, 1986*). It is now more a 'linguistic community' than a 'caste community'.

'Linguistic consciousness' of the Rajbanshis was stimulated in the 1950s with the formation of Andhra State in 1953 and the creation of the State Reorganisation Commission (1956). To give an illustration the Siliguri Zonal Rajbangsi Kshatriya Samiti (SZRKS) strongly supported reorganisation of Indian states along linguistic line. It demanded (in 1955) the merger of Purnea district of Bihar and Goalpara district of Assam (where the Rajbanshis have significant concentration as a linguistic community) to West Bengal on the linguistic ground.

Linguistic issue of the Rajbanshis was again raised in the 1960s by a few middleclass intellectuals. Sri Kalindra Nath Barman, a Rajbangsi social activist and poet (and founder of the Uttar Khanda Dal, 1969) brought the linguistic distinctiveness of the Rajbanshis to the fore in 1965. He argued that the language spoken by the Rajbanshis is distinct and deserves to have a distinctive identity with a separate state. Creation of Punjab and Hariyana in 1966 on linguistic ground had added strength to the linguistic identity of the Rajbanshis. Since 1966, they have founded several political organisations to utilise 'linguistic consciousness' of the Rajbanshis for collective action for the formation of separate state in North Bengal called Kamtapur. Among such organisations, mention may be made of Kamtapur Rajjya Sangram Parishad (1967), Uttar Khanda Dal (1969), Koch-Rajbangsi International (1984), Uttar Banga Gana Parishad, Kamtapur Peoples' Party (1995), Greater Cooch Behar Peoples' Association (1998) and so on, which have given maximum priority to the linguistic identity of the Rajbanshis as the foundation of state-hood movement in North Bengal. Statehood demand of the Rajbanshis has also categorically raised the question of economic and political subordination and cultural decline of the Rajbanshis along with the consequences of partition of Bengal (1947) and regional backwardness of North Bengal. It is interesting to note that this development has pushed the earlier 'caste consciousness' of the Rajbanshis to the back seat.

The Malo and Fishermen Movement: Being a smaller community, the Malos had only two MLAs in Bengal before the partition. But after the partition they lost all political representatives. However, the Malos and fishermen sections of the Poundras, Namasudras and Rajbanshis had received the partition in positive way. The East Bengali fishermen, after their migration to West Bengal, were looking for shelter in the river banks or even on the river beds. But their resettlement was not an easy task because of two major problems. First problem was the abnormal growth of fishermen population, i.e., engagement of more people in same source of income and secondly, all existing fisheries of West Bengal were not fit for fish production.

However, the fishermen tried their best to survive by their own efforts although in the initial stage some fishermen families got assistance from the government as 'camp- refugees'. The fishermen communities had taken some steps for forming cooperative societies as a practical tool for struggle for survival in post-partition West Bengal. Long tradition of 'co-operative type of production system' in fishing helped formation of fishermen co-operative societies (FCS) with modern concept.[7] We can get an idea about the efforts of the refugee fishermen from the very name of fishermen cooperative societies, such as, Falta Refugee FCS Ltd (24 Parganas), Chandannagore Bastuhara FCS Ltd., Rabindra Nagar Refugee FCS Ltd. (Hooghly), Raghunathpur Refugee FCS Ltd. (Hooghly), Kashiganj Bastuhara FCS Ltd., (Jiaganj), Jalpaiguri Refugee FCS Ltd. (Jalpaiguri), Kayakata Barman Colony FCS Ltd. (Jalpaiguri), Nirmala Colony FCS Ltd. (Cooch Behar), Media Government Colony Refugee FCS Ltd., (24 Parganas), Adi Saptagram Gar Colony FCS Ltd. (Hooghly) and so on. Struggle of the fishermen got a new dimension when 100 representatives of fishermen communities from eight districts of West Bengal met in a convention at Dumdum (Calcutta) in 1968 to form a state level organisation called the West Bengal Fishermen Conference (WBFC or *Paschim Banga Matsyajibi Samiti*) (*Bhagirathi,* 1969: 5). Under the leadership of the educated section of the Malos the WBFC got its final shape in 1969 in its first conference held in Calcutta (7-8 June) which had the following objectives:

(1) upliftment of lives, livelihood and economic status of the fishermen; (2) development of the water bodies and introduction of modern and scientific pisciculture in West Bengal to mitigate the fish crisis by increasing fish production; (3) upliftment of social and cultural status of the fishermen by spreading education and literacy campaign; (4) attainment and enjoyment of social justice and political right of the fishermen by uniting them; (5) to arouse the self-consciousness, social cohesiveness and fellow feelings among the fishermen communities; (6) establishment of financial organisation to assist the needy fishermen; (7) to make adequate employment of the unemployed and jobless fishermen; (8) to assist the brilliant but poor students of the fishermen communities to pursue their higher studies; (9) to highlight the contribution of the intellectuals, poets, laureates, educationists and artists of the fishermen communities in the Bengali literature and culture; and (10) to organise the cooperative movement by organising primary (local), secondary (district) and central (state) level cooperatives for production and proper distribution of fish (Paschim Banga Matsyajibi Samiti, 1969).

Throughout the 1970s and 1980s, the WBFC had agitated for the development of the fishermen through proper management of water resources of West Bengal. The WBFC had also pressed the demand for abolition of tank fishery provision of the *Estate Acquisition Act* (1953) what allowed the landholders to retain their possession over the big fisheries. This demand was particularly directed against the interest of the feudal class.

The second demand of the WBFC was more radical. It raised the slogan '*jal jar jala tar*', i.e., fisheries for fishermen. It can be compared with the popular slogan like 'land for the tillers' (*langal jar jami tar*). The WBFC had also mobilised the fishermen for abolition of toll tax (including *khutigary* tax) in Sundarban area, ban on the use of harmful pesticides, distribution of the technology of scientific pisciculture to the fishermen, and proper rehabilitation of the refugee fishermen in West Bengal. From all their efforts it appears that the fishermen of West Bengal were more concerned about their professional and class interests rather than their caste status as was evident in the *kshatriyaisation* movement of the Rajbanshis and other lowly ranked castes in the colonial period.

The Poundras: Towards Indigenous Identity: The Poundras, after the partition, were in dilemma. Since they had main concentration in 24 Parganas before the partition, the Poundras were considered to be lesser sufferers than other three caste communities. So the caste organisation of the Poundras had continued caste movement for a decade after the partition. The main outcome of movement of the Poundras was their recognition as Poundras instead of Pod. Under the *Scheduled Caste and Scheduled Tribe Modified Order (1956)* the demands of the Pods as Poundra got government recognition thanks to the efforts of Shri Sakti Sarkar, a Poundra MP. However, from the 1950s the Poundras of South West Bengal, more precisely of 24 Parganas, were divided along political lines as they became associated with political parties like Congress, Janata Party, CPI, CPI (M), RSP, and SUCI. Political disunity had its toll on the caste consciousness and caste unity of the Poundras. Caste consciousness thus became less effective in electoral politics at least among the Poundras. However, the Poundras founded a few new social organisations, namely, Poundra Kshatriya Unnayan Parishad (1970), Bharatiya Poundra Society (2003) and Poundra Mahasangha (2008) in the post-colonial context. All these organisations of the Poundras have rejected the 'fictitious Aryan Kshatriya origin' claim of their caste leaders in the colonial period. They now give more emphasis on the indigenous identity, especially on 'pre Hindu Buddhist identity' (Naskar and Halder, 2013). So instead of Kshatriya identity, the Poundras feel proud to be considered indigenous people of Bengal and as Scheduled Caste(Naskar, 2013; Haldar, 2013).

The Namasudras: From Caste to Sect: Post-colonial transition of ethnic consciousness of the Namasudra was quite different from that of other three castes. The Namasudras did not migrate to India immediately after the partition. Their leader Jogendra Nath Mondal, a cabinet Minister of Pakistan, preferred to stay in East Bengal/East Pakistan. But communal tension, violence, insecurity and atrocities on the minorities (including the Namasudras) and resignation of Jogendra Nath (1950) had brought about change in community perception; the disillusioned the Namasudras felt insecure in East Pakistan and started migrating to India. The political leaders of the Namasudras also migrated to West Bengal. The Namasudras along with the members of other minority communities migrated to the border districts of West Bengal, Assam and Tripura. The Namasudra peasants were also deported to Andaman and Nicobar Islands. Uttar Pradesh, Bihar, Orissa and Dandakaranya (Chhattisgarh) had also received the Namasudra (and Poundra) refugees in their settlement colonies and rehabilitation sites. Such widespread migration of the Namasudras in the post-partition period had weakened their caste based ethnic feeling.

Till 1956, the Namasudras had a few representatives in the Legislative Assembly of East Bengal. With the transition East Bengal into East Pakistan the Namasudras were transformed into a minority community in East Pakistan/Bangladesh and lost much of their political significance. With their large-scale migration to India and overwhelming concentration in 24 Paraganas district of West Bengal the foci of their movement had shifted to Thakurnagar (24 Parganas) under the leadership of P.R. Thakur (grandson of Guruchand).

Since 1952, the Namasudras have contested in different SC reserved constituencies of Legislative Assembly of West Bengal and Tripura and in Parliamentary seats. P.R. Thakur and Apurbalal Majumdar (as Congress), Charumihir Sarkar (Left), along with several others have played significant part in the politics of West Bengal. The fact of Jogendra Nath Mondal contesting election in 1967 with the left support motivated the Namasudras to join left political parties in West Bengal in large numbers. The Namasudras had established themselves as a strong political force in certain constituencies during the rule of Left Front Government in West Bengal (1977-2011). Simultaneously anti-left political forces of West Bengal and the BSP have also prepared their support base among the Namasudras in the recent years (Aikatan, 2011; Namasudra Mahasammellan, 2004).

Despite disunity and fragmentation in terms of political stands the Namasudras never forget their caste and Matua identity. With head quarters at Thakurnagar, the Matua Mahasangha works as a symbol of unity of the community and sustains the Matua ethnic identity. For its organisational acumen the Matua Mahasangha has brought all political parties of West Bengal to its feet; it has the power to negotiate with the political parties and set terms for extending its support (Aikatan, 211).

Conclusion

Social movement for formation of identity of the scheduled caste communities of Bengal had manifold dimensions. Firstly, the early social reform movements, which together can be termed *kshatriyaisation* movements, which claimed higher status in the Hindu caste hierarchy, were the by-product of the 'divide and rule' policy of the colonial rulers. The movements, however, did not challenge the Brahminic hegemony over the social order. Secondly, leadership of these social movements, with the exception of the Namasudra movement, remained in the hands of the educated and landed middleclass. The Namasudra movement till 1937 was controlled from the rural base while in other cases urban areas such as Calcutta, Dacca, Mymansinga, Rangpur, Diamond Harbour and so on were the epicentres of the movements. Thirdly, social reforms had reinforced the occupational mobility what contributed to the emergence of a 'lower caste middle class'. Fourthly, the social movement had generated self-respect among the caste groups of present study what eventually became an integral part of colonial politics and administration of Bengal. The Scheduled leaders had always been a part of the government led by the KPP and Muslim League. However, on the eve of the partition the people belonging to Scheduled Castes began to consider themselves as the essential part of nationalist (Congress) and class (Communist) based politics. In this process they lost their distinct political identity when they got politically fragmented and accepted the decision of partition of Bengal.

In the post-colonial scenario, the major scheduled castes of Bengal gave up much of their movements for social reforms and elevation of caste status as they took part in post-colonial democratic polity and nation building. In the new scenario, the Rajbanshis became interested in mobilising themselves not in the name of caste but more as an ethnic group in the mould of a cultural-linguistic group demanding a separate identity and a 'political place', a separate state in North Bengal. One can notice here the conflict between the nationalist-integrationist agenda of the government and aspirations of the marginalised ethnic feelings of the Rajbanshis. The fishermen section of the Malos, Poundras, Namasudras and the Rajbanshis of southern Bengal, being threatened by the water management policy of the government, have raised a slogan like 'fisheries for fishermen' (*jal jar jala tar*) instead of caste based social movement. However, all these castes have been divided in terms of their fragmented political support and allegiance and this has left a negative impact on their caste unity or solidarity. Despite constituting one-fourth of the state population, the Scheduled Castes collectively do not have a political organisation or party, they do not constitute a strong political force in West Bengal. However, in the recent years, the Matua Mahasangha of the Namasudras has emerged as some kind of a united force which is in position to bargain with the major political forces on issues of caste/community interest.

Notes

1. The *mangala* literature, particularly *Manasa Mangala, Annada Managa, Chandi Mangala* and *Gosani Mangala* composed in the late medieval Bengal, eulogised the worshiping of certain folk female deities by then trading and the ruling communities of Bengal, and also highlighted the socio-economic condition of the traditional fishermen communities of the region. The *charitas* or biographies of the Vaishanava saints of the late medieval period, particularly the biographies of Sankardeva and his

disciples, have vividly illustrated the lives of the lowers castes of Bengal and Lower Assam.

2. The Koches were the ruling community of Cooch Behar State. They had established a kingdom in the beginning of the sixteenth century (for more details see Barman 2007).
3. Gobinda Mohan Sarkar, Organising Secretary of the Samiti, Sri Madhusudhan Ray, a Lawyer of Jalpaiguri and the first president of the Samiti, Sri Kamini Kumar Singha Ray, *zamindar* of Dimla, Sri Harikishor Barma, zamindar of Simulbari, and many other Rajbanshi *zamindars* and intellectuals had actively collaborated with Panchanan Barma in founding the Rajbangsi Kshatriya Samiti.
4. Sri Prasanna Dev Raikat (of Jalpaiguri-cum-Siliguri constituency) was entrusted with the charge of the Department of Excise and Forests while Sri Mukunda Bihari Mullick of (Khulna) was given the charge of the Cooperative, Credit and Rural Indebtedness ministry.
5. Siliguri Anchalik (Zonal) Kshatriya Samiti in its First Annual Conference held on 8th April, 1955, supported the formation of linguistic state in India and stressed on the continuity of reservation policy for the Rajbanshis and implementation of reservations in the semi-government organisations. See resolutions passed in the First Annual Conference of the Siliguri Anchalik (zonal) Kshatriya Samiti in its First Annual Conference held at Haidarpara, Distt. Jalpaiguri.
6. Bangiya Rajbanshi Kshatriya Samiti was founded in 1943 in Calcutta and got registered in 1944 (See *Annual Report of the Bangiya Rajbanshi Kshatriya Samiti* 1986).
7. For more details see Barman, 2008.

References

Aikatan Sambad Patra, 4th Cultural News Issue. (April, 2011).

Azam, Kouser J., (ed.) 2001. *Ethnicity, Identity and the State in South Asia.* New Delhi: South Asian Publishers.

Bhagirathi 1 (1), 8th May, 1969.

Bandyopadhaya, Sekhar, 1997. *Caste, Protest and Identity in Colonial Bengal: The Namasudras of Bengal 1872-1947.* Surrey: Curzon Press.

Bandyopadhaya, Sekhar, 1998. *Changing Border, Shifting Loyalties: Religion, Caste and Partition of Bengal in 1947.* Asian Studies Institute Working Paper 2, Victoria University of Wellington.

Banerjee, Dilip, 1990. *Election Recorder.* Calcutta: Book Front Publication Forum.

Barman, Upendra Nath, 1985. *Sekaler Uttar Bangla O Amar Jiban Smriti*. Jalpaiguri.

Barman, Rup Kumar, 2004. '*Jati Parichiti Gathan, Uttarn O Elite Netrittya'* (in Bengali), in *Itihas Anusandhan 18*, Kolkata, West Bengal History Council.

Barman, Rup Kumar, 2012. *Partition of India and Its impact on the Scheduled Castes of Bengal.* New Delhi: Abhijeet Publications.

Barman, Rup Kumar, 2006. Malo Samjer Atma Chetana O Adwaita Malla Barman (Bengali), in Haldar, Susanta (ed.): *Bhasaman 8*, Kolkata, Adwaita Malla Barman Educational and Cultural Society.

Barman, Rup Kumar, *2008*. 'Caste and Class Awareness among the Dalits', *Voice of Dalits, Vol. 1, No. 1 (Jan-June)*.

Barth, Fredrik, 1969. *Ethnic Groups and Boundaries: The Social Organisation of Culture Difference*. Boston: Little, Brown and Co.

Brass, Paul, 1991. *Ethnicity and Nationalism, Theory and Conceptio*. New Delhi: Sage.

Chattopadhyaya, Gautam, 1984. *Bengal Electoral Politics and Freedom Struggle 1862-1947*. Delhi: Indian Historical Studies.

*Constitution of the Paschim Banga Matsyajibi Samit*i, 1969, Calcutta, Paschim Banga Matsyajibi Samiti.

Datta, P.S., 1978. 'Movement for Scheduled Status in a Poly-ethnic Society: The Case of the Koch-Rajbangsi's of Assam', *Journal of North East India Council for Social Science Research* II. (11).

Dirks, Nicholas B., 2001. *Castes of Mind: Colonialism and the Making of Modern India.* Delhi: Permanent Black.

Haldar, Benimadhav, 1983. *Jati Bibek.* Rangilabad.

Haldar, Megnath, 2013. Interview, Sonarpur, 26th June.

Hunter, W.W., 1984. *Statistical Accounts of Bengal.* Delhi.

Mitra, A.K., 1953. *The Tribes and Castes of West Bengal.* Alipore: West Bengal Government Press.

Martin, Montgomery, 1976. *The History, Antiquities, Topography and Statistics of Eastern India* (Vol. V). New Delhi: Cosmo Publications.

Maynaguri Declaration of the *Bharatiya Kamata Rajya Parishad*, *Circular No. KRP/dated* 8th *August, 1986.*

Namasudra Mahasammellan, 2004 (5-7 November).

Naskar, Dhurjati, 2013. Interview, Dakshin Barasat, 23rd June.

Naskar, Srimanata, 1887. 'Jati Chandrika', in Sanat Kmar Naskar *et. al.* (reprint. 2012), *Poundra Manisha*. Kolkata: Poundra Mahasangha.

Pakrasi, Kanti B., 1971. *The Uprooted: A Sociological Study of the Refugees of West Bengal, India.* Calcutta: Editions Indian.

Phadnish, Urmila, 1995. *Ethnicity and Nation Building in South Asia.* New Delhi: Sage.

Ray, Kunjabihari, 1389. *Rajbanshi Kshatriya Samitir Karyabibarani.* Jalpaiguri: Panchanan Smarak Samiti.

Risley, H.H., 1981. *Tribes and Castes of Bengal*. Calcutta: KLM Pvt. Ltd.

Sanyal, Hites Ranjan, 1981. *Social Mobility in Bengal.* Calcutta: Papyrus.

Singha, Kshetra Nath, 1940. *Ray Saheb Panchanan Barmar Jibani Ba Rangpur Kshatriya Samitir Itihas*. Rangpur.

Singh, Anita Inder, 1987. *The Origins of the Partition of India, 1936*-1947. Delhi: Oxford University Press.

Sinha Roy, Kalyan, 2007. 'Hari Buddha and the Namasudra Movement in Bengal', in Biswajit Chatterjee and Debi Chatterjee (eds.), *Dalit Lives and Dalit Visions in Eastern India*. Kolkata: Centre for Rural Resources.

Shills, David L. (ed.), 1968. *Encyclopaedia of Social Science* (Vol. 5). The Macmillan Co. and Free Press.

Tarkaratna, Panchanan, (ed.) 1314. *Brihaddharmma Purana.* Calcutta: Bangabasi Electro-machine Press, Part III, Chapter 13, pp. 29-56.

William, Raymond, 1976. *Keywords: A Vocabulary of Culture and Society*. London: Flamingo.

6

Protest and Power: The Matua *Sampraday* of Bengal

Kanchan Mukhopadhyay

Consciousness and Ideology of Protest

It has generally been accepted that the dominant groups in a society do not exert their domination through political and economic tools only; ideological domination is exercised largely through cultural hegemony. The hegemony, however, is never absolute; the members of the mass often challenge the domination with alternative ideologies. The consciousness of the 'active man-in-the-mass' might not be ordered and clear enough to explain his practical activities, it can historically be in opposition to his activities. He can be described to carry two contradictory consciousnesses in him. One of it is contained in his activities that unite him with his fellow-workers in transforming the real world; the other one is superficially explicit or verbal, which he has been handed down by the past and which he has absorbed uncritically. It is to be noted that the verbal consciousness holds together a specific social group and governs the moral conduct and thought process of the people. At times, the contradiction between these two levels of consciousness can be so strong that it can produce a condition of 'moral and political passivity' (Gramsci, 1971:333).

Some examples of anti-hegemonic consciousness are found in the religious thoughts of the masses. In North India followers of the *saguni* tradition are generally devotees of Krishna and Rama, two avatars of Vishnu. The followers of *nirguni* tradition, on the other hand, do not worship any avatar or anthropomorphic form of God. In most parts of North India, *nirguni* remained a subordinate and minority tradition; the Kabir-panthis or the followers of Gorakh Nath were mostly the non-privileged masses (Lorenzen, 1995: 3, 13).

Followers of the Kartabhaja or the Sahebdhani *sampraday* of Bengal, who are mostly lay householders and apparently remain indistinguishable from others, create a 'congregational space defined outside the boundaries of the dominant religious life, outside caste society or the injunctions of the *shariat*, but a space brought into active existence only periodically at thinly attended weekly meetings with the *mahasay* or the *fakir*, and at the three or four annual large festivals where sectarians perform the prescribed duties of allegiance to their preceptor and their faith, while numerous others come just as they would to any religious fair. The doctrines preached by the sect leaders often in a language which conceals under its surface imagery and esoteric meaning open only to initiates, will talk of their rejection of the Vedas and of caste, of idolatry and sastric or shariati ritual, but the greater their reach across caste hierarchy, the less strident is their critical tone and the more vapid their sentiments about the sameness of all faiths' (Chatterjee, 1989:193).

Genesis of the Matua *Sampraday*

In fourteenth century, Vaisnavism took a different shape in Bengal when Shri Chaitanya re-interpreted its basic tenets to accommodate the socially downtrodden sections of the society, including the lowly-positioned castes and the women. As many of them were debarred from participating in orthodox Brahminical rituals, Shri Chaitanya asked the oppressed sections of the society to perform simpler rituals.

After death of Shri Chaitanya, the spirit of equality in religious practices preached by him became dilute, the high-caste disciples brought back certain features of the old caste order like caste distinction and elaborate rituals; such reforms distanced the subjugated people to a large extent. As a result of marginalisation of the low-caste devotees within the mainstream of Bengali Vaisnavism, many of them established their own orders. Such groups had large following among the lowly positioned castes and each such group claimed to adhere to the original message of Shri Chaitanya (Banerjee, 2002: 86-88). The heterogeneity among the Bengali Vaisnavites became so wide and unmanageable that a conference was convened at Kheturi in Rajshahi sometime between 1576 and 1582, which was attended by representatives of about hundred Vaisnava groups from different parts of Bengal. The conference attempted to bring all disparate groups under the ideological tenets of the high-caste Gosvamis, but failed to assimilate or integrate the diverse Sahajiya Vaisnava Sampraday into the Gaudiya mainstream (Chatterjee, 1989:187). By the seventeenth and eighteenth centuries the varied interpretations of Vaisnavism in Bengal gave rise to a diverse array of sects, mostly founded and followed by the 'depressed castes' among the Hindu and Muslim population of Bengal (Banerjee, 2002: 119).

It may be noted that the varying ideologies and practices found among the lowly-placed people were not always placed in opposition to the ideologies of the dominant; often popular interpretations borrowed ideas and practices from the high-caste people and mixed the same with opposing viewpoints. Following Gramsci such phenomenon can be described as subaltern consciousness composed of contradictory and opposed elements—one autonomous and the other borrowed (Chatterjee, 1989: 174).

The Matua *sampraday* came into existence among one of the lowly positioned social groups of Bengal, the Namasudra, in earlier parts of nineteenth century. This *sampraday* has been rooted in the alternative ideologies of Bengal Vaisnavism, but it borrowed a lot from the Gaudiya tradition as well. Matua is one such *sampraday* that shows all those features; while the beliefs and practices are positioned on the sub-stratum of Bengal Vaisnavism, it claims itself to be the true inheritor of Vaisnavism as propounded by Shri Chaitanya, it moved away from the post-Chaitanya Brahminical dominance by accepting certain important tenets of *nirguni* religions like denouncement of elaborate caste based rituals and idolatry.

The term *sampraday* has been used to describe the group for certain reasons. The term sect cannot be used to describe them because a sect is understood to be a sub-group within a larger religious group. In this case if the Hindus are the larger group, the Vaisnavites can be described as one sub-group under it. So it becomes difficult to describe each of the groups that have originated from the alternative ideologies of Bengal Vaisnavism as a sect. The term *sampraday* is more neutral in the sense that it does not essentially denote whether a group is the larger umbrella group or a sub-group under the larger one. It can denote any collectivity holding some common beliefs and having some common practices related to those shared beliefs.

To understand the Matua *sampraday*, it is necessary to know the social group of the Namasudra, as the *sampraday* had its root in and majority of the following among this group. It may be noted that the term Namasudra was not present in Bengali literature or vocabulary before the nineteenth century; till that time the people were referred to as the Chandal. In late nineteenth century, four exogamous groups were found among them, but in eastern Bengal, the area of their concentration, there was only one *gotra* group among them, the Kasyapa. Thus, the *gotra* had no function in regulating marriages. However, a number of sub-castes were present among them, which were formed mostly on basis of occupations they used to pursue. The Namasudras of eastern Bengal had several such groups, which were: (1) Halwai, the cultivators, (2) Ghasi, the grass cutters, (3) Kandho, the palanquin bearers, (4) Karral, the fishmongers, (5) Bari, the carpenters, (6) Berua, the fishermen, (7) Baqqal, the traders and hucksters, (8) Pod, who were numerous in Hughli and Jessore but not found in Dacca, practiced cultivation, pottery and fishing. The landed gentry also employed them as lathiyal or clubmen (Risley, 1891: 185-86).

The area of Namasudra concentration was the low-lying swamps of Eastern Bengal. In the late nineteenth century they were the single largest community in six districts, Bakarganj, Faridpur, Decca, Mymensingh, Jessore and Khulna. It may be noted that this was the core area for the Matua *sampraday* as well.

As the Namasudras had a large numerical presence in the area and as they had some economic solvency, thanks to their usufruct right over cultivable land, the oppressive nature of the caste system was not felt much by the people. In comparison, many other caste groups in other parts of the country, and the Teor, Bagdi, Muchi, Dom, Hadi, Bhuimali in Bengal, were placed much lower and treated as *asprisya* in real sense of the term (Bandyopadhyay, 1997: 15-16).

Harichand Thakur founded the Matua *sampraday*; he was born in 1811 or 1812 in a Namasudra family in Safaladanga village of Gopalganj subdivision, Faridpur district. This was a Vaisnavite family, his grandfather Mochanram was a pious man, he was known as Thakur (master) in his locality. The family was engaged in cultivation and small-scale trade. Harichand was known as a religious person in the area, he soon became famous in the adjacent villages for his religiosity and supernatural healing power. He had a large group of followers and spent more time in religious activities than in trade or cultivation. He had a self-revelation and came to know of himself as the incarnation of God with a mission to bring salvation to the downtrodden. All the previous avatars, including Shri Chaitanya, were born in high caste families; so they could not do enough for the low-caste people. Harichand started preaching a simple ritualistic doctrine of *bhakti*; he denounced all rituals and said that the only way to salvation is through devotion to god, faith in mankind and love for living creatures. The simplicity of the doctrine and the denouncement of elaborate Brahministic rituals in fact challenged the power structure existing at that point in time; by questioning the supremacy of the Brahmans the doctrine attracted a large following among the lower orders of the society in a short span of time. Devotees were convinced that Harichand could bring about dramatic changes in their life. A thorough dislike of the life the devotees were living pulled them towards the charisma that involved a 'social endowment of power'. Such power was demonstrated when Harichand punished the oppressive zamindar or the *naib* (agent) of the zamindar (Bandyopadhyay, 1997:35-36).

Though the overwhelming majority of the followers of Harichand Thakur were members of the Namasudra community, the Matua *sampraday* was never co-terminus with that community. People from other depressed sections of the

Hindu society, the Kapalis for example, joined the movement in considerable number. There were some devotees of Harichand from among the high caste Hindus and the Muslims as well.

After death of Harichand in 1878, the Matua *sampraday* expanded further under leadership of his son Guruchand. He modified the doctrines of the *sampraday* to make them suitable for the needs of an emerging lower caste peasant community. According to Guruchand, pursuit of spiritual abstractions and mystical devotion is not for the hungry and the poor, for them food was the supreme god. He asked his followers to earn money, be educated and become respectable. Similarly, the *sampraday* gave importance to *garhasthya dharma*, seeking salvation as a householder, and not to the life of ascetics or celibates. Women in Matua philosophy were regarded as equal partners in family life (Bandyopadhyay, 1997: 37, 42-3).

The Matua *sampraday* had its own way of organising the followers. All members of the *sampraday* could be divided into four categories, bhakta, sadhu, gosain and pagol. While the first kind of people was the commoners, the general devotees, people belonging to the latter three categories were the preachers and organisers. The organisational structure persists till date, albeit in an amorphous shape.

Among the preachers, the sadhus stay with the people like any other householder. A gosain, on the other hand, is different from laity; he is supposed to be more educated in the religious teachings and practices and is expected to preside over all religious and social occasions in bhakta households. A pagol is more advanced in religiosity and spirituality than the rest, so much so that he need not take part in any ritual or get involved in mundane affairs of life. All these preachers are endowed with power of miracle healing; while others require some materials to cure people, a pagol can do so by his words.

Social and Political Initiatives

The Namasudra followers of the Matua *sampraday* were opposed to the ideology of caste hierarchy but at the same time were trying to assert their position in the same hierarchy. Since long the Namasudras were emphasising their Brahman origin. They were performing *shraddha* or funeral ceremony on eleventh day of mourning, as is the practice among the Brahmans. Later some Namasudras started wearing sacred thread, adopted the practices of child marriage and widow celibacy and replaced bride price with dowry. Such a contradiction was possible because by late nineteenth century and early twentieth century the Namasudra community was not an assemblage of landless rural poor and small land-owning farmers any more, by that time some upwardly mobile individuals and families came in existence among the Namasudras, who had different interests, motives and aspirations from the peasants. While the ascending section of the community was more accommodative, the peasants were asking for an ideology of protest.

As the Matua *sampraday* had both the sections in it, the contradiction was obvious (Bandyopadhyay, 1997: 48-9).

The emphasis of the upwardly mobile section of the Namasudra community on raising the ritual status of the people soon shifted to more secular agenda, education and share of political power. It was realised that in a colonial situation status conferred by the *pundits* was not enough, the new role models were the high-caste urban educated elite. The Namasudra leaders were now discussing the evils of child marriage or were taking initiatives to get the young widows of the community get remarried. The most important programme for uplifting the community was not donning sacred thread, it was educating the people.

However, in spite of sustained efforts, much progress could not be made to educate the Namasudra community. It was believed that stiff competition offered by the better equipped higher castes was responsible for this slow progress. The elites felt that state intervention could help the community to counter the disadvantages. This attitude brought the Namasudra leaders closer to the colonial government and the Christian missionaries, the latter were perceived as representatives of the government. The same attitude furthered their distance from the nationalist movement led primarily by the high-caste Hindu *bhadralok*.

The people were trying since long to be recognised as Namasudra instead of the derogatory and abusive term Chandal; the government obliged by changing the nomenclature in the list of communities for census operations.

The Namasudras and the Muslims, representing two major communities of peasants in Eastern Bengal, opposed the *swadeshi* movement. They also disagreed with the nationalists, when the latter opposed the partition of Bengal in early twentieth century. The Matua leaders took the lead, they tried to keep the Namasudras away from the movement, and if necessary, to resist the movement actively in alliance with the Muslims. The nationalist political forces made several attempts to win the Namasudras over, but they had no political programme to address the issues the Namasudras were raising. When they could not persuade the Namasudras to support them, on many occasions they tried to coerce them.

In subsequent years, the Namasudras took more and more active part in institutional politics, though their basic stance towards the government and the nationalists remained the same. But it was not the Namasudras alone, depressed classes in other parts of the country were speaking in similar voice, it was only a matter of time when the Namasudras joined hands with them to find a much wider political platform. Though the Matua leaders of Orakandi were not much involved in such activities, they sometimes supported certain candidates contesting for posts of district unions. Such a process, however, created factions among leaders of the community (Bandyopadhyay, 1997: 110).

The Namasudras were probably the most politically active community in Bengal, they had five out of ten representatives in the Bengal Legislative Council in 1930; but they failed miserably on another count. The leaders of the community objected to extension of voting right to the women of the community; they were of the opinion that the womenfolk would not be able to understand their responsibilities in political administration of the country as they were illiterate and steeped in religious superstition. Ironically, the high-caste Hindus were using the same logic to keep the entire bulk of depressed classes away from political mainstream (Bandyopadhyay, 1997: 141, 144). The stand taken by the Namasudra leaders made it clear that the Matua philosophy of equality, including gender parity, was not their guiding principle anymore.

It has been acknowledged that the social movement of the Namasudra revolved around the Thakur family of Orakandi; Mahatma Gandhi described Guruchand Thakur as a great guru in a personal letter written to Pramatha Ranjan Thakur. However, with death of the guru in March 1937 the prime ideologist responsible for keeping the movement away from the Congress led nationalist force was gone. Within a year his grandson Pramatha Ranjan could see reason behind coming closer to Congress (Bandyopadhyay, 1997: 180, 182). Thereafter it was a story of building alliances and coming out of them, of factionalism among the leaders and gradual alienation from the masses they once led.

During 1930s and 1940s, the Namasudra masses on the other hand were torn between preferences. They had alliance with the Muslim peasants against the gentry, which was based on class identity; they were rioting with the Muslim peasants over issues of community honour, which was opposed to class identity (Bandyopadhyay, 1997: 236). Though most of these Namasudra peasants in eastern Bengal belonged to the Matua *sampraday* around this time, 'gradually the sect and its belief system absorbed many elements of established Hinduism or of the more orthodox trends within the *Bhakti* tradition and thus lost much of its distinctiveness as well as its subversive edge' (Bandyopadhyay, 1997: 210).

The Post-partition Situation

Partition of the country in 1947 devastated much of the gain achieved by the Namasudra community during all these years. Two major factors helped the people to consolidate their community identity and solidarity; it was their distribution over a contagious area where they had a numerical preponderance, and then by bringing this area under cultivation the community could abandon their previous diversified occupational callings and could earn some economic foothold as land-owning peasants. Such economic status was a prerequisite for their quest for social and ritual status.

After the country was partitioned, the entire Namasudra concentration area became part of East Pakistan. In that country, the Namasudra found them to be in a disadvantageous position in comparison to the Muslims, their one-time allies. In the changed situation many of the Namasudras preferred to leave the land for India. Within a decade a large number of Namasudra families crossed border to enter India, there they were initially accommodated in transit camps before being rehabilitated in different parts of West Bengal and then in the states of Odisha, Madhya Pradesh, Uttar Pradesh, Maharashtra and the Andaman Islands. It was estimated by Kapilkrishna Thakur, an important leader of the Matua *sampraday* that by 1964 one fourth of the Namasudra population of Eastern Bengal shifted to India (see 'Introduction' in Sarkar, 2007: 10). The exodus continued through the next decade, the Indian government continued to settle them in different places of the country. After a lull new immigrants started entering India in 1971 in the wake of the Bangladesh Liberation War or *Muktijuddho*. A large number of war refugees, many of whom were from the Namasudra community, decided to stay back in India. This time, there was no government scheme to rehabilitate such people, they settled down on their own.

Under such circumstances the social and political gains that the community could garner all these years took a severe jolt. Unlike the pre-partition days when the Namasudra mass rallied around the identity of the community and perpetrated acts to protect that, the refugee population was struggling hard for mere survival. Still, they tried their best to maintain community solidarity; the Matua *sampraday* helped them by offering an identity marker and a reason for assemblies and congregations.

Shifting Priorities

It has been mentioned earlier that social and political movements of the Namasudra in eastern Bengal in the pre-partition years remained closely connected to the Thakur family of Orakandi; it was the leaders of the *sampraday* who tried to keep the Namasudras away from the nationalist movement led by the Hindu higher caste gentry. The decision to oppose those leaders matched with the aspiration of the general Namasudra people, who were looking for uplifting their social status. It can be argued that the stance would have resulted in further consolidation of the popular support enjoyed by the leaders of the Matua *sampraday*. The same argument can be furthered to say that by compromising the political argument put forward by Guruchand Thakur by later day leaders of the *sampraday*, who joined hands with the gentry and shared political platform with them since 1938 would only have distanced them from the people.

The Matua *sampraday* took a formal and institutional shape for the first time when it was registered in 1943 as Matua Mahasangha in the office of the Registrar of the Companies with its registered office at Sree Hari Guru Chand Ashram, Thakurnagar alias Labanchora, Khulna. Education for the children of the community was the priority in those days, so hostel facilities were created at the Khulna Ashram. This was in parity with the aspiration of the educated upwardly mobile sections of the Namasudra community and the Matua *sampraday*; they were not looking any more for raised ritual status for themselves. Their primary objectives were more education, higher share of white collar jobs and a larger share of political power.

In post-1947, period the president of the organisation decided to shift the headquarters to some place in India. A location in the district of 24 Parganas of West Bengal was identified for the purpose and the new Thakur Bari (house of the Thakurs) and a temple complex came up there. This new headquarters also was named Thakurnagar. It may be noted that the new Thakurnagar in Bongaon sub-division, now falling in North 24 Parganas District.

It is noteworthy that the new headquarters in North 24 Parganas was not built after the Ashram at Khulna. Like the Thakur Bari at Orakandi in Faridpur District, there is a *gaddi* or seat of the master at the new headquarters and a pond called *Kamana Sagar* where devotees take bath and pray for wish fulfillment. The members of Matua *sampraday* and other devotees assemble at Thakurnagar in hundreds of thousands on the occasion of the birth anniversary of Hari Chand Thakur as they used to gather at Orakandi village on this day. In the biography of Guru Chand Thakur, there is a description of the *mela* or fair that took place at Orakandi in the initial years; the congregation and the fair are still organised at Orakandi. On the same day, the events are organised at Thakurnagar too where people gather in large number and take part in chanting, ritual bathing and worshipping. It is widely believed that the water of Kamana Sagar has magical healing power. There is a temple complex at Thakurnagar; other than temples devoted to Harichand, Guruchand and Pramatha Ranjan, there are temples containing idols of major and lesser Hindu deities.

The primary objectives of the leaders of the *sampraday* shifted from educating the children or preparing them for honourable occupations, the Thakurnagar centre is not much known for its educational facilities, the important tasks were establishing a network of the devotees and the likeminded people and creating a space for their congregation. This became necessary because the partition of the country and subsequent population migration resulted in dispersal of members of the Matua *sampraday* and of the Namasudra people over a large area in two countries. The elitist programmes had to make room for populist programmes; regaining contact with common people in terms of their beliefs and aspirations became essential.

Matua Organisations

In their effort to consolidate the network, the leaders of the *sampraday* took several steps. A constitution was created for the Matua Mahasangha in 2004, which was more elaborate than the memorandum of association registered in 1943. The constitution is, in fact, a guideline for the devotees and the members of the organisation; therefore it deals with both religious and secular subjects. It summarises the teachings of Hari Chand and Guru Chand Thakur for the devotees and for persons seeking membership of the Mahasangha. It describes the shape and colour of the festoon and flag to be used by the Matuas and explains their significance. It elaborates the rights and duties of the members, of the branch committees, of the office bearers of the organisation at different levels. In the section on structural arrangement, it describes what would be the functions of the Mahasangha. The spheres where the organisation envisages acting are spiritual, educational and cultural, social welfare and social service, socio-economic and political, youth and women welfare.

The institutional structure of the *sampraday* asserts its control over the preachers, who were part of the traditional or non-institutional organisation of it. Thus, the principal advisor is authorised to award the Matua sadhu, gosain and pagol with *chhota* and any title. *Chhota*, the commanding baton carried by the leader of a group within the *sampraday*, is a symbol of authority. By controlling the power of distributing the symbol of authority, the eventual authority over the *sampraday* could be consolidated. The 1943 memorandum of association made no effort of bring the sadhu, gosain and pagol under its gambit.

In reality, the Matua Mahasangha does not enjoy the allegiance of all the Matuas; quite a few other organisations function independently with their own objectives. Shree Shree Hari Guru Ashram has its headquarters at Ghutiari Sharif in South 24 Parganas District of West Bengal and several branches in other parts of the state of West Bengal. This organisation functions independently of the Mahasangha. Another organisation located at Bagula in Nadia District, West Bengal, was founded to carry out relief work among people affected by natural and other calamities and to do social welfare activities round the year. Then there is the Guru Chand Sena or the army of Guru Chand, which was established in 2001 as a political outfit. Often followers of Matua *sampraday* in both rural and urban areas form local bodies to organise different activities in their respective localities; generally the most important activity for them in a calendar year is organising a religious gathering sometime within one month from the day of *mela* at Thakurnagar. Often devotees from other places are invited to attend such congregations. Such local bodies can be guided by one of the larger bodies like Matua Mahasangha, but it is not necessary that all such local bodies would have their allegiance to one of the larger bodies.

Then there are many members of the Matua laity who live their life without bothering much about the organisations discussed here. However, they have their own ways of organising them at the village level.

In a village where there are followers of Matua *sampraday* in sizeable number, they form a *dal* or group. The concept of *dal* is important among the

Matua, Guruchand Thakur once commented – '*jar dal nei, tar bal nei*' – people who do not have their own organisation have no power.

Generally, the *dal* in a village bears the following structure; it is headed by Sabhapati or President. The Sabhapati is one of the senior experienced villagers, who acts as the chief advisor of the *dal*. The Saha Sabhapati or Vice President is the accountant of the *dal*. The principal executive office bearer is Dalapati, who is expected to be a good organiser with considerable popularity among and command over the general villagers. The Dalapati is assisted by general members to organise different Matua events; some of them act as messengers to inform the villagers about forthcoming events. The general members of a *dal* are known as *bhakta* or devotee or simply as Matua.

The *dal* acts as a group within the village, the members of a *dal* are supposed to act as a cohesive group with a sense of solidarity. They are supposed to meet regularly, especially on Wednesday, which is the weekly congregation day for the Matuas. The congregations are organised at homes of different devotees in rotation. Members of the *dal* in the village help the householder in organising the event.

Quigmire of Power

Earlier in this article it has been mentioned that in pre-partition Bengal, especially around 1930s, the Namasudras were considered to be one of the most politically active community. It has also been argued that the organisational ability of the Matua leaders was largely responsible for the electoral success of the community. The political closeness of the Namasudras with other 'lowly positioned' Hindu communities and with the Muslim peasantry and their opposition to high caste Hindu gentry was an approximation of the social and class identity of the Matua followers.

The support base and the political momentum worked in favour of Pramatha Ranjan Thakur, who joined Indian National Congress in 1938 and later became a Member of Parliament. In post-partition India the Matua *sampraday* or the Namasudra community were deprived of those advantages, those who could rise to the position of leadership in political parties were often considered to be representing the refugees and not any socially disadvantaged section of the society.

The Matua organisations, especially the largest one among them, the Mahasangha, were trying to reach out to their followers in West Bengal and in other parts of India for several decades. The Mahasangha has its branches in different states and union territories of the country where Bengali refugees were rehabilitated. It may be noted that the leaders of the *sampraday* were not nurturing much political ambition themselves; in places beyond the state of West Bengal they have not tried to convert their following into political support. But the story was different in the state of West Bengal, particularly in the districts of North 24 Parganas, Nadia and the adjacent areas, where they have a large following. The Motua population in West Bengal was estimated by some to be more than ten million strong and that the *sampraday* could determine the fate of twelve assembly constituencies located in North and South 24 Parganas and Nadia (*The Times of India*, 8th December, 2010). The estimated numerical strength of the *sampraday* or of the influence they could exert was not uniform; another report stated the population to be five million strong and they could cause swing in seven assembly constituencies (*The Times of India*, 20th April, 2011). According to another estimate, the Matuas could decide the fate of 74 constituencies and be a decisive factor in determining which party wrests political control of the state (*The Hindu*, 31st March, 2011).

The major political parties of West Bengal have traditionally stayed away, at least in public, from identifying and organising voters on basis of their religious affiliation or on caste identity. But there was no such compulsion for Bahujan Samaj Party, a political outfit that highlights its commitment to stand for emancipation of backward sections of the Indian society, who have been the victims of the Manuwadi or Brahminical system, and the minorities. They approached some of the Matua leaders in early years of the present century and tried to strike an alliance but received a rather cold response.

The situation started changing in recent years when the left parties experienced a major setback in the high concentration areas of the Matua *sampraday*. In early 2009, some newspapers reported that the Matua Mahasangha was responsible for the debacle of the left in Bongaon Assembly by poll and the panchayat elections in that area. The Matuas, the analysts claimed, turned away from the Left in retaliation to an incident that took place in 2007. That year the Matua devotees demanded a college named after B.R. Ambedkar be re-christened after the Matua masters Harichand and Guruchand. The protest meeting convened by the Matuas was disrupted by Communist Party of India (Marxist) activists, reported *The Times of India* (April 20, 2011).

Reportedly, the Communist Party of India (Marxist) was trying to reach out to the Matuas since late 2010. One step towards that direction was laying foundation of a college in the North 24 Parganas named after Harichand and Guruchand Thakur by the then Chief Minister of West Bengal, Buddhadeb Bhattacharjee. Soon after Kapilkrishna Thakur, the head of All India Matua Mahasangha, received the Thakur Harichand-Guruchand Award from the Government of West Bengal for his contribution to the uplift of Dalits.

The Trinamul Congress was not lagging behind, the then Railways Minister Mamata Banerjee announced the Thakurnagar railway station will be converted into a model station. Another leader of the party, who was a Member of the Legislative Assembly, spent a large part of the money from the fund for local area development to repair roads in Thakurnagar and renovate Kamana Sagar, the sacred water body. The party fielded one member of the Thakur family, Manjulkrishna Thakur, as a Trinamul Congress candidate for the 2011 Assembly elections. He won the election and was made the minister in charge of refugee, relief and rehabilitation.

The Matua Mahasangha tried to stay clear of controversies of realpolitik. In a pre-election statement it was stated that the Mahasangha is a socio-religious body and not a political outfit. Pramatha Ranjan Thakur, who is a cult figure for the present day Matua Mahasangha leadership, represented Congress in state legislative assembly and also in parliament. He never issued any diktat to the Matuas asking them to vote for him or for his party. The Mahasangha is opposed to the idea of handing out political endorsements (*The Times of India,* 20 thApril, 2011).

Some Other Equations

Eagerness of the political parties to gather support of the Matuas *en bloc* must have convinced the Matua leaders of the potential strength in form of a large vote bank under their control. In a possible reaction to such a realisation, the Mahasangha set out to take stock of their might. Each devotee family was being issued identity card by the Mahasangha that mentioned names and number of the family members and their address. Poor farmers were also enrolled in groups (*The Times of India,* 25th January, 2009).

A senior leader of the Mahasangha stated that the leadership follows the teachings of Harichand Thakur and Guruchand Thakur. It was the latter who advised the Matuas to move close to *rajshakti*, the state power, in the interest of the downtrodden. But in his opinion, the Mahasangha has learnt some lessons from the past. Whenever a Matua has joined a political party, the party has demanded that the person be primarily loyal to the political ideologies and programmes of the party at the cost of interests of the Matuas or other oppressed sections of the society. The present leadership or at least a section of it feels that even Pramatha Ranjan Thakur, with his influence over the party men, could not do anything effective for the people he was representing. They do not find the contemporary situation to be different; the political parties pick up a few persons from among the Matuas but do not bestow them with decision making authority. The Mahasangha has noticed all these and is in the process of assessing its own strength. The leadership of the organisation is not thinking in terms of West Bengal alone, they are aware of the support base in other parts of the country as well. The Mahasangha is considering converting the popular support into political might, possibly independent of the existing political groups.

It has been mentioned earlier that there are other organisations in the Matua *sampraday* with their own objectives. Most of those organisations are too small in their strength of following in comparison to the Mahasangha, but the fact that those organisations exist suggests the Mahasangha does not enjoy allegiance of all sections of the Matua *sampraday*. In fact, many such organisations were formed because all members of the *sampraday* did not feel that their aspirations and expectations were being fulfilled by the Mahasangha. Then there are people who revere Harichand Thakur and Guruchand Thakur and have faith in the Matua philosophy, visit Thakurnagar once or twice a year but do not subscribe to any of the organisations. Even if the Mahasangha asks the *sampraday* to act in a given way, for people having little or no allegiance towards the Mahasangha or its leaders, the decree would have very limited effect.

The perception of the Matua *sampraday* as a potential vote bank is a rather recent phenomenon among the major political parties of West Bengal; it change in discernment took place a few years before the 2011 assembly election in the state. It can be counted as a success on part of the Matua organisations, especially the Mahasangha. The *sampraday* appeared to others as a cohesive body only when the Mahasangha could bring the people in their elaborate and well defined network decades after their migration and dispersal.

However, perceiving the *sampraday* as a collection of people who behave alike in all matters of life is in all probability driven by some oversimplified views. In fact the people described as a *sampraday* here are not known exclusively by their Matua identity; each individual member of the collective bears several other identities. It looks improbable that their political behaviour will remain insulated from their other identities or affiliations. Looking at the issue from another way, it can be said that during last few decades the members of the Matua *sampraday* have not voted differently from their immediate non-Matua neighbours. This is evident from the result of the 2011 assembly poll of West Bengal. The way the major political parties of the state have fared in the core area of Matua concentration was not in much variance from the neighbouring areas.

The districts of Nadia, North and South 24 Parganas have been considered to be the core area of Matua concentration. In Nadia, there were seventeen assembly seats and the Trinamul Congress bagged fourteen (82.35 per cent) of those seats. In North 24 Parganas the number of seats were thirty three and Trinamul Congress candidates were elected in twenty eight (84.85 per cent) of those. In South 24 Parganas, there were thirty one seats and the Trinamul Congress could win twenty six (83.87 per cent) of those seats. The above eighty per cent rate of success for Trinamul Congress in those districts was in tune with the success rate of the same party in the neighbouring districts of Howrah (100 per cent) and Hooghly (88.88 per cent). The latter two districts are not known for high concentration of the Matuas.

As the members of the Matua *sampraday* are mostly from the Scheduled Caste communities, it can be prudent examine the success rate of Trinamul Congress in the seats reserved for Scheduled Caste candidates. This rate also showed a similar trend in all the five districts of Nadia (100 per cent), North 24 Parganas (85.71 per cent), South 24 Parganas (66.66 per cent), Howrah (100 per cent) and Hooghly (75 per cent). The observations validate the argument that the Matuas did not behave differently from their co-citizens.

Transformations and Contradictions

The core ideology of the Matua faith remained opposed to inequality in the form of caste hierarchy or gender disparity. It has been discussed how the emphasis on egalitarianism was compromised by claiming Brahman origin or by arguing against voting right for the women. This shift can be equated with transformation of a section of the marginal cultivators into landed, educated and upwardly mobile group in late nineteenth and early twentieth century. The group of elites was not much interested in improving their position in a rural caste based society; for them becoming part of an urban secular social milieu was more important. Arguably, the clash of interest resulted in a fissure between the peasants and their leaders.

After partition of the country the leaders were compelled to build their support base once again, they shifted back to the popular elements of the faith. Putting education on back burner, more attention was given to building temples, organising annual festivals and establishing contact with the rural populace on regular basis.

The sustained efforts on part of the leaders started yielding some result when the *sampraday* was recognised by many as an organised group of people who listen to the commands of their leaders and can possibly act as a vote bank. The leaders of the *sampraday* might not have worked for decades to get this kind of recognition, but it is a reality that the *sampraday* is not known to many for what it once stood for, a philosophy of protest, but it has been perceived as a group of voters who can be manipulated.

Neither the Matua philosophy nor the members of the Matua *sampraday* remained monolithic and static entities in their history of existence; both have been subjected to various opposing forces from inside and outside. A group of people have been perceived as champions of protest against domination of the dominating forces and at the same time were imagined as a collection of persons whose thoughts can be dominated by the dominant groups. The contradiction is generally not limited to the popular images of the people as held by others; it is often manifest in form of opposing consciousness among different sections of the people.

References

Bandyopadhyay, Sekhar, 1997. *Caste, Protest and Identity in Colonial India: The Namasudras of Bengal*. Surrey: Curzon Press.

Banerjee, Sumanta, 2002. *Logic in a Popular Form: Essays on Popular Religion in Bengal*. Calcutta: Seagull Books.

Chatterjee, Partha, 1989. 'Caste and Subaltern Consciousness', in Ranajit Guha (ed.) *Selected Subaltern Studies VI.* Delhi: Oxford University Press.

Gramsci, Antonio, 1971 (1986). *Selections from Prison Notebooks.* London: Lawrence and Wishart.

Risley, H.H., 1891 (1981). *The Tribes and Castes of Bengal,* Vol. I. Calcutta: Firma K.L. Mukhopadhyay.

Sarkar, Tarakchandra 2007 (1916), *Shree Shree Harileelamrita* Thakurnagar. Published by Binapani Thakur.

The Hindu, 31st March, 2011, 'Why the Matuas Matter'.

The Times of India, 25th January, 2009, 'Membership Cards and Fee for Matuas, CPM Style'.

The Times of India, 8th December, 2010, 'CPM Reaches Out to Motua Community'.

The Times of India, 20th April, 2011, 'A Sect That Can Swing It'.

7

Search for Identity of a Tribe through Administrative Reform: The Case of the Lepchas of West Bengal

D.C. Roy

Introduction

Apart from other problems the tribes of the world are facing today is a kind of identity crisis due to change in demographic composition, structural set up, social formation, religious faith, administrative outlook, and the like. Such problems are more volatile and acute with the small communities who are fighting hard for their existence and against all forces of marginalisation. Living under a constant threat from outside, the small tribes and communities, with weak resistance power and insignificant control over the material resources, are busy working out strategies for survival. They may not be assimilating themselves completely with the comparatively stronger communities but many of the elements of their culture are getting lost and they are at a loss to find the means to sustain their cultural identity. In this uneven competition or interaction with the powerful, the marginalised communities construct the 'other' while articulating their demands and grievances.

The present paper aims to highlight the long unresolved problems of the Lepchas of Darjeeling hills and their recent movement for setting up the 'Lepcha Development Council' within the state of West Bengal. The article has four sections—the first section deals with the short history of the Lepchas and their land; the second section narrates the long standing problems of the

Lepchas; the third section describes the recent movement of the Lepchas for separate Council and the last section concludes the study.

Short History of the Lepchas

Lepchas are the aboriginals of the southern part of the Eastern Himalayas consisting of the present day Sikkim, Darjeeling district of West Bengal, Illam district of Nepal and Western part of Bhutan. Before the Tibetans occupied Sikkim in 1642 and British occupied the Darjeeling area in 1835, the whole area the Lepchas were the only inhabitants. All the scholars and the writers on the region and its people have unanimously admitted that the Lepchas were the early settlers of the place. Different adjectives, which have been in use for the Lepchas such as 'aboriginal' (Rowney, 1882; O'Malley, 1907; White, 1909; Kawagachi, 1909; Dozey, 1922; Nebesky, 1956), 'original' (Hooker, 1854; Hunter, 1876; Gorer, 1938; Siiger, 1967; Lepcha, 1979; Sen, 1989; Choudhury, 1999), 'oldest' (Risley, 1928), 'autochthonous' (Gazetteer, 1980); 'indigenous' (Tamsang, 1983), and so on, unequivocally support the claim.

In the bygone days the Lepchas not only lived but also ruled the land which they called *Nye Mayel Renzong Lyang* or in short *Mayel Lyang*. Mainwaring (1876), Risley (1891), Namgyal (1908) and others have mentioned about the Lepcha *Pano* (king) who ruled the Lepcha land. Among them there were Tarvey Pano and his successors, namely, Tur-Sang Pano, Tur-Ageng Pano and Tur-Ayek Pano. In Sikkim Namgyal dynasty had started through a Blood Brotherhood Treaty between Khye-Bumsa, the Tibetan leader and Thy-Kung Tek, the Lepcha leader. Bhutan occupied the whole of Sikkim including Damsang area (present day Kalimpong) by killing King Gaeboo Achyok Pano, the last king of the Lepchas in 1700.

History of the Lepchas and their land has never been written properly. But from the Lepcha folktales and folklore it can be found that the original Mayel Lyang (Lepcha land), was spread over a larger geographical area, larger than the present day Sikkim and where the Lepchas used to live as freely. From the existing literature it appears that in the latter period the Lepchas lost the northern Chumbi Valley to Tibet and Thang La to Bhutan. In the east they lost the entire boundary to Bhutan. In the west Lepcha land was spread up to Tamor River, Arun River and Koshi River. They lost it to Nepal. The southern tract had been shared by Nepal, Bangladesh, West Bengal and Bihar. In a word, all the neighbouring countries and states have expanded their territories by encroaching into the Lepcha land.

At present the Lepchas are residing in the state of Sikkim and in the hilly region of Darjeeling district of West Bengal. Due to the rearrangement of their land some Lepchas are still found in the eastern part of Nepal and in the western part of Bhutan. The spread of Lepchas over the three countries is not due to their migratory character but due to the political shuffling of the old Lepcha land by the respective countries. The important Wars, Treaties and

Agreements which are responsible for the loss of Lepcha land are Blood Brotherhood Treaty of 13th century, Bhutan War in 1700, Gorkha War in 1791, Segauli Treaty of 1815, Treaty of Titalia of 1817, Darjeeling Grant of 1835, Treaty of Tumlong of 1861, Treaty of Sinchula of 1865, and the British-China Convention of 1890. But except Blood Brotherhood Treaty Lepchas were neither involved nor ever been made a party to any of the agreements by which their land was handed over to the third party.

Since 1951 the Lepchas of West Bengal have been enlisted as one of the Scheduled Tribes (STs) in India. The SC, ST Orders (Amendment) Act 1976 recorded the Lepchas as one among the thirty eight STs of the state. But much before this Constitutional recognition as ST, Lepchas were identified as 'Primitive Tribe' (Hunter, 1876; Porter, 1931; Hutton, 1931) at extremely under-developed stage (SC/ST Commission, 1960). Cultural Research Institute, Government of West Bengal, had recommended for inclusion of Lepchas in the category of 'Primitive Tribes' of India. But only three communities, Birhor, Toto and Lodha, from among the tribes in West Bengal, have been included in this category in 1979. Considering their backward socio-economic condition and land alienation problem, the Constituent Assembly Debate (Proceedings) Vol. VII dated 4th November, 1982 remarked: 'There may be other areas which the provincial Governments may like to bring under special administration. This can be done by the provincial Government in their discretion. For the protection of land of Tribes like the Lepcha in Darjeeling the provincial Government could make the appropriate provision of the chapter relating to the Scheduled areas applicable to the area concerned' (Government of West Bengal, 1982).

Marginalisation of the Lepchas

Over the years the Lepchas have come in contact with more powerful alien forces, which, in turn, have left the Lepchas marginalised in different walks of their life. In this section I have brought to focus some such areas where the Lepchas have been subjected to marginalisation.

Demography: The story of demographic marginalisation of the Lepchas in their own homeland started with the immigration of large number of the Tibetans from Tibet in the 13th century, which continued until China occupied Tibet in the middle of twentieth century. During and after Gorkha War, a large number of Nepalese had settled in this hill tract. The situation aggravated when the East India Company in 1835 took control of Darjeeling area and when Sikkim merged with India in 1975 because with such developments a good number of people from Nepal and the plains of India migrated into the Lepcha dominated areas in Darjeeling hills.

Before the Tibetans came and settled in these places, Lepchas were the only inhabitants of the hills. They not only controlled the vast land spreading all over the southern part of the Eastern Himalayas but they were the rulers of their land and people. There were no other communities other than the Lepchas in this tract. Now the area has turned multi-ethnic since a large number of migrants from the neighbouring countries of Nepal and Tibet and many others from the plains of India have settled. In the process, the Lepchas have been reduced to a small minority; they now comprise very negligible portion of the total population of the area. The Lepchas now comprise around 2.07 per cent of total population in Darjeeling (Census of India, 2001), seven per cent in the state of Sikkim (Govt. of Sikkim, 2006) and 0.03 per cent in Nepal (Niroula, 1988).

Although demographic picture of the Lepchas in West Bengal is very confusing (Roy, 2005) the available figures put the Lepcha population to a negligible proportion of the total population of Darjeeling district. The figures available from 1911, 1921, 1941 and 1971 censuses give a picture of negative growth of Lepcha population. The share of the original inhabitants of Darjeeling has been reduced to 2.07 per cent of total population of the district over the last hundred and sixty years. Due mainly to the British policy of inviting and encouraging immigrants the Lepchas in their own homeland have become an insignificant minority.

Education: The Lepchas have their own language, script and rich literature but they have never been given an opportunity to study in their own language. In the pre-British period as such there was no system of formal education in this area for any community and not for the Lepchas. What they used to learn was either to enrich themselves with the knowledge of their surroundings or the religious knowledge from the monasteries. The Gazetteer of Darjeeling (1980) states: 'The earliest attempt to reach modern secular education to the Hill people was made around A.D. 1850 by Revd. W. Start, a private missionary, who added to his record of good work in Darjeeling by opening a school for Lepchas. After him came a band of German missionaries, one of whom, Mr. Neibel, devoted himself specially to school work, prepared some Lepcha primers and gathered some boys together into schools.'

But within two decades, all the Lepcha medium schools have converted either into English or Nepali medium schools and the Lepcha language started losing all its relevance in the school curriculum. In Sikkim, the heartland of the Lepchas, Lepcha language has been recognised as a medium of instruction up to the degree level. But the Lepchas on the other side of the hill are debarred from learning in their mother tongue notwithstanding a good number of languages like English, Nepali, Hindi, Bengali, Tibetan, Dzonkha, China, Khasi, Mizo, etc., are being taught in the different ICSE, CBSE, State Board Schools. At present under the guidance and initiative of the Lepcha Association about forty Night Schools have undertaken a massive task of imparting education to the Lepchas in their mother tongue. But this gigantic work is hard to continue long without direct support from the state.

Loss of Land: Another factor that has affected the Lepchas badly is the loss of land. The Britishers were very much concerned about the transfer of Lepcha land to the non-Lepchas. As early as in 1921, Philpot in his Survey and Settlement Report on Kalimpong Estate noted: 'one of the main considerations in the management of the estate has been the protection, so far as possible, of Lepchas and Bhutia population, especially the former, from the consequences of their own extravagance, and to prevent them from being displaced by their thriftier Nepali neighbours. Ordinarily no sales of land held by Lepchas or Bhutias are permitted except to a Lepcha or a Bhutia.' The West Bengal Land Reform (Amendment) Act, 1965, fails to retain lands in the hands of the Lepchas. Poverty is the root cause of transfer of land from the Lepchas to others. It has been reported that in most cases the non-Lepchas evaded the Land Reform Rule by marrying the Lepcha girls and buying the Lepcha land in the name of their Lepcha wives. The land alienation is a century old problem for the Lepchas as over the years they have become landless in their homeland. The process of land alienation fastened with the division of existing land among their descendents. At present, most Lepchas are either landless or are small and marginal farmers.

Loss of Religion: Religious conversion is another major problem of the Lepchas which leads to their identity crisis. Originally Lepchas are nature worshippers and they worship different objects of nature like mountain, hill, river, lake, sun, wind and so on of the region. Kanchanjunga is their divine deity and it is believed that their primogenitors had originated from the virgin snow of this mountain peak. They generally believe that *Bongthing* and *Mun*, the Lepcha priest and priestess, act as the mediators between the common Lepchas and the spirits, good and bad. It is also believed that only *Mun* can take the soul of departed person to *Poomju,* the resting place to meet their ancestors. All rituals are simple, nature-based and are performed by the *Bongthing or Mun*. In course of time, the Lepchas were the first to be converted to Buddhism and then some of them again converted to Christianity. Buddhists to some extent follow their traditional rituals but the Christians have moved far from their traditional beliefs and practices (Roy, 2012).

Culture and Custom: Changes can be noticed in the traditional customs and culture of the Lepchas. Lepcha culture bears testimony of their rich heritage and high level of mental and spiritual development. Lepcha culture is religion based and is much close to nature. Lepchas are God-fearing and most their religious rituals are performed by the *Bongthing* and *Mun.* Loss of land and inflow of outsiders have impacted the Lepcha culture badly and they have adopted alien culture and customs in the process. *Moo*, the Lepcha clan, is another identifying marker of Lepcha society. It keeps the special identity of the women but it has been mismanaged and misused in modern times. The rhythmic tune and typical musical instruments have been part of their rich cultural tradition. But the wave of modernisation and globalisation has washed out the Lepcha culture. Religious conversion and incidents of intermarriage with other communities are the two major forces that have affected the Lepcha culture drastically.

The traditional material culture of the Lepchas has been nature-based. Lepchas traditionally used wood, bamboo and cane in construction of house, bridge, utensils, ornaments, agricultural implements, hunting implements, carrying containers, musical instruments and so on. *Doo-Kye-Moo-Lee*, the traditional Lepcha house, is made with wood, bamboo and thatch. Not a single imported item like nail or screw was used in its construction. The house was earthquake proof, flood proof, landslide proof, warm in winter and cool in summer. The cane and bamboo bridges used to be made by the Lepchas exemplified Lepcha knowledge of engineering and architectural skill. Musical instruments of the Lepchas were made of bamboo or wood which were nature-based. Lepchas used to use all bio-degradable items which are collected from nature. The Lepcha material culture in the form of all these artifacts has undergone drastic changes in modern times.

Dumpraa and *Dumdem,* the Lepcha dress for men and women, were typical of the Lepchas and the identifying marker of the Lepchas. *Thyaaktak*, the Lepcha hat was typical of the community and was an illustration of their excellent craftsmanship. *Baan-pak* and *Banhoor*, the knives used by the Lepcha men and women, were unique in shape and had wide-range use in hunting, agricultural operation, house construction and for protection from wild animals and enemies. With the passage of time Lepchas have been influenced by the material culture of the dominant neighbouring communities and modernism and, as a result, they are on the verse of losing much of their traditional culture and distinctiveness.

Political Life: Lepchas, in course of time, have lost the power and authority they had enjoyed earlier in their own state, which included Darjeeling hills. Once the rulers of the land are now ruled by others. Lepchas have lost their say in making policies and implementing them for their land and people. They were not even made a party when their land changed hands in different historical points. Excepting the Blood Brotherhood Treaty by which Lepcha land was handed over to the Tibetans, Lepchas were never made party to any Treaty by which their land has been divided and distributed among the foreigners. During the colonial rule the Lepchas were never chosen at the higher administrative positions. In post-colonial democracy the Lepchas have lost significance because of their insignificant numerical strength. The Lepchas now live as second and even third grade citizens in their own land. No ministerial port folio in state government has ever been enjoyed by any Lepcha. In the state and central legislative assemblies they have had only token presence when the mainstream political parties wanted. In two local level administrative arrangements, namely Darjeeling Gorkha Hill Council (DGHC), and Gorkhaland Territorial Administration (GTA) they Lepchas have only a token presence. The longing for a greater political space might have prompted them to demand a separate Lepcha Development Council within the state of West Bengal.

Economic Life: Traditionally the Lepchas were the hunters and gatherers, depending heavily on forest and other natural resources. But the Land Settlement Act and the Forest Reservation Act had completely transformed the Lepcha economy and they were compelled to settle down in terrace cultivation on the hill slopes. The lords of nature thus have been restricted to small plots of land and in course of time many of them have been reduced to the status of landless labourers (Roy, 2005). A few of them have been absorbed in different white-collar jobs. The meager amount of land that the Lepchas control and low level of productivity of their land, because of ecological constraints, they have been largely confined to what can be termed as 'subsistence economy'. In the absence of 'surplus' of any kind they have to dependent heavily on their physical labour. Their failure to make much headway in terms of human resource development has also contributed to their economic backwardness.

Recent Movement of the Lepchas

The Lepchas are involved in a united movement since 2010 under the leadership of their Association for a Separate Administrative Identity with a demand for the creation of Lepcha Development Council. The Lepcha ethnicity in Darjeeling hills is the outcome of a long course of their marginalisation in their own land which has found articulation in the movement for a development council. In order to understand its genesis, we have to look into the recent political developments in the hills. The Darjeeling Gorkha Hill Council (DGHC) was formed out of a violent movement by the Nepalese in 1988 and was a step towards recognition of Gorkha identity in India. In 2009 the Gorkha Jana Mukti Morcha (GJMM) launched a statehood movement which ran for nearly two years. In 2011, a political entity namely Gorkhaland Territorial Administration (GTA) was created through a tripartite agreement between the Central government, State government and the leaders of the GJMM.

The nomenclature of the new politico-administrative setup upset the Lepchas and they started feeling insecure in their own homeland where they were in majority and the rulers in bygone days. One memorandum in this effect was submitted to the Chairman, National Commission for ST, New Delhi on 18th January, 2010. In a letter to the Union Home Minister, the Chairperson of the Commission (dated 18. 01. 2010) wrote: "It has been stated that the Lepchas are the original indigenous tribe of Darjeeling District of West Bengal and any political settlement of the Darjeeling Hills (in context of demand for creation of a separate Gorkhaland) should not be in favour of a particular community and any such arrangements should be based on blending of all communities to ensure equal opportunities to all of them. It has been stated that the nomenclature Gorkhaland will threaten the existence of Lepchas and it will be very difficult for them to save their community and its unique ancient language, literature, culture and tradition from extinction... As Chairperson of this commission I feel that the apprehensions of the Association are quite genuine as the name of the new political settlement should not be in the name of a particular community. If the demand for political resettlement of Darjeeling Hills is conceded by the Government and the new settlement is given the name of Gorkhaland, there is every possibility that Scheduled Tribes belonging to Limbu and Tamang communities who are Gorkhas will get an opportunity to dominate over the Lepchas and to corner away the benefits available for Schedule Tribes as the Lepchas are not considered as Gorkhas as per Government of India's instructions dated 10-09-2004."

The feeling of insecurity among the Lepchas also finds reflection in their memorandum submitted to the Government of West Bengal in August 2010. The memorandum states: "The political turmoil of Darjeeling district for last three decade has put more pressure on the community. The community due to uncertainty has been more marginalised and has plunged into deeper poverty. Darjeeling Gorkha Hill Council was a big eye-opener for the Lepchas as Lepchas were treated as non entity. Till 1988 we all were one community that is hill community, but as the functioning of the Council started we realised that the nomenclature itself meant the Council was for another community. Several appeals were out rightly rejected just because we were from different community. The direct disparity was established. Not a single Lepcha festival was declared a holiday as compared to numerous holidays did not sanction for majority community festivals nor single fund were allotted for the Lepcha festivals compared to crores of rupees spent for promotion of the culture. The nomenclature of Council gave advantage to one community and welfare of other communities was directly overlooked. Today in Council there are more than six thousand employees and out of which less than three per cent Lepchas work in the Council. Day to day disparity and treatment of our community members in Council offices were intolerable during the time of the elected Council. Several attempts were made to erase the historical facts attached with the land. The practice of distorting or renaming the names of the villages, streets and monuments having Lepcha names were profoundly practiced. The statues of the Lepcha heroes of olden days were systematically removed from public eyes to obscure places. In the name of the development the lands of the Lepchas were targeted. Lepchas were forced, coerced and lured to donate lands."

Nature of Movement

The movement for the creation of the Lepcha Development Council was started by the Rong Ong Prongzum, the youth wing of the Lepchas. Later a separate wing by the name Lepcha Rights Movement was formed specifically for spearheading the movement for the creation a Lepcha Council. But both the wings have worked under the guidance, supervision and direction of the Indigenous Lepcha Tribal Association (ILTA). Some representatives of either *Thom Shezoom* or *Poom Shezoom* attend all demonstrations, protest rallies, *dharnas* and other programmes to keep control over the movement.

The movement has been kept democratic and confined to meetings and deputations with the top bureaucratic and political leaders, both at the central and state. The Lepchas have been organising protest rallies, holding *dharnas,* courting mass arrest pressing the demand for formation of Lepcha Development Council. The movement demonstrates that the Lepchas in Darjeeling hills are conscious of their distinctive culture and ethnic identity which they are serious to preserve. They do not want to be submerged into the predominant Gorkha identity which constituted the ideological backbone of the long-standing demand for a Gorkha state in Darjeeling hills.

With reference to the on-going movement for setting up of Gorkhaland the ILTA delegation met the Chairperson, National Commission for ST, Government of India at New Delhi, on 18 January, 2010 and submitted a memorandum spelling out their objections to the nomenclature of Gorkhaland as follows:

A letter dated 22nd December 2010 of the Administrator, Darjeeling Gorkha Hill Council, addressed to Joint Secretary Hill affairs Department, Government of West Bengal, mentioned three demands of the Lepchas and request for appropriate measures to be taken by the government. The three demands are: (a) nomenclature of the new set up, (b) representation of the Lepchas in the new setup, and (c) formation of Lepcha Development Council.

A delegation of the ILTA and Rong Ong Prongzum met District Magistrate, Darjeeling on 11th May, 2011 and submitted memorandum regarding nomenclature of proposed Gorkha Territorial Administration, formation of Lepcha Development Council, and so on. The District Magistrate, in turn, stated the demand as genuine and forwarded the case to the Administrator DGHC on the following day. The ILTA sent delegations to meet the Commissioner, Jalpaiuri on 14th May, 2011, and different state government officials and ministers between 21st and 25th June, 2011 to submit memorandums articulating their demands and grievances. A Lepcha delegation met the Governor of West Bengal at Raj Bhawan, Kolkata, on 14th July, 2011 and discussed the matter of Lepcha preservation, protection and safeguard. The Lepchas of Darjeeling sat in a *dharna* for twenty five days from 9th August, 2011 at Kolkata in support of their demand for separate Council within the state of West Bengal. Different renowned personalities (Like Mahasweta Devi, a renowned Bengali writer and social activist), Trade Unions, Associations and NGOs extend their support for the Lepchas at the *dharna* site. In support, the Lepchas of Darjeeling expressed their solidarity with the movement by sitting in round the clock *dharna* at the SDO office premise, Kalimpong, for four days from 1st September, 2011.

About seventy Lepchas were arrested in Kolkata for violation of Prohibitory Orders on 22nd August 2011 but were released on bail later. In protest the Lepchas of Darjeeling assembled in front of Kalimpong Police Station and demonstrated. They also announced hunger strike in demand for unconditional release of the arrested Lepchas. On 16th November, 2011, Lepchas assembled at Baghajatin Park, Siliguri, in support of their demand for the creation of separate Council for the Lepchas. They thanked the Chief Minister of West Bengal for her announcement on 2nd September, in the assembly and reiterating the same on 12th October, 2011 in Darjeeling for the creation of Lepcha Development Council.

Lepchas are demanding for a separate democratic institution in the name of council, board or agency in the name of Lepcha Development Council or Mayel Lyang Development Council. The Council is proposed to be formed within the state of West Bengal and will be operational in the district of Darjeeling where the Lepchas are residing in majority. The basic aim of the Council will be to protect the Lepcha language and culture along with development of the community. The proposed Lepcha Council will be a democratic body and will run as per the traditional *Shezoom* System of the community with three tiers: (a) Village Council or *Kyong Shezoom*, (b) Cluster of Villages Council or *Thom Shezoom* and (c) Executive Council or *Poom Shezoom*. The powers and functions of the three *Shezooms* will be mutually inclusive will be distributed in a hierarchical order of a bureaucratic structure. It has been stated that the Council will ran as par the typical Lepcha Customary Law. The Council is proposed to have different Cells: Language Cell, Cultural Cell, Traditional Cell, Handicraft Cell, Games and Sports Cell, Museum Cell, Administrative cell and so on and all of which will operate to protect the language, culture and custom of the Lepchas.

Besides protecting language, culture and custom, the Council is proposed to take initiatives for the all-round development of the community. The main areas of intervention of the Council would be agriculture, horticulture, animal husbandry, tourism, cottage industry, micro-finance and infrastructural development. Fund for the Council is expected to be allocated by the Government on annual basis and the Executive Council under the *Poom Shezoom* will remain responsible for preparing the annual budget allocating funds under different heads. The audit system will be according to the norms and regulations of the State Government.

Conclusion

Historically the Lepchas of Darjeeling hills represent a typical case of a ruling tribal community being reduced to a minority and marginalised community by the immigrants into their territory. The marginalisation is evident in areas like demography, language, power structure, control of resources, material and human, culture and so on. The on-going movement for a separate Gorkhaland since mid-1980s has seen formation of Gorkha identity by most Nepali speaking people in the hills but the Lepchas have largely refused to be a part of this identity. In order to protect their traditional culture and identity the Lepchas have launched a separate movement for setting up a Lepcha development council, which they think will save them from extinction as an ethnic community. The Lepchas have kept the movement democratic and peaceful and the movement has yielded a strong sense of unity among different segments of the community. The youth, both boys and girls, men and women, the elderly members—all have come forward in support of the movement. In spite of cultural differences both the Buddhist and the Christian Lepchas have joined hands for the cause of the community. The prospect of learning through their mother tongue, preservation of their traditional culture, economic development and recognition as community is being highly valued by the members of the community. Love for fellow members and pride to be Lepcha have been reflected in their urge to be governed by their customary laws.

Since 1925, the Lepchas of Darjeeling are fighting for measures to preserve their language, culture and custom. The Lepcha Association has organised movements on various ethnic demands in different historical points but few of their demands have been met. Against this backdrop the Lepchas in Darjeeling hills have welcomed with great hope and enthusiasm the announcement of the Chief Minister of West Bengal on 2nd September, 2011 on the floor of the Legislative Assembly of West Bengal. The dominant Gorkha community has spent no time in dismissing the announcement as a move to create divisions among the hill people. One has to wait and watch whether the proposed Council succeeds in fulfilling the aspirations of the Lepchas by arresting their further marginalisation and bringing them back to the path of development. Also to watch what ramifications it has for the volatile politics of culture in Darjeeling hills.

References

Ananda Bazar Patrika, 7th August, 2011.

Choudhury, N., 1999. 'Darjeeling-Sikkim Himalayan Region: An Ethnographic View', in Sanjib Sarcar (ed.) *Glimpses of the Eastern Himalayan Culture*. Calcutta: Centre for Communication and Cultural Action.

Dozey, E.C., 1922 (1989). *A Concise and Complete History of the Darjeeling District since 1835 with a complete Itinerary of tours in Sikkim and the district.* Darjeeling: Jetsum Publishing House.

Gorer, G., 1938 (1996). *The Lepchas of Sikkim.* Delhi: Gyan Publishing House.

Government of India, 2001. *Census of India.* West Bengal, CD on Schedule Tribes.

Government of Sikkim, 2006. *State Socio-economic Census*. Gangtok: Department of Economics, Statistics, Monitoring and Evaluation.

Government of West Bengal, 1980. *West Bengal District Gazetteer: Darjeeling*. Calcutta.

Government of West Bengal, 1982. *Planning for the Scheduled Tribes and Scheduled Castes: A West Bengal Perspective*. Kolkata: Cultural Research Institute. Schedule Caste and Schedule Tribe Department, Government of West Bengal.

Himalayan Darpan 3rd September, 2011; 6th September, 2011.

Hooker, J.D., 1854 (1980). *Himalayan Journal*. Delhi: Today and Tomorrows Printers and Publishers.

Hunter, W.W., 1876 (1984). *A Statistical Account of Bengal* (Vol. X). Delhi: Concept Publishing House.

Hutton, J.H., 1931 (1984). *Census of India with Complete Survey of Tribal life and System*. Vol. 1. Delhi: Gyan Publishing House.

Kawagachi, E., 1909 (1979). *Three Years in Tibet*. Nepal: Ratna Pustak Bhander. Nepal.

Lepcha, S.W., 1979. *The Process of Detribalisation of an Indian Tribe and the Problems of Modernisation: A Sociological Study of the Lepchas of Darjeeling District* (Unpublished Ph. D. Thesis). Bhagalpur University, Bihar.

Mainwaring, G.B., 1876 (1985). A *Grammar of Rong (Lepcha) Language*. New Delhi: Daya Publishing House.

Namgyal, T. and Maharani Dolma of Sikkim, 1908. *History of Sikkim*. Unpublished Typed Manuscript.

Nebesky, W.R.V., 1956. *Whether The Gods Are Mountains: Three Years Among the People of Himalayas*. (Translated from German by Michael Bullock). London: Weildenfeld and Nicolson.

Niroula, B.P., 1988. 'Caste/Ethnic Composition of Population of Nepal', *CNAS Journal*, Vol. 25, No. 1, January, Kathmandu. Nepal.

O'Malley, L.S.S., 1907 (1989). *Bengal District Gazetteers: Darjeeling*. Delhi: Logos Press.

Philpot, H.C.V., 1925. *Final Report on the Survey and Settlement of Kalimpong Estate (1919 -1922)*. Calcutta.

Poter, A.E., 1931 (1987). *Census of India: Bengal and Sikkim Part II*. New Delhi: Usha Jain for Usha Publication.

Risley, H.H., 1891 (1981). *The Tribes and Castes of Bengal: Ethnographic Glossary*. Vol. II Calcutta: Firma KL Mukhopadhyay.

Risley, H.H., 1928 (2001). *The Gazetteer of Sikkim*. Delhi: Low Price Publications.

Rowney, H.B., 1822 (1974). *The Wild Tribes of India*. Delhi: B.R. Publishing Corporation.

Roy, D.C., 2011. 'Kaaden-Moo-Lee: The Traditional Lepcha House', *Aachuley* (A Quarterly Lepcha Bilingual News Magazine), Vol. 15, No. 2.

Roy, D.C., 2005. *Dynamics of Social Formation among the Lepchas*. Delhi: Akansha Publishing House.

Roy, D.C., 2009. Status of *Women among the Lepchas*. Delhi: Akansha Publishing House.

Roy, D.C., 2012. *Lepchas: Past and Present.* Siliguri: N. L. Publishers.

Sen, J., 1989. *Darjeeling: A Favoured Retreat*. Delhi: Indus Publishing Company.

Siiger, H. and J. Rischel, 1967. *The Lepchas: Cultural and Religion of a Himalayan People*. Part I and II. Copenhagen: The National Museum of Ethnographic Series.

Tamsang, K.P., 1983 (1998). *The Unknown and Untold Realities of the Lepchas*. Kalimpong: Mani Printing Press.

The Bengal Post, 2nd September, 2011.

The Telegraph, 23rd August, 2011.

White, J.C., 1909 (2005). *Sikkim and Bhuta: Twenty One Years on the North East Frontier: 1887-1908*. Varanasi: Pilgrims Publishing.

Risley, H.H. 1891 (1981) The Tribes and Castes of Bengal: [illegible] Glossary, Vol. II. Calcutta: Firma K.L. [illegible]

[illegible] 1998, 2001 [illegible]

[illegible] 18[illegible] (1934) [illegible] Delhi: B.R. Publishing Corporation.

Roy, S.C. 2011 [illegible] The Traditional [illegible]
[illegible] Quarterly [illegible]

Roy, D. 2005 [illegible] Delhi: [illegible] Publishing House.

Roy, L. 2009 Status of Women among the [illegible] Publishing House.

[illegible] Past and Present. [illegible]

[illegible] Delhi: [illegible] Company.

[illegible] 1968 [illegible] Peoples Part I and II [illegible] Monograph Series.

[illegible] K.R. 1983 (1998) [illegible] Publishing Press.

The [illegible] Post, 2nd September 2[illegible]

[illegible] 23rd August 2014

[illegible] 1991 (2005) [illegible]
[illegible]

8

Santals, the Victims of Academic Ethnicity: A Note on Baganpara (South) Santiniketan

Dipak Piplai

Prologue

Baganpara (South) is the name of a locality situated in the *Surul mouza* in Birbhum district of West Bengal. The locality is adjacent to Visva-Bharati, Santiniketan, which is the only Central University of the State. The word *Baganpara* has been derived from two Bengali words, Bagan (garden) and *Para* (hamlet), which has come up on the land of a *Bagan*. Earlier, the locality had a mango garden, known as *Kartick Babur Bagan* (the garden of Kartick Babu). *Baganpara* is *Santal* settlement now. The present-day settlers are the descendants of early *Santal* inhabitants of Birbhum, who have been living in this area for nearly three hundred years. The long social and economic intercourse between the *Santals* and the non-tribal and 'civilised' people of the area is a part of the local history. Visva-Bharati was established only ninety-four years back. But the recent activities of Visva-Bharati are threatening the physical, cultural, economic and religious life of the *Santal* settlers. The question of *ethnicity* is assuming a new meaning here, which is of immense anthropological interest.

The present paper is the outcome of a search, which has been conducted by the present author over a period of last 13 years. For collection of data I have used (1) observation, (2) conversation, (3) questionnaire, (4) document study, and (5) visual recordings methods.

Santals of Baganpara (South)

Everyday life of the *Santals* of *Baganpara* (South) was traditionally tied with the land of the area: (1) they were the cultivators of the nearby paddy-fields; (2) the adjoining land (which was previously called *Kumirdangar Math* and now known as *Binoy Bhabaner Math*), was (a) the regular grazing ground of their domesticated animals, (b) the 'road' for the boys and girls to their schools, (c) the 'road' for the patients to go to the doctors, (d) the play ground for the boys and girls, (e) the place for evening chatting, i.e., reciprocal verbal communication between men and women, and (f) occasionally used as the 'hunting ground' (at the time of *Bandhna* festival); (3) only three out of total twenty-three households (i.e., 13 per cent) have their own toilets while the remaining 20 families (132 persons) use this land for defecation.

In the last 13 years, the Santhals have planted 10 types of trees on the land. The fruit, flower, leaf, branch and twig, bark, and gum of these trees are used by them for various purposes, including medicinal use. The Santhals volunteered their labour to dig a pond on the said land. They used the soil, thus dug out, for various household purposes, including the maintenance and plastering of their mud-built huts. The pond partially helped sorting out the acute water crisis of the area. The pond was the source of drinking water and for washing utensils and the domestic animals. The pond gradually became the epi-centre of village culture; the Santhals used to do bathing and swimming, community fishing in the pond. It was an example of eco-friendly 'sustainable development' with peoples' initiative from the below.

Visva-Bharati: Tagore and After

Visva-Bharati was established in the year 1918 (Tagore 1919). But much before it came into being the basic philosophy of Visva-Bharati was conceptualised and expressed by Rabindranath Tagore in 1902 in *Naibedya as thus*:

- Where knowledge is free;
- Where the world has not been broken up into
- Fragments by narrow domestic walls …

In 1916, Tagore wrote: 'The Santiniketan school should be upheld as the bridge of communication between India and the rest of the world—we should aim to establish a centre of international humanities (*saarbajaatik manushwatyacharchaa*) there… It is my aspiration to make that place beyond all ethnic and geopolitical boundaries—there the first flag of the victory of all humanity will be waved' (Tagore 1916). This idea of *saarbajaatik manushwatyacharchaa*, centering Santiniketan, ultimately led to the establishment of Visva-Bharati. Throughout his life, Tagore maintained this ideal as a distinction on the soil of Santiniketan.

In 1930, he said at Santiniketan: 'Human beings have a natural characteristic features, which is sociability. He finds his/her ideal place inside the society by means of connecting with each other... When the human connections are spread over among his/her surrounding neighbours or inside his/her own abode and outside of it, the immensity of the link then derives pleasure in its own' (Tagore, 1930). In the last but one year of his life (1940), at a public meeting at Bankura Rabindranath said:

> I have transplanted myself from Kolkata to Santiniketan. The place is surrounded by villages... The local people—Santals—are bold in truth and beautiful in simplicity. I love them. I have roamed around villages at ease. There were no hindrances... (Tagore, 1940).

Largely because of this philosophical foundation, Visva-Bharati was a boundary-less institution in its early years. This was the fabric of Visva-Bharati till the 6th decade of the 20th century.

From the 1970s its various *Bhavans* (departments) started to separate themselves from others, creating fencing around themselves. Lastly, from the 1st decade of this century, Visva-Bharati started construction of brick-walls around the campus. Thus, by making it a well-demarcated, rather secluded academic centre, physically detached from the *Santal* villages, so far identified as its closest, oldest and trusted neighbours. Hence, the institution has rejected its novel and founding-philosophy of human oneness. Now, the 15 kms. long boundary wall has symbolically 'imprisoned' Visva-Bharati from its surroundings.

Two important observations may be made in this context.

1. At present, a total of 21 (i.e., 17 per cent) boys and girls of *Santal* community of *Baganpara* (South) are school children. All of them are the students of *Srinanda High School* (SHS) and which is situated very close to the Visva-Bharati. Out of nearly 1, 300 students of SHS, approximately 16 per cent are *Santals* (Goswami 2012). None of the *Santal* students from Baganpara is, or was, a student of Visva-Bharati. One of the former Vice-Chancellors of Visva-Bharati wrote: 'It is necessary to assess that how far we are trying to spread education by Visva-Bharati, to the surrounding villages' (Datta, 1980). But the culture of academic ethnicity is still withholding the task of spreading-education to the 'surrounding villages', of which the adjacent *Santal* village, *Baganpara* (South) is one.

2. At the Birth-Centenary Celebration function of Sadhu Ramchand Murmu, in the year 2000, none of the senior faculty like Barkha Soren or the Santal students of Visva-Bharati was invited even at the seminar. Altogether 15 tribals had participated and they were from Purulia and Jharkhand while the function was inaugurated by a Santal Minister of Central Government (Halder, 2009).

Local *Santals* are, *de facto*, considered as 'academically untouchable' by the Visva-Bharati authority. The origin of this academic ethnicity of Visva-Bharati may be traced back to the early 1940's. After the death of Rabindranath Tagore, in a meeting on the future of Santiniketan, Mohandas Karamchand Gandhi proposed to ban the 'outsiders' from getting education at *Pathabhaban*, i.e., the school section of Visva-Bharati (op. cit.). This is, perhaps, the earliest sign of formation of academic-ethnicity, which has culminated into the construction of the present-day boundary wall. The 'fighter' against social-untouchability became the tragic initiator of academic-ethnicity at Visva-Bharati.

Two Sides of the Wall: 'Legal' and 'Moral'

The south-western side of the boundary wall near *Baganpara* (South) has been witness to some 'development' activities within the 'legal' area of Visva-Bharati. The pond dug by the Santals has been filled up and in that place a sports complex has come up in the last few years. The north-eastern part is experiencing the immoral degradation of human life, a *de facto ghettoisation* of the *Santals*.

With the wall in place the *Santals* can no longer access the adjacent ground and pond, and they also had to forego their *traditional rights* over the aforesaid land. One can term this development as a kind of colonisation of the area. While the *Santals* bear the consequence of the Wall they have had no say on any of the decisions that have been taken. All of the Santal inhabitants, from a child to the aged, female and male, now sit by the road side, outside the enclosure of their houses to relieve themselves. The wall has destroyed the harmony of life of the Santals.

Moreover, the 'ownership' of Visva-Bharati over all the portions of its 'own land' is not beyond dispute. In a court-case centering an 'acquired' land of Visva-Bharati (which is nearly 25 *bigha*, i.e., approximately 3,60,000 sq. ft. in area), the Officer on Special Duty (Estate), Visva-Bharati, (in a Petition No. 749/C/2006) in the Court of the Civil Judge (Junior Division), First Court of Bolpur, Birbhum, pleaded on 05. 12. 2000 that the said land was 'acquired' on 02. 02. 1946 (L.A. Case no. 1/46-47). But, The Additional L.A.O. apprised on 24. 03. 2008 that no such 'acquisition' of land (J.L.No. 104, Dag No. 2393 and 2395) took place in favour of Visva-Bharati (Sarkar, 2011). The *Anamika Boys Hostel*, built by Visva-Bharati over a piece of land, had to be demolished and the total land (measuring 42 Cottas, i.e., 30, 240 sq. ft.) was returned to the Legal Owner, *Rajrajeswari Jew Trustee*, in accordance with a Court-order, in the year 2007 (Mitra, 2011).

'Legal' justification of the aforesaid newly constructed wall contradicts the moral basis of the relevant law which says: 'Whoever, not being a member of a Scheduled Caste or a Scheduled Tribe ... interferes with the enjoyment of his rights over any land, premises or water, ... shall be punishable with imprisonment for a term which shall not be less than six months but which may extend to five years and with fine' (Act, 1989).

Legality-morality dichotomy of the activity of Visva-Bharati has endangered the very existence of the *Santals* of Baganpara (South)! Back in 1932, Tagore said at Visva-Bharati: 'This time when I arrived from Kolkata, the people of the neighbouring village took me with them—being inside their own circle pleased me immensely, that we are kin to them, people have acknowledged' (Tagore 1932). After 80 years, today, the *Santal* villagers of the nearest Baganpara (South) are openly saying: 'They (i.e. Visva-Bharati) do not consider us as human beings!'

Visva-Bharati has spent at least Rs 4, 30, 96,627 for construction of 14.65 km. long 'boundary wall at various places within the premises of Santiniketan and Sriniketan' (Khastgir, 2010). Had Visva-Bharati spent less than one per cent of their total boundary-expenses not only the *Santals* of Baganpara (South) but all the 400-odd *Santal* families of adjacent five villages, i.e., *Baganpara (South), Baganpara (North), Balipara, Pearsonpalli* and *Kalidanga,* could have had their own sanitary toilets, and could have avoided the inhuman and undignified life-style.

While constructing the wall in total disregard to Tagore's philosophy and the institution's social responsibility towards its closest and oldest neighbours the present-day Visva-Bharati authorities did not feel it necessary to conduct an impact-assessment of the project on tribal life. Despite having a wing for rural reconstruction (*Palli Samgathana Vibhaga* – PSV), and a centre for social studies and rural development (*Palli Charcha Kendra*) the university authorities have not bothered to take a look at how the wall has impacted the life of the wretched Santals on the other side of the Wall, whom Tagore considered his own kin.

Consolidation of Santal Ethnicity

The *Santals* of Baganpara (South) maintained their social, cultural, political and religious life in many ways despite penetration of exogenous forces of change. They have largely retained community fishing, forestry, hunting (at the time of *Bandhna Parab*), dance, musical performance, meeting for selection of *Sardar*, worshiping of their own deities and so on. The vast ground adjacent to their habitation has facilitated continuation of these activities.

Erection of the aforesaid wall has impacted their various socio-cultural and even religious activities. This development has hurt their collective self and aroused a sense of anger among the *Santals* at the community level. They now talk about the 'dignity of the *adivasis*' and want to have a piece of 'own' land where they could perform their religious and other cultural activities. As an expression of their anger they have already smashed the wall twice, in two places, despite the possibility of police action.

Opinions of both the male and female members of the Santal community are reflections of their sense of insecurity or threat-perception, which, in turn, is strengthening a sense of ethnic (tribal/*adivasi*) identity. Let me place here how the Santals perceive the encroachment of 'development' activities into their space and existence.

Nitai Marandi, Male, 61 years (*Sardar*) said: 'We are gradually being encircled by the newly constructed buildings. Our access to the ground is now gone. Where will we go? Where will we graze our cattle? How will they survive? Can they live consuming rice?' Ramu Soren, Male, 45 years (a priest) said: 'Yes, going and coming through the ground is no more possible; it is a serious problem. But more serious problem is the loss of privacy. Henceforth the relatives will not come; they will not stay in our house. Where will they go for toilet? There will be no more dignity of the *adivasis*. Indu Marandi (55 years), male, said: 'The government is telling us to give school-education to our children. But the boys and girls cannot go to the school due to the wall. They are children and cannot cross the high wall. Nanda Hansda (31 years), male, said: 'The boys can no more play on the ground. Now we cannot bring the leaves and twigs easily through the ground.' This is what Dhana Marandi, Male, 42 years, had to say: 'We have to demolish the wall. There is no other alternative. If they want to arrest us, let them do that.'

The same anger and frustration found expression in the voices of many others. Meno Soren, Female, 42 years, said: 'For the construction of the wall, they have demolished the water-tap as well. They did not spare even a small piece of land for our use, not even a place for drying paddy. There is no other place for us to go; we have to stay here. We do not know, what will be our fate!' Sunati Murmu, a woman of 48 years of age, echoed the collective feeling saying: 'in the absence of a proper place relieving ourselves has become a nightmare. How can I bring the twigs at home through the ground which is full of filth?' Phulmoni Membram, another woman of 60 years of age, said: 'We cannot go for toilet; cannot move through the ground; cannot go to the hospital, without taking a long route. Our movement is problem because of this wall.' Basanti Tudu, a 22 year-old girl said: 'The wall has brought us miseries, the worst being the problem of lavatory.' Repeating the concern Saraswati Marandi, a woman of 57 years said: 'It has become a problem even to go to the health centre. The children are being forced to cross this high wall for going to school, which involves a great deal of risk for them.' And thus echoes the collectively shared concern of the Santals Baganpara in many more voices.

Conflict and Co-operation: Conflict in Dominance

It appears, from the above, as if the two neighbourly ethnic groups—the *Santals* and *Visva-Bharati* are alien to each other and are at logger-heads. Anthropology needs 'observation and more observation' (Bose, 1972) to understand the dynamics of the relations between the two conflicting communities. While the two neighbourly communities would have been in a friendly cooperation a relation of conflict, as we observe today, could have been avoided.

Not too long ago the whole area was full of *shal* forest, and the *Santals* were the sole inhabitants of the region (Acharya, 1982). The Santals of Baganpara (South) continue to celebrate the *Baha* festival after the blooming of *shal* flower in every year. Some elderly members of the *Santal* community specify the mango-garden near their village (and under the disputed 'legal' jurisdiction of Visva-Bharati), as *sarjom bagan*, i.e., shal forest. These facts are very much suggestive of the rootedness of the *Santals* in this area. But, despite their repeated request, the Visva-Bharati refused to pay any hid to the deepest pain of the *Santals.* Their written appeals might have been thrown into the waste-paper box. The illegal, unethical and inhuman construction of the wall—defying the law of the land—has totally been rejected by the Santals because of its telling effect on their life. The ethnicity of Visva-Bharati community is so dominant that none of its '8,000 strong members' has raised a voice of sympathy for the marginalised Santals. There has been no voice of resistance to the move of the university authority from any corner of its fraternity—faculty, research scholars, students and general staff of the university.

Marginalisation of the *Santals* at Baganpara (South) seems to be a fait accompli. The author noticed *Bursi Sengel* (fire with husk) among the *Santals* in Baganpara (South).

Epilogue

Ethnicity is a highly elastic concept and the process of its formation and dissolution is an important area to the social scientists (Calhoun, 2002). The Academic Ethnicity of Visva-Bharati, the intrusion by the dominant into the physical and cultural space of the people on the margin, is arousing frustration and anger in the latter, encouraging them to unite in the name of tribal (Santal) identity, where class and ethnic identities coalesce. The boundary wall that the university authorities have constructed is read as both real and symbolic wall between the dominant community of the university and the marginalised Santals, whom Tagore considered his kin. 'Tribal' ethnicity of the *Santals* here is markedly proportionate to the Academic-ethnicity of Visva-Bharati.

'Scientific observation' and dispassionate and objective description are the declared standards of Anthropology or any other scientific discipline. But there are scientists with human concern who stress on embeddedness. Every possible intervention in the 'life of suffering humans' (here, the *Santals*), is an obligatory duty of the 'science of man'. To be active to minimise the travail of *Santal*-life is also a part of our many obligations.

References

Acharya, Buddhadeb, 1982. *Surul–Sarkaarbaari O Maharshir Santiniketan* (in Bengali). Rarh Santiniketan: Gabeshana Parsad.

Act, 1989. *The Scheduled Castes and the Scheduled Tribes (Prevention of Atrocities) Act, 1989 and Rules, 1995*. Hyderabad: Gogia Law Agency, 2005: 2-3.

Bose, Nirmal Kumar, 1972. 'Methods in Anthropological Study of Indian Society', *Journal of the Indian Anthropological Society*, Vol. 7, No. 1.

Calhoun, Craig, 2002. *Dictionary of the Social Sciences*. Oxford University Press: 148.

Datta, Amlan, 1980. Cited in Arun Majumder, 'Visva-Bharati Samaaje Asaamaajik Upaachaarja' (in Bengali), in Pathik Basu (ed.) *Byaktitwa O Samajbhabna* (An Anthology of the Personality and Social Thinking of Professor Amlan Datta). Kolkata: Samatat Prakashani, 2000: 25.

Goswami, Gouranga, 2012. Verbal Communication with Shree Goswami, the Teacher's representative in the Managing Committee, Srinanda High School, Bolpur.

Halder, Niranjan, 2009. 'Visva-Bharati O Adivasi Samaajer Durabasthaa' (in Bengali), *Adivasi Sambad*, Volume 1, 15th Nov., 2009.

Interview with Mitra, Siddhartha 2011. Social activist, Santiniketan.

Khastgir, Shyamali, 2010. Information under the RTI Act, provided by Visva-Bharati, dated 06. 08. 2010 (Courtesy: Niranjan Haldar).

Sarkar, Madhab, 2011. Papers of the Court-case and related information provided to the present author by Sri Madhab Sarkar, Member of the *Surul Barabaari Debottar Trust*, on 19-20 March, 2011, at Surul village, Birbhum.

Tagore, Rabindranath, 1902. *Gitanjali*, with an introduction by W. B. Yeats. Kolkata: East India Publishers. (E.I.P. Edition): 35, (Original Bengali version in *Rabindra Rachanabali*, Vol. 1. Calcutta: Government of West Bengal, 1980, p. 994)

—, 1916. *Visva-Bharati* (in Bengali). Kolkata: Visva-Bharati Grantha Bibhag, 1396 B.S. (1989), p. 170.

—, 1932. Speech at Annual Meeting of *Visva-Bharati Parisad Sabha* (1339 B.S.); in: *Visva-Bharati*.

—, 1930. *'Grambasider Proti'*, in *Russia'r ChiThi* (in Bengali), Visva-Bharati Granthan Bibhag, Kolkata, 1411 B.S. (2005), p. 128.

—, 1940. *Rabindra Rachanabali* (in Bengali), Vol. 13. Calcutta: Government of West Bengal, 1990, p. 814.

9

Timelessness in Identity Politics and Reincarnation of Ethnic Movements: Constructing Ethno-histories of Rajbangsi People in North Bengal

Rajib Nandi

Introduction

India since independence has experienced a series of movements based on 'identity politics' demanding separate states and reorganisation of its internal state boundaries. The contemporary discussions find the uneven development and unequal access to power accelerated by regionalism and linguistic fanatism responsible for these movements.

A close look at today's Kamatapur movement by the Koch-Rajbangsi people (or popularly known as Rajbangsi), certainly shows that there is more to it. It would be a uni-dimensional analysis to single out the elitist nature of regionalism in these movements or post-independent politically hasty decisions to demarcate states as solely responsible for today's separatist movements. Nor would it be enough to explain these movements as an outcome of economic deprivations and underdevelopment alone but are more complex in nature. Clifford (2004: 9) argues, 'today's indigenous movements complicate dichotomous, arguably, Eurocentric conceptions of 'cultural' verses 'political' or 'economic agency', which can be seen in the present Kamatapur movement as well.

I argue, in this paper, that the ethnic movements display a timeless quest of people and their aspirations which is reflected in their deep sense of history, where their present and future lies in the past. Here the past which is continually constructed and re-constructed and each time it is contextualised within the contemporary socio-political setup. In other words, people's unique sense of history or 'historical imaginations', are each time contextualised within their particular aspirations/quest. Today's 'separatist movements' might be couched in a more contemporary and secular language of socio-economic injustices and socio-cultural differences yet they are rooted in people's 'historical consciousness'. Socio-economic injustices are more often seen as a continuation of past history in the present and the future. Thus, a certain historicity is evoked, at a certain moment in time, allowing contemporary social relations to be understood and interpreted in terms of the past.

Based on my field work carried out from 1993 onwards in Darjeeling, Jalpaiguri and Cooch Behar districts of West Bengal this paper explores Kamatapur movement as a struggle for regaining a lost land, a lost culture and language and most importantly the 'true identity' of Rajbangsi people. I argue that the Rajbanshis are not only making and re-making their past 'both as actors and narrators' (Trouillot 2003: 12) but there is a constant dialogue taking place between the past and present. Nandy (2001: 1) comments, 'This idea of the past has some curious implications. First a study of the past becomes not merely a conversation with archives, but also the creation of new and unique dialogues with those who live with their distinctive pasts.' He further observes that Indians have a unique 'concept of "cyclical" time where the present, past, and future blend into a static "timeless" absolute, and where progress and material well-being bear no direct relationship to progression in time' (Nandy 2001: 24). Perhaps, this is because people tend to construct their past history and present identity simultaneously. Today the Rajbanshis of North Bengal are creating a 'new past' and a new identity. They are glorifying their 'ancient Kamata civilisation' on the basis of an argument 'we had established a strong civilisation before you came here' (Clifford, 2007: 197) and simultaneously crafting a contemporary 'Koch-Rajbanshi' identity which is a blend of colonial ethnography on one hand and Rajbangsi mythographies on the other. Here I raise an important question—can the past or the present for that matter be understood in complete isolation from one another? Thus, questioning the dichotomy that apparently exists between the past and present as pointed out by Comaroff (1985). The paper also argues that identity as a category of practice is not born on a particular situation. It is rather a timeless practice. However, the historical moments make this practice spectacular and eventful.

Hermann's (2005) study of the Banabans in central Oceania later resettled in Fiji raises similar questions. It is an excellent example of how people create specific consciousness of history that transforms themselves and their relationship with the others through awareness of their ethnicity, both in the past and present. Interestingly, Hermann also points out how emotions shape and structure the Banabans historical consciousness by highlighting particular events of the past as relevant.

Questions of indigeneity on the other hand, are often seen in the context of historical consciousness which also has an inherent element of power relations. Thus discussions on the ideas of 'indigenous' people (Béteille 1998; Childs and Delgado-P, 1999; Kuper, 2003) revolve around ethnic activism and indigenous people's fight over land, culture and administrative authority (Escobar, 1998; Jackson and Warren, 2005; Morgan, 2007). Hirsch and Stewart (2005) particularly clarify this by arguing the importance of local political strategies in shaping the micro histories where both past and present overlap in forming people's identity in a global context. Several authors have also raised questions on people's sense of historical continuity with pre-colonial societies and the nature of historicity that is being invoked. However, it has also been argued that there is an apparent arbitrariness to the historicity because it depends on a key moment in history. Hence, 'indigeneity' is not simply a historical relationship of 'we were here before you' but the perduring power relations that arise out of a sense of historical injustice rather than simple historical priority (Canessa, 2008). De la Cadena and Starn (2007: 3) contend that the structures of power and imagination of indigeneity demands its recognition as a relational field of governance, subjectivities, and knowledge that involves both the indigenous and non-indigenous. 'To be or not to be indigenous is to be in a position, usually of relative powerlessness but it is always a claim to justice and a claim to justice based on an historical relation. Indigeneity is about history and power.' Often indigenous people are seen as inheritors of a colonial situation which has continued over time with altered symbols of power and oppression. Canessa (2008) argued that continuity lies in the historical consciousness rather than specific cultural forms, where the 'historicised consciousness' is fundamentally based on contemporary social relations rather than a romanticised attachment to the mythical past.

Comaroff and Comaroff (1992: 11) argue that historical imagination is culturally crafted. They propose a 'neomodern' framework to construct imaginative sociologies emphasising on one hand, the need to include human maneuver, ambivalence and historical indeterminacy as 'meaning is always, to some extent, arbitrary and diffuse, that social life everywhere rests on the imperfect ability to reduce ambiguity and concentrate power.' On the other, micro/local histories which are partial and hidden must be contextualised within the wider worlds of power that give them meaning or they stand in danger of remaining stories (Comaorff and Comaroff, 1992). If we look at Kamatapur movement as creation of micro/local histories with the issue of identity at its heart we certainly cannot overlook the larger political context in which it is being shaped.

Identity formation and politics based on identities in India and other developing countries are seen as effects of globalisation and development in contemporary studies (Appadurai, 1996, 2003; Tomlinson, 1999). Their view of identity and belongingness, which is fluid as well as constructed, raises questions about the idea of nationalism in a continuously changing world. On the other hand, Pathak (2006) argued that India has always been characterised by intense identity politics. Consequently, centralising Hindu-nationalism has been contested time and again by diverse ethnic groups of this vast country.

It is understood that in India a cultural nationalistic hegemony co-exists with politics of difference. India's democratic institutions have encouraged the culture of centralised politics and at the same time created different socio-cultural identities. The emergence of identity politics in present-day India combined with socio-political conflicts and conflicting sentiments is thus contextualised within new economic and social issues, which is a part of global democratic scenario.

The term identity is 'too ambiguous, too torn between hard and soft meanings, essentialist connotations and constructivist qualifiers, to serve well the demands of social analysis' (Brubaker and Cooper, 2000: 2). Identity is formed with varying levels of centrality for the individual and the group in reference to an 'other' (Croucher, 2004) whereas, identity politics is treated as normative political evaluation geared toward social change, which is primarily descriptive rather than explanatory (Bernstein, 2005). In the present-day global era, 'identity politics' might have acquired a new meaning and visibility as a political practice with the corresponding literature and a large number of analysts as well as protagonists. Chatterjee (2009) argues that identity politics or the ethnic politics in recent time could be connected with the new forms of political mobilisation in which people actually expect government to provide them with some kind of basic services like education or employment without any primordial loyalties as understood in 'old anthropology'.

Under such circumstances, it is not surprising that the emergence of regional identities as forms of social and political movement have strengthened. The presence of a centralised force that acts simultaneously to counter the 'politics of otherness' is evident, too. The issues have formed a vital aspect of political campaigning in India during the past sixty years, and the trend perhaps grew steadily stronger since 1980s as a more consolidated political strategy. Here identity acts as a vehicle of socio-political mobilisation and strengthen the forces of differences bringing back with it historical identities and differences in opinions.

It is often argued that identity politics of the minorities is contextualised in a modern global context because they challenge national narratives of social cohesion and homogeneity (Appadurai, 2006). Clifford (2004: 9) points out that under the conditions of globalisation, self-determination is less a matter of independence and more a practice of managing interdependence, inflecting uneven power relations. Moreover the present day subaltern strategies are 'flexible and adapted to specific post-/neocolonial, globally interconnected contexts', which is 'not an entirely new predicament as indigenous movements have always had to make the best of bad political-economic situations.'

The Kamatapur movement has brought to life the identity issue in this region. It is a part of an age old tradition of broader north-east region of India where the people have always felt marginalised and never accepted the categories imposed by the dominant groups (Baruah, 1999), nor it ever accepted the formalised categorisation developed by the state. Through the social movements of Rajbanshis, I explore their history and ethnography to establish my argument that, 'historicised consciousness' is not evoked suddenly but haunts people's emotions, which may not be visible but remain subtle. It gains visibility when a key moment of history is celebrated in a spectacular manner through people's movements marked by a re-interpretation, re-writing and re-documenting of the past, real yet imagined, time bound yet eternal. I attempt here to understand the ethnography and the history in making of the Rajbanshis at one hand. On the other, I try to grasp and relate the different contexts with different underlying power relations in which the Rajbangsi ethnography and history is being made.

The paper relies on narratives collected from a range of people belonging to numerous local communities, primarily Koch-Rajbangsi and Bengali. I have paid attention to pre-colonial folk scriptures, colonial survey reports and accounts, pamphlets, souvenirs, letters of different organisations and political parties and contemporary vernacular literature written by the local people discussing the history and society of North Bengal as they offer a wealth of data for the events and periods considered in the paper. Since, the Rajbangsi people's historical self is not just confined to the pages of colonial ethnographic documents, pre-colonial folk scriptures or vernacular literature but extends much beyond it—to poetry, stories, legends and myths, which have also provided me with rich data.

The History of Kamatapur: The Journey from Pragjyotisha to Cooch Behar

The history of Kamtapur, written and documented since the colonial period or even before, is often found disjointed and obscure. It presents a pre-colonial past of North Bengal or North-East on the whole which was dominated by different groups of Mongoloid and semi-Mongoloid people and their indigenous cultures. Although their cultures, at times, apparently seem inseparable from one another, have different yet unknown origin and history. The cultural and political boundaries of North Bengal not only gave birth to different people with different languages but also at the same time paved way for cultural exchanges and resistances. Over time the region has emerged as a cultural frontier on the margins of the Gangetic Hindu civilisation and the myths and folktales on their origin and culture time and again tell and re-tell their interactions with and resistances to greater Hindu societies.

Diverse myths and folklores of Koch, Rajbangsi and other indigenous people on their origin, naming, movement and struggle indicate towards a greater cultural interaction on one hand and cultural instability on the other. The continuous change of names of the people and the places can be interpreted as repeated cultural makeovers in defence of culture and cultural resistances. It is understood that affiliations among the people have been effective at different points of time. Consequently, 'identity' was always a concern for this cultural frontier. On the other hand, historicity of Pragjyotisha always set in the context of 'acceptance' by the greater Indian society.

The emergence of Koch kings as a power centre in the region in the 16th century and its protest against the mighty Mughals certainly tells a story of their great political resistance (Chatterji, 1974). Colonial North Bengal on the other hand experienced a different form of dissent-witnessing an era of emergence of Rajbangsi identity, as a separate and dominant cultural entity, as a resistance to colonial development and colonial categorisation, documentation and publishing of history, geography, economy and culture of the local people, followed by large-scale peasant movements. It is popularly believed that the present-day backwardness and social tensions in the region is rooted in its colonial legacy.

The History of Colonial Development: A Bengali-Marxist Version

Many contemporary discussions tend to locate the present Kamatapur uprising in the colonial history of North Bengal. They argue that the moment British brought Dooars and adjacent Darjeeling Terai region under their direct control in 1860s drastic changes took place. Within a few years of its annexation Terai-Dooars became an important timber supplying zone for British India. Subsequently, railways were introduced. The British brought the four 'T's—timber, tea, tribe and tilling as they were interested in generating revenues from the natural resources. They set up the forest department and demarcated huge forestlands as reserve forests. In the process, the forest-based communities—*Koch, Mech, Garo, Rabha*, and so on—were thrown out of these areas. Secondly, large forests were cleared for tea plantation and plough cultivation. European and Indian planters established hundreds of tea estates, entirely new to the local people and hundreds of thousands of tribal people were brought here from Chotanagpur to work as tea coolies. A few of the local forest-based communities were also engaged as forest labourers. Thirdly, the Rajbanshis from Rangpur and neighbouring districts started settling here as cultivators. They were believed to be hard working and more enterprising in comparison to the local Rajbanshis. They took large holdings from the government on lease for cultivation and then leased large parts of these lands to sharecroppers. The big land holders were termed as '*jotedars*'.

Rajbangsi *jotedars* were the primary architects of modern North Bengal by extending agriculture as a revenue generating trade. People from other districts of Bengal too came in search of land and livelihood because land was in abundance here. They were encouraged to extend agriculture by clearing forests. Several land settlement surveys were conducted to regularise this process. As a result, bigger agricultural markets developed quickly. The outcome of agricultural development led to the crystallisation of sharecropping. The skewed distribution of land among the big and small cultivators and exploitation of landless poor peasants resulted in a series of peasant movements from 1940s onwards by the sharecroppers of North Bengal.

At the same time, colonial developments attracted a large number of people since 1860s. With the development of agriculture, forestry and tea plantation, in such a short span of time, people from other parts of Bengal started pouring in. In addition, with the establishment of new government offices, courts, schools and so on, many Bengalis came here as teachers, lawyers, clerks and businessmen, for the white-collar jobs. People came in search of new opportunities. Finally, the partition of Bengal in 1947 broke all barriers. Thousands of Bengalis from East Pakistan (now Bangladesh), the Bengali refugees or *bhatias* settled everywhere in North Bengal that too within a decade. Many of them bought land from the local Rajbanshis. Gradually, a large share of the economy was taken over by a group of Bengalis.

The contemporary readings of Rajbangsi history largely reflect not only a Marxist perspective of the present Kamatapur movement but also the underlying power dynamics between Begalis vis-à-vis their Rajbangsi neighbours in a very subtle way. Bengali culture is largely represented by a Calcutta centric Bengali culture which has evolved in the past one and a half century by the English educated *Bengali Bhadraloks* (Bengali gentlemen). Highly influenced by European education during the colonial period it got strengthened in the twentieth century through literary practices, artistic expressions, social movements, and anti-British resistances. All of which gave birth to a political culture of Bengal that at times was criticised as exclusive, hegemonic and ethno-centric. The regional Bengali culture more often acted very submissively towards this 'Bengali nationalism' with usual resistances on occasions. Even the Marxist ideology of Bengal is regarded as Bengali culture or rather as their hegemonic political culture by others in the region, nurtured and shaped by the Calcutta based leaders and intellectuals.

Rajbanshi *Kshatriyaisation* Movement: Contouring the Past and Shaping the Present

Identity movements, as already mentioned, are not new to North Bengal. Perhaps, in modern times the issue gained prominence with Rajbangsi *Kshatriyaisation* movement. The agitation started with the publication of the first Indian Census Report in 1882, when the British administration clubbed

Koch and Rajbangsi as 'same tribe'. The Rajbangsi intelligentsia protested vehemently against this categorisation. This not only initiated a debate on the origin and social status of Rajbanshis but also a reform movement in Rajbangshi society of Bengal.

The clubbing of Koches and Rajbanshis in the census might have been an outcome of several ethnographic surveys that considered Rajbanshis as more Hinduised Koches, having semi-Mongoloid origin. A few on the other hand argued that Rajbanshis were ethnically linked to Dravidians. But Rajbanshis opposed both these views and claimed to be *'vartya kshatriya'* or down-trodden Kshatriyas as opposed to Koches who they believed to be a semi-Hinduised tribe, who still practice profane rituals and consume prohibited meat. The main demand of Kshatriyaisation movement was to be recognised as Kshatriyas and be given a separate status distinct from the Koch.

Oommen (2010) argues that in India caste, religious, linguistic and tribal movements are primordial in nature. If one follows his arguments, Kshatriyaisation movement was seeking symbolic goals through the redefinition of status and privilege of Rajbanshis. Social movements of twentieth century in India could be better understood within the reformist, transformative and revolutionary framework as coined by Rao (1979). Most social movements in India are substantively historical and should be seen within the processes of social change. The Rajbangsi Kshatriyaisation movement consolidated itself during the upsurge of movements in an epoch of social transformation in colonial India. The movement, on the other hand, was 'separatist' in nature if one re-looks at the Rajbangsi effort in establishing themselves as different or distinct from the Koches. The nature of the movement was in tune with the dominant Hindu-Brahminical order in Bengali society and the reforms were done in accordance with the existing Hindu caste system on the basis of purity and pollution. Taking clue from the argument made by Clifford (2004), this was an effort to reconstruct history to adjust in the dominant discourse of that time and reviving the past.

However, since 1940s with the emergence of Dalit politics the Kshatriyaisation movement gradually faded. Rajbangsi leadership started showing more interest in understanding the legal and constitutional rights of the Rajbangsi people as a 'scheduled caste' group. Though Kshatriyaisation ceremonies continued and mainstreamed within the Rajbangsi culture, it lost its earlier enthusiasm and remained as merely ritualistic. However, the relevance of Kshatriyaisation movement cannot be undermined. The movement was an attempt not only to ascertain a higher status for the Rajbanshis but also to find their 'true identity'. In the process they not only celebrated the sacred-thread wearing customs but also recreated a past for themselves through this movement but reiterating and celebrating it in their everyday practices. It also spawned a time and space where they re-documented their history by the re-reading and re-interpretation of their folk ballads, Puranas and tantras.

The making of history never ceases. The celebration and making of history has once again at the end of the twentieth century captured the central stage of Rajbangsi social life but this time it is not exactly on the same lines compared to the beginning of the century. This time it is in the guise of a movement for a separate state. Now, Rajbangsi people are fighting for a greater social and political authority on the basis of another past, partly based on colonial documentations and partly on their reconstructed history. Nevertheless, the historical imaginations have been fine-tuned, sharpened and re-contextualised within contemporary socio-political setup and secular language.

Rajbangsi Kshatriya to Koch-Rajbangsi Kshatriya: Another Past, Another Resistance

Departing from their earlier arguments the Rajbanshis are now trying to ascertain that Koch-Rajbanshis were not Kshatriyas by birth but by their *karma* (deed). However, Rajbangsi Kshatriyaisation movement, which is less than hundred years old, has been totally subverted by the ethnographic present of the Rajbanshis. The Rajbangsi historicity is formed strategically in accordance with contemporary Indian society and polity. The Koch and Rajbangsi dichotomy is strategically muted by highlighting another dichotomy between the Rajbangsi and the Bengali.

The historical land which the Rajbanshis are creating is widely believed to be put together by the Koch kings. As far as the documented history is concerned, a state called Kamatabehar with its capital in Kamatapur was established by the Khen king Sandhya Roy in early 13th century. Since 16th century it was ruled by the Koch kings, who once again reorganised the kingdom and renamed it as Cooch Behar in 17th century. The present Kamatapur movement in its attempt to create a Koch-Rajbangsi identity not only recreates the history of this region but gives a certain historical perspective to the movement. By which I refer to the unique process of historicising their identity and place that draws a connection between the identity of the people, their culture, land and history.

The Rajbangsi historicity has clearly taken a different shape within a gap of hundred years. The contradictions and discontinuities between those two versions of history are wide and distinct. Consequently the Rajbangsi identity has been re-configured from Kshatriya to Koch in a fascinating manner. The reference points have been changed from *Puranas* and *Tantras* to colonial administrative ethnography. It is understood that the shift has been brought over due to the changed social and political environments of present day India. The dalit politics in India has changed the overall political scenario and social compositions to a large extent. However, one is surprised to see that the Rajbangshis themselves have forgotten their much celebrated Kshatriyaisation movement. The strategic silence on the Kshatriyaisation movement seems to be a desperate attempt by the present Rajbangshi leadership to disconnect the present movement from the earlier one. Perhaps, they understand that two different Rajbangsi pasts as discontinuous which are non accommodative in a single history.

If one looks at the key players in this whole drama, not much change could be noticed here as Koch, Rajbangsi and Bengali remain in the centre of discussions. The earlier battle lines were drawn between the Koch and the Rajbanshis where the Bengali was placed as a catalyst but an isolated factor. On the other hand, this time it is between the Rajbanshis and the Bengalis where Koch has been rediscovered as an intimate historical associate. However, one cannot deny that the core fight between the Rajbanshis and the *bhadralok* Bengalis of Bengal continues.

The thread of resistance continues against the forceful categorisation by external authorities, either colonial government or the Indian state. Identity here serves as the source of political organisation for the Rajbanshis, where they are presented as victims of social and political hegemony. If one looks at this strategic construction and re-construction of Rajbangsi identity within a broader historical perspective, it could be interpreted as an endless process of re-configuring strategy marked as historical moments in Rajbangsi history.

A closer look at the history of Rajbangsi social movements in pre- and post independent Bengal reveals a shift yet the quest for Rajbangsi identity is very much at its core. The Rajbangsi Kshatriyaisation movement in pre-independent Bengal in early twentieth century was essentially a reformist cultural movement which gradually gave way to a transformative political movement in the post-independent India at the end of the century through the Kamatapur movement. The shift of identity from 'Rajbangsi Kshatriya' to 'Koch Rajbangsi' is articulated through a more intense political action ruptured with an ambiguous historicity and a paradoxical strategic dilemma. Consequently, the Rajbangsi social movements have been affected with strange identity crisis. The strategic essentialist nature of the movement influenced by the contextualised social, cultural and political factors strengthens and at the same time weakens the Rajbangsi social movements, as these paradoxes remain conflicting and unexplained.

The interpretations made by the Rajbanshis of their history and identity are a blend of colonial ethnography on the one hand and Rajbangsi mythographies on the other. Here the past not only overlaps with the present but the ahistorical with the historical as well. Thus, suggesting the complex nature of their historical consciousness and imaginations, which is at times ruptured, contested and fluid. They go beyond and in making of their identity they reconstruct an ancient history of the Koch-Rajbangsi that is simply a celebration of history through creation of histories, both real and imagined.

Interestingly, both versions of Rajbangsi imaginations derive legitimacy from their historical past which is merged with a mythical past. The conflicting articulation between the two pasts is not due to the lack of history but many histories. The articulation and practice of historicity change with every re-telling. Identity as a category of practice was not born in a particular situation but is rather a continuous quest making it a timeless practice. It is the historical moments that make this practice spectacular and eventful.

Through the study of the social movements of Koch-Rajbangsi people in North Bengal, the paper argues that these movements display a timeless quest and aspirations of people that is rooted in their deep sense of history. People's unique sense of history or 'historical imaginations', are contextualised within the secular language of socio-economic injustices and socio-cultural differences celebrated in a spectacular manner through these movements marked by re-interpretation, re-writing of the past, real yet imagined, time bound yet eternal. The conflicting articulations between different pasts are not due to the lack of history but many histories. The temporal practice of historical memories changes with every re-telling. The paper argues that identity as a category of practice is not born on a particular situation. It is rather a timeless practice. However, the historical moments make this practice spectacular and eventful.

References

Appadurai, A., 1996. *Modernity at Large: Cultural Dimensions of Globalisation.* Minneapolis London: University of Minnesota Press.

Appadurai, A., (ed.), 2003. *Globalisation.* Durham: Duke University Press.

Appadurai, A., 2006. *Fear of Small Numbers: An Essay of the Geography of Anger*. London: Duke University Press.

Banarjee, S., 1980. *In the Wake of Naxalbari – A History of the Naxalite Movement in India*. Calcutta: Subarnarekha.

Baruah, S., 1999. *India against Itself: Assam and the Politics of Nationality*. Delhi: Oxford University Press.

Bernstein, M., 2005. 'Identity Politics', Annual *Review of Sociology*, Vol. 31, pp. 47-74.

Béteille, Andre. 1998. 'The Idea of Indigenous People', *Current Anthropology*, Vol. 39, No. 2, pp. 187-192.

Beverly. H., 1872. *Report of the Census of Bengal 1872*. Calcutta: Bengal Secretariat Press.

Brubaker, R. and F. Cooper, 2000. 'Beyond Identity', *Theory and Society*, Vol. 29, No. 1, pp. 1-47.

De la Cadena, Marisol and O, Starn (eds.), 2007, Indigenous *Experience Today*. London: Berg.

Canessa, A., 2008, 'The Past is not Another Country: Exploring Indigenous Histories in Bolivia', *History and Anthropology*, Vol. 19, No. 4, pp. 353-369.

Chatterjee, Partha, 1975. 'Bengal: Rise and Growth of a Nationality', *Social Scientist*, Vol. 4, No. 1, pp. 67-82.

Chatterjee, Partha, 2009. 'Towards a Post-colonial Modernity', Interview with Partha Chatterjee, [online] Available at: http://www.asiasource.org/news/special_reports/chatterjee.cfm

Chatterji, S.K., 1974. *Kirata Jana Krti The Indo-Mongoloids: Their Contribution to the History and Culture of India*. Calcutta: The Asiatic Society.

Childs, J.B. and Delgado, P.G., 1999. 'On the Idea of Indigenous', *Current Anthropology*, Vol. 40, No. 2, pp. 211-212.

Clifford, J., 2004. 'Looking Several Ways: anthropology and Native Heritage in Alaska', *Current Anthropology*, Vol. 45, No. 1, pp. 5-30.

Clifford, J., 2007. 'Varieties of Indigenous Experience: Diasporas, Homelands, Sovereignties', in M. de la Cadena and O. Starn *(eds.) Indigenous Experience Today*. Oxford: Berg.

Comaroff, J., 1985. *Body of Power Spirit of Resistance: The Culture and History of a South African People*. Chicago: The University of Chicago Press.

Comaorff, J. and J. Comaroff, 1992. *Ethnography and the Historical Imagination*. Colorado: Westview Press.

Cooper, A., 1980. *Sharecropping and Sharecroppers' Struggles in Bengal 1930-1950*. Calcutta: K.P. Bagchi.

Croucher, S., 2004. *Globalisation and Belonging: The Politics of Identity in a Changing World*. Lanham: Rowen and Littlefield.

Das Gupta, R., 1992, *Economy, Society and Politics in Bengal: Jalpaiguri 1869-1947*. Delhi: Oxford University Press.

Debnath, S., (ed.), 2007. *Social and Political Tensions in North Bengal (Since 1947)*. Siliguri: N.L. Publishers.

Escobar, A., 1998. 'Whose knowledge, Whose Nature? Biodiversity, Conservation, and the Political Ecology of Social Movements', *Journal of Political Ecology*, Vol. 5, pp. 53-82.

Hermann, E., 2005. 'Emotions and the Relevance of the Past: Historicity and Ethnicity among the Banabans of Fiji', *History and Anthropology*, Vol. 13, No. 3, pp. 275-291.

Hirsch, Eric and Stewart, C., 2005. 'Introduction: Ethnographies of Historicity', *History and Anthropology*, Vol. 16, No. 3, pp. 261-274.

Hunter, W.W., 1876. *Statistical Accounts of Bengal: Districts of Darjilling and Jalpaìguri, and State of Kuch Behar, Vol. X*. London: Trubner and Co.

Jackson, J.E. and K.B. Warren, 2005. 'Indigenous Movements in Latin America, 1992-2004: Controversies, Ironies, New Directions', *Annual Review of Anthropology*, Vol. 34, pp. 549-573.

Kaviraj, S., 2000. 'Modernity and Politics in India', *Daedalus*, Vol. 129, No. 1, pp. 137-162.

Kuper, A., 2003. 'The Return of the Native', *Current Anthropology*, Vol. 44, No. 3, pp. 389-402.

Martin, R.M., (ed.), 1838. *The History, Antiquity, Topography and Statistics of Eastern India.* Londin: W.H. Allen and Co.

Mitra, A., 1954. *West Bengal District Census Handbooks: Jalpaiguri*. Calcutta: Govt. of West Bengal.

Morgan, R., 2007. 'On Political Institutions and Social Movement Dynamics: The Case of the United Nations and the Global Indigenous Movement', *International Political Science Review*, Vol. 28, No. 3, pp. 273-292.

Nandy, A., 2001. *Time Warps: The Insistent Politics of Silent and Evasive Pasts*. New Delhi: Permanent Black.

O'Malley, L.S.S., 1999 [1907]. *Bengal District Gazetteers: Darjeeling*. New Delhi: Logos Press.

Oommen, T.K., (ed.), 2010. *Social Movements-I: Issues of Identity*. New Delhi: Oxford University Press.

Pathak, Avijit, 2006. *Modernity, Globalisation and Identity: Towards a Reflexive Quest*. Delhi: Aakar Books.

Rao, M.S.A., (ed.), 1979. *Social Movements in India*, Vol. 1. New Delhi: Manohar.

Tomlinson, J., 1999. *Globalisation and Culture*. Chicago: University of Chicago Press.

Trouillot, M.R., 2003. *Global Transformations: Anthropology and the Modern World.* New York: Palgrave Macmillan.

10

Modes of Identity Formation of the Rajbangshis

Nandini Basistha

Identity formation is not one-day event that can be done just switching on one's idea in one direction. It sometimes takes several years as it has in the case of the Rajbangshis. Literary, the word 'Rajbangsi' means the 'Royal Community'. But, what's in a name? The Rajbangshis are now a largely a marginalised ethnic community; their backwardness is evident in the spheres of education, employment, income and over-all development. Their despair and disappointment have found expression in agitations and movements of various forms. The movements by different groups of Rajbangshis have taken various routes despite they having same anthropological and historical past, being a part of the same dynasty, common 'Kamtapuri language' and same culture and same sufferings; they have demanded an ethnic state carving out from more or less same geographical area.

Separatist movement, backed by different ethnic groups, is not a new phenomenon in India. With the merger of different communities with Indian nation this kind of movements started at every nook and corner of India. Many groups of people with the same stock, language, religion and culture get mobilised and started claiming their own 'homeland'. But, as aforesaid, the case of Rajbangshis is different. We can identify as many as two different streams of movements, which are led by Rajbangshis for their separate homeland.

After getting united and mobilised by the *Kshatriyaisation* movement, one group of common Rajbangshis has started movement for Rajbangsi-led homeland in form of a separate Kamtapur state, under Union of India. This is generally a proletariat movement fought for the socio-political upliftment of the group status. Although all Kamtapur-supporters are generally following non-violent democratic way, one segregated group of Kamtapur movement waged guerrilla warfare under the banner of Kamtapur Liberation Organisation (KLO) for the sovereign Kamtapur state. Rajbangshis of Lower Assam also striving for this same purpose through their own organisational initiatives. Second stream of movement is mainly backed by the middle class intelligentsia in demand of the proper implementation of Merger Agreement 1949 and to regain separate entity of Cooch Behar as a Union Territory under the control of Central Government.

Obviously, their movements of divergent interests never become too powerful to reach destiny. For becoming numerically stronger, time to time some attempts of joint collaboration have taken place. But these are too fragile. So, never their movement succeeded to fulfill their aim. However, every movement has some genesis and modes of operation, which generally arises out of people's grievances. In the following paragraphs, I want to discuss that point.

Both of the movements of Rajbangsi's (viz., Kamtapur and Greater Cooch Behar) have repeatedly called for regaining control over the geographic areas of the historical Kamata and Koch kingdom. Established by Prithu in twelfth century, Kamata kingdom comprised the tract of land bounded by the Karotoya in the west, the Brahmaputra in the east, and the Dooars in the north and the Padma-Brahmaputra basin in the south. The last Kamata king, Nilambar (1480-1498) expanded the kingdom to include the present Cooch Behar districts of West Bengal and the undivided Kamrup and Darrang districts of Assam and northern Mymensing in Bangladesh as well as eastern parts of Dinajpur district. Sometimes after the fall of the Kamata kingdom, indigenous Koch ruler, Biswa Singha established Koch Kingdom in the same tract. Despite several attacks from Mughals and British, these Koch-Rajbangsi rulers maintained their separate political identity and independence up to 1949.

But, in the meantime, the social identity of Koch-Rajbangshis faced a crisis. Although Hindu Brahmins christened Kshatriya status to the Koch ruler Biswa Singha, Koch-Rajbangshis got 'Tribal' or low-caste status in the British Census. After the marriage of King Nripendra Narayan with Suniti Devi (the daughter of Brahma Samaj-leader Keshab Chandra Sen), the Koch royal family, however, drifted gradually away from the caste rigidity and caste-based identity. Moreover, they felt pride in introducing themselves as Koch (Debnath, 2007: 44). So, under the leadership of Rai Saheb Panchanan Barma, educated and affluent Koch-Rajbangsi intelligentsia had started Kshatriyaisation movement, which eventually acted as the base of the various ethno-political movements in North Bengal (Barma, 2007: xii). To regain the lost social status of the Rajbangsi community in Hindu society, Thakur Panchanan established Rangpur Kshatriya Samiti in 1910. Very soon it acquired the status of a central association of the whole Rajbangsi community. To achieve its immediate objective, Samiti had taken two-fold activities; one is to prove that the Koches were inferior to the Rajbangshis in social status, in the hope that this would legitimise their demand for inclusion in the Kshatriya Varna; other is to intensively incorporate Brahmanical values and practices for a purified social image. Such social uplift movement organised by the Kshatriya Samiti not only consolidated caste solidarity among the common Rajbangshis but also created consciousness of a separate identity among the educated youth of the community in particular (Sarkar, 2006).

Samiti took various initiatives to unite Rajbangshis. This includes bringing out a monthly journal called Kshtriya, in which many provocative writings were published against the Bengali upper-caste hegemony and advised the community members to sever all socio-political ties with these castes. Even the intellectual sections henceforth discontinued their association with the literary organisations of Bengalis. In spite of that the movement got confined into a particular section of the Rajbangshis, who were mainly land-owners, jotedars and autochthonic population. The leaders of the Kshatriya movement were equal to other caste Hindu Bhadraloks in matters of education, profession, dress and manners and felt quite acutely the odium of belonging to a low caste in Hindu society due to their low social origin (Mukhopadhyay, 2009). So, the rural poor, who constituted the bulk of the Rajbangsi peasantry, were unable to identify themselves fully with those people of their community who belong to the high strata of the society. Thus, the class solidarity of the Samiti got fractured under the weight of class contradictions and ultimately the Samiti failed to crystallise a distinct 'social identity' for the Rajbangshis.

Although this movement started with the declared aim of caste upliftment, we cannot fully ignore some leaders' personal interest behind such moves. There is no denying fact that the Cooch Behar royal family had always in the grip of the outsiders and all privileges were exercised by non-Rajbangsi people. In that situation Panchanan Barma failed to secure any post other than that of a Hostel Superintendent and, for his criticism of the Royal family, he was declared unwanted in Cooch Behar. Being treated ignominiously, he jumped into the Kshatriya movement already begun by predecessors, like Haramahan Khajanchi and Harikishore Barma.

However, to survive in the new colonial socio-economic structure, in which British counted them as semi-tribal, Rajbangsi gentry forced to start movements for their lost power and status. But the leaders of the Samiti, however, later realised that just adoption of the sacred thread and upper-caste practices could not help in raising the social status of the Rajbangsi masses whose economic condition was extremely bad. Then they started looking for being accommodated in the government-approved institutional arrangement of 'protective discrimination', especially in matters of education and employment. To avail this, they were ultimately granted Scheduled Caste status in Bengal. Therefore, the social movement of the Rajbangshis, which initially began for achieving a superior status in the caste hierarchy was ultimately reduced to a mere real politic for getting reservation in government services, which later on created certain confusion in the question relating to the identity of the Rajbangshis. The offshoots of Koch-Rajbangshis got different status in different provinces, like Other Backward Classes in upper Assam, More Other Backward Classes in lower Assam, Scheduled Tribe in Meghalaya and simple Backward Classes in Bihar. This led to India-wide fragmented identity of this ethnic group.

Though the Kshatriya Samiti started its way mainly as a social organisation, but from the second decade of the 20th century, it began to partake in national politics. The Samiti gave candidates in all the four elections held in Bengal Legislative Council from 1920 to 1929 under 1919 Act and achieved striking electoral success. The Samiti placed their candidates against the all-India party candidates because they considered the Indian National Congress (INC) and the Communist Party of India (CPI) as associations of the upper caste Hindus. The candidates of the Kshatriya Samiti won in the Assembly election of 1937 and 1946 against the candidates of the INC and CPI. The elected candidates formed the Independent Scheduled Caste Party in 1938 along with Scheduled Caste representatives of East Bengal. But, against the background of the constitutional negotiations continuing since the appointment of the Simon Commission, the Kshatriya movement became involved in the issue of political and economic reforms and improvement of ritual and social status was given the back seat. Later on, this movement dried up with the death of Panchanan Barma in 1935 and merger of its leaders with Congress and mainstream politics.

However, from the election results, it should be clear that Kshatriya movement had considerable influence on the political life of Jalpaiguri and its neighbouring districts of Rangpur and Dinajpur. Although it did not gather momentum in the princely state of Cooch Behar as any kind of movement was not allowed there. Only exception was Hitasadhani Sabha, under which we can see the rise of second stream of Rajbangsi-led movement.

According to some historians, Hitasadhani Sabha was established in 1918 for the development of the indigenous (*deshi*) people of Cooch Behar (Varman, 2008: 85). But this student-oriented party was banned by Prince Nityendra Narayan in 1921. In 1942, Cooch Behar Legislative Council was formed in response to the persistent clamour for responsible government in the princely states throughout the country. After contesting election primarily on the issue of awareness and rights of the Rajbangsi people and winning all the seats, aspirations of the Rajbangsi members got a big fillip. Kings' administration was so long run by the educated, non-Rajbangsi, upper-caste Hindus and there was no Rajbangshis although the king himself was belonged to the same caste (Dakua, 2007: 54). The participation in administration through this democratic medium raised hope amongst the commoners that *deshi* people can be able to capture the power of administration at last and they can achieve the ultimate goal of being administered by themselves. So they started movement against the *Bhatias* (outsiders).

In mid 1940's, Hitasadhani Sabha was, formally, established by *deshi* (Rajbangsi Hindus and Muslims) elites and jotedars—like Satish Chandra Singha Sarkar, Khan Chaudhury Amanatulla, Gajendra Narayan Basunia—for the Hita (good) or welfare of *deshi* people. Although the exact date of its foundation is not known, its presence felt in the historic meeting of 19th May 1946 in the field of Rashmela of Cooch Behar. The communications were not so developed at that period. Still the people came by bullock's carts or on buffaloes, by bicycles and on foot (Barman, 2007: 73). In a state of around five lakhs people, this meeting was attended by around two lakhs of people. Here, the Sabha-leaders raised the proposal of keeping Cooch Behar under the Central Government of Indian Dominion for the interest of the development of the local people.

Although political activities were illegal in Cooch Behar, it got registered by the Cooch Behar dynasty. In 26th July, 1948, Radhakanta Sarkar wrote about Hitasadhani Sabha that – '…a most reactionary group has been formed, formulated and patronised by the Maharaja of Cooch Behar, to serve his own personal purpose of dominating and ruling the people for his own exploitation to the detriment of the interest' (Varman, 2008: 99).

In the meantime, it was made clear that India would be free but Pakistan would emerge as a new state out of the divided parts of India. The native states were allowed to join with either of the two states. The King of Cooch Behar was in a Horns of Dilemma to join (Das, 2007: 101). The people of Cooch Behar came to learnt that the king's going out of democratic ideas would be prevailing in near future. So, they wanted to rule Cooch Behar for the all round development through the local representatives of the people as per democratic system. So, Hitasadhani Sabha, along with Independent Scheduled Caste Party raised the first demand of a separate homeland for the Koch-Rajbangsi community. This proposed state, Rajasthan, was comprised of Siliguri, Purnia of Bihar, Goalpara of Assam, North-eastern side of Rangpur, Jalpaiguri and Dinajpur districts. Although the-then princely state, Cooch Behar, was not included in the proposed state, it was supposed that it will be naturally merged with the Rajasthan state, after signing the merger agreement by the existing king. This demand of 'Rajasthan' was popularised by the—then Central Minister Jogendra Nath Mandal in the mass meeting in Darjeeling, Jalpaiguri and Dinajpur in 4th, 6th and 7th May, 1947 respectively.

However, the demand of Rajbangsi people was never taken seriously and Cooch Behar was joined in the Indian Union as a Part 'C' state. After India's independence, the Hitasadhani Sabha took the name of Cooch Behar State Praja Congress. On the question of joining of the native state Cooch Behar into the Indian Union, the Sabha demanded for the proclamation of Cooch Behar as a separate state. A part of the Rajbangsi Hindu and Muslim Jotedars of Dooars were also inspired by the Cooch Behar State Praja Congress and they preferred to stay under the umbrella of proposed 'Cooch Behar' state. But their demands were, again, looked down upon.

In spite of the hindrances of the demand of a separate state raised by the Hitasadhani Sabha, their movement did not obliterate completely. On 30th October, 1949, the representatives of Cooch Behar State Praja Congress, along with Darjeeling Gorkha League, Sikkim Praja Sammelon and Jalpaiguri Gurkha League assembled at Darjeeling. In this gathering they called for separate state styled as Uttarakhand Pradesh Sangha. Malda and West Dinajpur were not included in the propôsed Uttarakhand Pradesh Sangha, but Sikkim was there. The demand for the establishment of Uttarakhand Pradesh Sangha was raised before the then Prime Minister Jawaharlal Nehru in 1952 when he came to Darjeeling. But he did not given any importance.

In the meanwhile, with the signing of Merger Agreement between Government of India and Maharaja of Cooch Behar on 28th August, 1949, Cooch Behar lost its separate existence and, ultimately annexed with West Bengal as a mere district on 1st January, 1950. This had evoked discontent amongst the native dwellers; one of its effects is rise of Uttarkhand movement. 'Uttarkhand' as a nomenclature of a separate state in North Bengal was first used in a conference in Darjeeling in 1949. A view in support of the Uttarakhandis for giving the name of Uttarakhand to their movement was that a large number of labourers, working in the tea gardens of Jalpaiguri Dooars, Malda, and West Dinajpur were sympathetic towards the Jharkhand movement. To acquire the support of the tea garden labourers, the Uttarakhandis preferred to take 'Khand' from Jharkhand and gave the name of Uttarakhand to their party (Ghosh, 2007: 182). Although their movement was popularly known as Uttarakhand movement, they named their proposed state, Kamtapur, following long historical tradition.

Out of the Uttarkhand movement, the Uttarakhand Party came out after a procrastinating historical process. On 5th July 1969, the Uttarakhand Party was formed in the historical Jalpesh temple of Mainaguri of Jalpaiguri district. Panchanan Mallick, Harimohan Barman, Kalidranath Barman, Wazuddin Ahmed, Suma Oraon, Sitanath Roy and the priest of the Jalpesh temple, Jogendranath Bhattacharya were witnesses of the auspicious moment. Panchanan Mullick was the key theoretician and mobiliser; and after his death, Jugal Kishore Rai Bir of Jateswar ran the work of the Party. The main slogan of the Uttarakhand Party was Bande Mataram and Jai Hok. According to the version of the Uttarkhandis, the Sannyasis were the first to adopt this slogan in North Bengal in 1763 and as a successor of the Sannyasis they took Bande Mataram as their catch word. Their song was Uttar Bangla Janani Amar (The Constitution of Uttarakhand Party, 15th August, 1980).

The prime aim of the Uttarakhand Party was to set apart North Bengal from South Bengal and create a state called 'Kamtapur' in order to protect the people of North Bengal from the exploitation of Calcutta-centric capitalist leaders. The Uttarakhandis were determined to create a separate 'Kamta' state out of West Bengal, comprising five districts of West Bengal—viz. Malda, Paschim Dinajpur, parts of Darjeeling, Jalpaiguri, and Cooch Behar. In their version, this wider area of 8,384 square kilometers would be much greater than many Union Territories of India in regard to area, population and natural resources. In justification of their movement, they exemplified the creation of several states—like Maharashtra, Gujrat, Nagaland, Haryana, Meghalaya and Andhra Pradesh—according to language and culture. Moreover, according to the Uttarakhandis, the name of any part of India can be changed by the amendments of the Constitution. Therefore, according to the Uttarakhandis, their demand for a separate state is legitimate from all respects. The Uttarakhandis also gave assurances that in their proposed new state the people would reside peacefully irrespective of caste, class and creed.

But, in the eighties, the Uttarakhand Party started the *Bhatia Khedao* movement. They called Bengali refugees and immigrants from Bangladesh as *Bhatia* and started agitation against the burgeoning Bengali settlement in the North Bengal area. Confrontations started between them because the Namasudra farmers began to protest by buying lands of the Rajbangsi peasants who on the other hand became landless.

However, it could not make stable organisation in West Dinajpur and Malda and had its influence mainly in Jalpaiguri, Cooch Behar and in the plains of Darjeeling district. But, here also this movement saw decay and gradual dismemberment. In the General Election, held on 10th March, 1971, the Uttarakhand Party contested in Maynaguri, Dhupguri, Sadar, Falakata seats of Jalpaiguri District and one Lok Sabha seat of Jalpaiguri (Ray 2007: 119). But their candidates were defeated. Ultimately, the party got splitted.

In the intermediary period between the decline of the Uttarkhand Dal and the emergence of the Kamtapur movement, an auxiliary organisation named *Uttarbanga Tapasili Jati Upajati Sangathan* (UTJUS) had been formed. They continued '*Bhatia Khedao*' movement with a strong mass base in the rural and tea garden areas of Dooars. The so-called autochthonous people, mainly the Rajbangshis, became the torch-bearer of a movement of anomalous type with explicit demands for the redress of their socio-economic and educational grievances, but more with the objective of dormant political design and ambition including the one against the citizenship of the Bhatias after 1971.

After the liberation of Bangladesh in 1971, a large section of the Bengali refugees, who came to North Bengal from Bangladesh, were Namasudras.

To protect themselves from the flame of the Bhatia Khedao movement, the Namasudras also started to unite themselves to maintain their own existence. All of a sudden, at the time of a big Central Conference of UTJUS, the Bharatiya hoodlums, consisting members of different clubs and the activists of different political parties, opened the pandora's box of their brutal force and hundreds of people were injured. The police took no cognisance of the crime. On the contrary, the Bengali people of Alipurduar gave the account that the leaders of the UTJUS delivered provocative speeches asking the audience to reclaim those plots of lands even of Alipurduar town which once had been grabbed by the immigrant Bhatias. They further added that no plot of land was grabbed; the Bhatia's had to buy lands in the prices as were prevalent from time to time. In this chaos of mutual blaming of disrupting peace, the real reason of that unfortunate incident still remains unsearched and a matter of impartial investigation. But this, instead of terrorising, further inspired those Rajbangshis in political involvement who so far maintained aloofness from political involvement. So, from the ruins of this disastrous incident, the full-fledged Kamtapur movement was resurrected.

In later part of the decade, the Uttarakhand Party came to be known as Kamtapur Gana Parishad. It rose on the lines of the All Assam Students Union and the Asom Gana Parishad. Following the oriental philosophy, its President, Sri Panchanan Mallick hoisted its icon, the triangular flag on 21st October., 1986, which proclaimed the firmness to reach their democratic ideas to a definite goal by totally non-violent democratic way. This triangular reddish flag with meridional white sun in its middle meant triguna- the three characteristic primal qualities of man and other creatures. The red colour is the symbol of power and the white colour is the symbol off knowledge. Knowledge and power prepare the way for development.

In 1980s, the break-up of the Russian, Yugoslav and Czechoslovak states into a number of new nations raised hopes amongst Rajbangsi nationals also that perhaps they would now be able to secede from West Bengal. This injected new valor in the Kamtapur movement. As an offshoot of Kamtapur Gana Parishad, Kamtapur People's Party was constituted in 1992.

Although it was formed as a democratic party, the realisation that their culture, tradition, customs and language were being pushed to a point of no return induced them to choose the path of protest. Although the leaders denied that the Kamtapur People's Party was piling up arms, their protest movements turned violent over the past years. The activities of this party came to the limelight and drew public attention in the 1990s, when its plans and programmes were designed under the banner of the Kamtapur Progressive Party, established in 1995. This party was recognised by the Government of India on 18th July, 2005.

However, territorial demands and demarcation of the proposed Kamtapur state has yet not been clarified. While Kamtapur People's Party demanded that the separate state should be created out of the Rajbangsi community dominated areas of Cooch Behar, Jalpaiguri, Darjeeling, North and South Dinajpur and Malda districts of West Bengal and four contiguous districts of Assam—viz., Kokrajhar, Bongaigaon, Dhubri and Goalpara. But, later, Atul Roy, the leader of the Kamtapur Progressive Party, has stated that the prospective state is supposed to correspond with the limits of Kamata-King Naranarayan's empire; thus it may extend from Kamrup Kamakshya temple to Purnia, and Kishangaj of Bihar is included within Kamtapur.

We can underline dichotomy also in the ideology of the KPP. In past, under the leadership of Nikhil Roy, the Kamtapur People's Party has put forward a charter of demands containing eleven demands—like carving out a separate state of Kamtapur comprising several North Bengal districts; recognition of their vernacular, Kamtapuri; establishing a separate university; development of education and so on. Thus, KPP contend that they carry a distinguished tradition—a history, social existence and culture distinct from the Bengalis and hence demand formation of a separate state on the basis of recognition of these distinctive features. But, later the leader of Kamtapur Progressive Party, Atul Roy confesses that there are leaders with myopic view and limitations in the party but as they believe in democracy, therefore, after the attainment of separate statehood, other people are bound to be involved through electoral politics. However, in the charter of demands placed by the KPP, the basic issues of the development of common people were conspicuously missing.

Thus, the differences between the two leaders, Atul Roy and Nikhil Roy, have been brewing for a long time, with roots traced back to 2001. However, in spite of that, Kamtapur movement showed its presence by peaceful protest-sittings, economic blockades and participation in the electoral politics under the banner of KPP.

Allegedly KPP had an armed wing, Kamtapur Liberation Organisation (KLO). Although KPP and KLO have different political agendas, but interrogations with the captured militants of KLO have confirmed the financing of the KPP by KLO. However, both ideology and path of these two outfits are different.

KLO was formed on 28th December, 1995 as an over-ground organisation of Koch-Rajbangsi tribes to carve out a separate Kamtapur State comprising six districts of West Bengal (viz., Cooch Behar, Darjeeling, Jalpaiguri, Malda, North and South Dinajpur) and four contiguous districts of Assam (viz., Kokrajhar, Bongaigaon, Dhubri and Goalpara). At its inception, KLO addressed problems such as large-scale unemployment, land alienation, perceived neglect of Kamtapuri language and identity, and grievances of economic deprivation. But soon, it got linked up with United Liberation Front of Assam (ULFA) and it waged guerrilla warfare in demand of sovereign Kamtapur state (Kamtapur

Liberation Organisation (KLO), [Online: web] URL www.satp.org/satporgtp/countries/india/states/.../Klo.htm).

According to the another source, the origin of KLO can be traced to the attempts of certain members of the Rajbangsi community belonging to the All Kamtapur Students' Union (AKSU) to organise an armed struggle for a separate Kamtapur State. For this purpose, they approached ULFA, who reportedly agreed to train them in order to gain foothold outside Assam, in the other geographically contiguous Indian States, to use them as transit routes. ULFA's line of thinking was that, it would not only facilitate the movement of its cadres to their base camps in Bhutan but also provide a safe haven for the injured or sick cadres. Decision to prop-up a Rajbangsi insurgent outfit was taken by the ULFA in December 1995 at the initiative of Raju Baruah, the deputy leader of the outfit military wing. The ULFA entrusted the then Chairman of its Darrang district Unit, Ajit Kachari with the task of setting up a Koch-Rajbangsi Organisation (KRLO) in lower Assam. Subsequently, the KLO was formed in North Bengal following a meeting at Kumaragram. KRLO became defunct after a brief spell of activity and most of its cadres joined the ULFA. Time to time, KLO also maintained link with the Tiwa National Revolutionary Front (an insurgent outfit based in the Nagaon district of Assam), the National Socialist Council of Nagaland-Isak-Muivah (an insurgent outfit of Nagas), National Democratic Front of Bodoland, the Maoist insurgents of Nepal and Pakistan's Inter Services Intelligence (ISI).

However, without going to the debate about the origin and linkages of KLO, we can say that ULFA transformed the character of KLO. Their cadres got training in a string of ULFA-led camps in the Bhangtar and Lhamoisingkha areas across the Wangchu River in Bhutan in using many sophisticated weapons like AK-series rifles, United Machine Guns, Chinese Grenades, Self-loading rifles, carbines and pistols. Tamir Das alias Jibon Singha was the Chairman of the KLO. Some other prominent KLO insurgents, who could be in positions of decision-making, were Milton Burman alias Mihir Das, Tom Adhikary alias Joydeb Roy, Bharati Das, Suresh Roy, Hiten Roy, Ravi Rajbangsi, Rahul Roy and Kajal Roy. At the time of its formation, its cadre strength was an estimated 60. However, subsequently, it is said to be operating with approximately 300 active cadres. For assured manpower, they had to depend a lot on the poor local people, who lived in the border areas. Apart from manpower and food supplies, the militants were in dire need of medicines as malaria and diarrhea were rampant in their jungle hideouts.

Then, like a typical insurgent outfit, which requires a regular flow of finances to buy arms to support its cadre and to maintain its effectiveness, started extortion for income. Like the ULFA, for its purpose, it has targeted the tea gardens in North Bengal, especially in the Dooars region. In the initial stages, the KLO insurgents used to come directly to the tea garden managers and demand money instead of sending demand notes and very often, the garden managers, in a bid to buy peace, came to a settlement rather than informing the police. However, this brand of extortion soon paved way for a more serious and organised mode of operation. Loot of garden remittance in various attacks on the National Highway-31 passing through the heart of the tea belt, abductions, demand of huge ransom, theft of gardens' properties like green tea leaves, costly irrigation implements and even fence wiring became the common modes of acquiring finance. The situation has reached such a level that the tea industry in the region, spread over nearly 300 tea gardens, had started contemplating in terms of raising a private protection force on the line of the one in Assam. However, according to a source in the Dooars tea industry, 'No extortion or ransom notes were received by the established tea gardens. It was the small tea growers and local businessmen who had invested in small gardens who were the victims of the KLO' (Chattopadhyay, 2004). There are hundreds of such gardens in the Maynaguri, Changra Bandha and Islampur regions. One tea garden at Rajgunj is reported to have paid Rs 1 lakh a year. Annual rates for other businessmen and tea gardens varied from Rs 10, 000 to Rs 15, 000. KLO cadres became most active in Alipurduar in Jalpaiguri and the Siliguri sub-division of Darjeeling. According to police sources, those who resisted were abducted. In at least two cases, the victims never returned.

Obviously, government got worried in such moves of KLO. So, they thought about counter-insurgency operations to tackle this problem. Police in West Bengal were not geared up to deal with the KLO cadres. So, representatives of the Governments of Assam and West Bengal met on 23rd May, 2000 and decided to jointly tackle the problem of cross-border insurgency. In the second half of the year 2000, Central Reserve Police Force (CRPF) was deployed to deal with the situation. Royal Bhutanese Army also promised to destroy KLO hideouts in Bhutan.

When Operation Flushout started on 15th December, 2000, the entire 150-km border between West Bengal and Bhutan was sealed. However, there was no slackening of the security arrangements on either side of the border. All vehicles were checked, and heightened intelligence and security measures were taken up by the police and the armed forces. By December 17, the two main gateways at Pheuntsholing and Samtse were opened. KLO had suffered a major setback with the Royal Bhutanese Army destroying its camps in the India-Bhutan border and capturing five of its most senior leaders. On 21st, December, the RBA handed over to the Indian authorities KLO founder-members Joydeb Roy alias Tom Adhikari and Milton Burman alias Mihir Das, and other important leaders such as Sanjoy Adhikari alias Vicky, Bhim Dakua alias Jayanta Das and Pabitra Singha alias Biplab Singha. The capture of Tom Adhikari and Milton Burman is also a psychological setback for the KLO. Just as the two were feared among the business community and the tea industry in the region, they were revered by a large section of Rajbangsi youth. Apart from being the organisation's main fundraiser, mostly through extortion, Tom

Adhikari was in charge of recruitment. The organisation does not have enough resources to regroup and stage a comeback.

In a well-timed gesture, the CPI (M)-led Left Front government in West Bengal has taken up a programme to rehabilitate the surrendered militants. Five such militants, including Madhusudan Das, who had surrendered following Chief Minister Buddhadeb Bhattacharjee's appeal, were reported to have been given Rs 12, 000 each and the licence to start trade in river bed materials. This offer is likely to encourage those insurgents who are on the run to give themselves up to security personnel and return to the mainstream of society.

In the meanwhile we can see the second stream of movement, led by common Koch-Rajbangsi people of Cooch Behar. This movement can be called a legacy of the Hitasadhani Sabha and Merger Agreement between King Jagaddipendranarayan of Cooch Behar and Government of India. According to that Agreement, Cooch Behar should be a Union Territory under the direct control of Central Government. But, on 1st January, 1950, it was merged with the state of West Bengal as a mere district and Cooch Behar lost its separate entity.

Denial of the promises of the Merger Agreement (28th August, 1949), coupled with the underdevelopment and Kolkata-centric rule of the non-Rajbangshis has fuelled the grudge of the Cooch Beharis and they spearheaded Greater Cooch Behar movement. Started under the institutional banner of the Greater Cooch Behar People's Association (GCPA), his movement got into its highest fettle in 2004-05 under the leadership of Bangshi Badan Barman, who was a disenchanted CPI(M) activist. According to the manifesto of this association, they want to form a separate state, Greater Cooch Behar, comprising areas of preset 'Cooch Behar' along with the parts of South and North Dinajpur, Jalpaiguri, Darjeeling and Assam. This state will be under the purview of Central government of India. Following to the history, cultures and tradition of ancient Cooch Behar, they want 'Kamtapuri' or 'Cooch Behari' as the state language.

GCPA had started the Greater Cooch Behar movement quite peacefully. They placed their demands to the Central Government. But the Central Government refused to pay attention to it. So they started non co-operation movement with the state government. This activism includes refusal of paying governmental *haat* tax by vendors in several weekly markets, refusal in paying bus fares and boat fares, refusal of paying entry fee in the Cooch Behar King's palace and so on (Bhattacharyya, 2005). But the situation got complicated on 20th September, 2005, on the day of a mass fasting programme in order to place their demands in front of democratic government.

The State Government of West Bengal handled the situation with the policy of oppression. Police exercised unrestrained suppression on the fasting crowd, in which one GCPA activist got killed. Naturally violence arose.

The demonstrators retaliated on the police by taking lives of two persons in uniform including a deputy superintendent of police. Such an unprecedented and un-preconceived reaction from the demonstrators compelled the police to go berserk for a few weeks in nabbing the activists from whether they could be found and sighted. Mr Bangshi Badan Barman, the leader of the GCPA, with a large number of his supporters were sent to Cooch Behar jail.

Afterwards, for the continuous legal pressure of the court and atrocities of the police, the GCPA got succumbed and its strength soon crumbled and evaporated. However, the cry for their demand is far from dying out. So, in retaliation, the GCPA opened a political fraction, the Greater Cooch Behar Democratic Party. They have now decided to participate in the electoral politics to place their demand in the Parliament legally.

The third stream of movement of the Rajbangshis can be seen in lower Assam. Unlike the Rajbangshis of Bengal, they were not included in either Scheduled Caste or Scheduled Tribe category. So, they failed to avail special benefits of 'protective discrimination'. Moreover, from 1950s, Bodos have started fighting for their own homeland. In spite of having same anthropological origin like Bodos, Rajbangshis have separate language, culture and social traits. So, they never thought of being stayed in a Bodo-dominated state. Therefore, when the Plain Tribal Council has proposed Udayachal in 1967, the Koch-Rajbangshis faced a serious crisis of existence as well as identity in the lower Assam. So, in response to the Bodo's demand, king of Sidli (in Goalpara of Assam), Ajit Narayan Deb demanded a separate state, 'Kamtapur'. They started their movement under the banner of Kamtapur Sangram Parishad. To weaken their movement, Government of Assam had appointed Ajit Narayan Deb as the Chairman of the Oil and Natural Gas Commission. In lack of competent leadership and a concrete plan for future steps, Kamtapur Sangram Parishad lost its ground within a few years.

But the Bodo demand for the separate state was not ended; it was increased day by day. And finally they got the Bodo Autonomous Council in the Sixth Schedule frame of the Indian Constitution. Moreover, six states (viz. Manipur, Nagaland, Arunachal Pradesh, Meghalaya, Tripura and Mizoram) were formed in Northeast India out of Assam on the basis of language and ethnic identity. But the status of Koch-Rajbanghshis remained same and their frustration have reached its optimiser point. Reversing Sarat Chandra Sinha's ideas of assimilation and accommodation, they started advocating that Rajbangsi is a separate ethnic group with distinct language, culture and historical past. For criticising the policy of the Assam Sahita Sabha, All Assam Students Union and the Government of Assam, large number of the ethnic based political, social, cultural, students and women's organisation has been formed. However, the most vocal, powerful and largest organisation is All Koch-Rajbangsi Students Union. According to Biswajit Roy, who is the President of this umbrella organisation, they are planning to step up their movement for a separate Kamtapur state and the Scheduled Tribe status for the Rajbangsi's in the following days with establishing connection with Kamtapur Progressive Party and Greater Cooch Behar Democratic Party of North Bengal.

The result of their thinking has given the birth of an umbrella organisation, the Greater Kamta United Forum in 2006. It is consisted of the All Koch-Rajbangsi Students Union of Assam and Kamtapur Progressive Party and Greater Cooch Behar Democratic Party of North Bengal. It is undoubtedly a turning point in the history of Rajbangshis of independent India, who, for the first time, formed a united organisation of the Rajbangshis of Assam and West Bengal. They have understood the ground reality of numerical strength and have usefully sorted their difference and are trying to remove it. It is true that the founders of the Greater Kamta United Forum are not politically heavy weights but still by taking the initiative for a joint organisation they have done the work of a pioneer. According to the Atul Roy, President of KPP, his organisation along with allies, the Greater Cooch Behar Democratic Party and the All Koch Rajbangsi Students' Union, would do everything possible to achieve the common goal of a separate state for Rajbangshis. 'Apart from the paramount statehood demand we would press the Centre to stop infiltration from across the Bangladesh border and to bestow a Constitutional recognition to the Kamtapur language,' he said (Roy, 2003). How much it will be workable is a different issue. At least they have succeeded burying the divided identity which created a hurdle for the growth of the united identity or community solidarity.

So in conclusion, one can say that, behind every demand of separatism, there has been some hidden issue of injustice. When injustice is projected as the reason for full or partial autonomy, there also remains some hidden interest of a small group of people. That's why most of the newly-created autonomous units fail to secure justice to the commoners and the disillusionment woos disgruntlement in the form of another movement. Governmental science admittedly produces multiplicities, yet the irony is that it wants to handle this multiplicity on a homogeneous scale, by a homogeneous standard, at a homogeneous level. The concepts of development, progress and modernisation are assumed to be embedded in a system of dominance and, in turn, to be contributing to that dominance. Rajbangshis got trapped in this state hegemony. However, it is true that mere statehood is not satisfactory in eradicating politics of secessionism. In fact, re-organisation of states on ethno-linguistic grounds has opened up the Pandora's Box of statehood demands. In other words, the state becomes an 'active contributor to identity politics through the creation and maintenance of state structures which define and then recognise people in terms of certain identities.' So, it is necessary to take a neutral look over the identity of Rajbangshis and act for their betterment as well as their area. A positive outlook to this ethnic group must be taken to stop their alienation from resources and marginalisation in society and politics.

References

Barma, Sukhbilas (ed.), 2007. *Socio-political Movements in North Bengal: A Sub-Himalayan Tract*. New Delhi: Global Vision.

Bhattacharyya, Debashis, 2005. *Cooch Behar Burning – The Struggle Threatens to Intensify in November*, [online: web], URLSunday, October30, 2005http://www.telegraphindia.com/1051030/asp/opinion/story_5414649.asp].

Chattopadhyay, Suhrid Sankar, 2004. 'A Ruthless Hit Squad', Frontline, Vol. 21, No. 1.

Debnath, Sailen (ed.), 2007. *Social and Political Tensions in North Bengal (Since 1947)*. Siliguri: N.L. Publishers.

Kamtapur Liberation Organisation (KLO), [Online: web].

Mukhopadhyay, Rajatsubhra, 2009, '*Social Formation of the Rajbangshis and the Emergence of the Kamtapuri Identity*', in N.K. Das and V.R. Rao (eds.), *Identity, Cultural Pluralism and State: South Asia in Perspective*. Kolkata: Anthropological Survey of India.

Routray, Bibhu Prasad, N.D. *Kamatapur Liberation Organisation* (KLO), Institute for Conflict Management Database on Armed Groups in South Asia.

Roy, Barun, 2003. 'KAMTAPUR: Kamtapur Party Plans to Step up Statehood Movement, Weekly Assessments and Briefings', *South Asia Intelligence Review*, Vol. 1, No. 39, [Online: web], URL http://www.satp.org/satporgtp/sair/Archives/1_39.htm.

Sarkar, I., 2006. 'The Kamtapur Movement: Towards a Separate State in North Bengal', in Govind Chandra Rath (ed.) *Tribal Development in India: The Contemporary Debate*. New Delhi: Sage.

The Constitution of Uttarakhand Party (15th August 1980) URL www.satp.org/satporgtp/countries/india/states/.../Klo.htm.

Varman, Lalit Chandra, 2008. *Rajyar Dabite Uttarbange Andolon* (in Bengali). Assam: N.L. Publishers.

11

Marginalisation, Alienation and Ethnic Identity Formation: The Case of the Adivasis in Dooars and Terai Regions of North Bengal

Sanjay K. Roy

Introduction

Nearly fifteen lakh tribal people (2011 Census) belonging to more than 30 distinct tribal groups inhabit the contiguous areas in Jalpaiguri and Darjeeling districts of North Bengal (in West Bengal), popularly known as the Dooars and Terai regions. The tribes of North Bengal constitute one-third of the total tribal population in the state, which is close to 45 lakh. Each of these tribes has its distinctive origin, language and culture and identity, which the members of that particular tribe jealously maintain and reproduce in their social life. Rigid adherence to clans and clan exogamy, tribal endogamy, language, religion (Animism, Hinduism or Christianity) and a sense of hierarchy help immensely in reproducing distinct tribal identity and maintain tribe-based ethnic boundaries. The tribal communities which have central India (Chhotanagpur) origin and who now inhabit all the districts of North Bengal, particularly the Terai and Dooars regions of Darjeeling and Jalpaiguri districts respectively, favour being commonly known as *adivasis*, while cultivating a sense of tribal unity drawing from their common root, some common racial features, common *lingua franca* (Sadri), and having to confront similar politico-economic and cultural 'other'. Adivasi identity, for the central Indian tribes, is, therefore, a 'constructed' (and strategic) inclusive identity, which helps them put up a united face against the systemic forces that are out to fragment them and subject them to marginalisation and 'othering'. Asked about their identity the tribals, whatever specific tribal community they might be belonging to, would answer they are *adivasis* and not Santal or Oraon. If an ethnographer insists further then only they would reveal their specific tribal identities (such as Santal, Oraon, Munda, Kharia, Mahli, and so on). Strategic articulation or construction of identity thus varies at three distinct levels, when they act (1) with reference to the members of their own distinctive tribe, (2) with reference to the members of the tribes other than their own, who often are their neighbours, and (3) with reference to those in the locality who are the members of many non-tribal communities and who for the *adivasis* constitute the 'other'. The 'other', for the tribal communities, are the members of the dominant communities (the Nepali, Bengali, the Rajbangsi, the Muslim) the tea garden management, the 'outside' leaders of the trade unions and of dominant political parties, the people in bureaucracy and in administration, the police and all other systemic forces which at the same time marginalise them and make efforts to 'integrate' them into the dominant political-economic order.

Although, economic and cultural othering of the tribal population continue at the hands of the dominant systemic forces (the tea-garden owners, the landlords extract surplus value out of tribal labour and the caste Hindus and Muslims maintain a clear cultural distance from them) the latter would always want them to be 'politically integrated' into the liberal democratic order while converting them into 'active citizens' (Habermas, 1992), the active agents of state-sponsored development or at least to 'peaceful supporters' of the political parties and trade unions which, in turn, would ideologically bind them with the order. Caught in this paradox, the tribal communities in this region, and also in other parts of India, try to organise them in search of an *adivasi* self or ethnic self—a process that could be termed 'ethnicisation' of the tribal communities. An ideal illustration of the process called 'ethnicisation' is the ongoing tribal movement for formation of a tribal autonomous district comprising parts of Dooars, Terai of Jalpaiguri and Darjeeling foothills and the northern blocks of North Dinajpur district.

The formation of a common *adivasi* identity, which found expression in the organisation called Akhil Bharatiya Adivasi Vikas Parishad (ABAVP), an ethnic outfit of the central Indian tribes particularly of those living in Terai and Dooars, epitomises an expression of no confidence in the organs of the systemic forces and a search for an *adivasi* self, which, according to a large section of *adivasis*, would be realised through establishing a self-rule over a territory where they have been living for more than one and a half century and where they have a substantial numerical presence, if not domination.

The key to understand the ongoing *adivasi* movement for self-rule is to unravel the systemic forces that work at tandem to integrate them yet end up alienating them. The purpose of this essay is two-fold; first, to point to the inefficacy of the systemic forces in integrating the 'population' that gets marginalised in the process of state-sponsored 'development' and second, whether it is possible for the *adivasis* to preserve their unity when put under the shrewd strategies of governmentality (Foucault, 1991) by the systemic forces and maintain the much needed autonomy, for an effective power bargain with the order.

The Tribes of North Bengal and Their Marginalisation

Fifteen lakh people who constitute the *adivasis* in North Bengal are the migrants from the Chotanagpur region of central India, who moved out of their original abode in the second half of the 19th century in search of a living or a better life and their descendants. In their places of origin they experienced widespread exploitation by the *dikus* (aliens), land loss, loss of forest rights, imposition of land rent and the colonial oppression, particularly in the aftermath of the Santal Rebellion of 1855-56. The expanding tea gardens in the Dooars and Terai regions (along with parts of Assam) offered them livelihood opportunities although they found themselves into another highly exploitative and oppressive economic and power arrangement. The expanding *zamandari* estates in the districts of the region, particularly in Malda, Jalpaiguri, Darjeeling Terai, two Dinajpur districts and the adjacent districts of erstwhile East Bengal in the latter half of the 19th and first half of the twentieth century also accommodated these migrants, primarily as agricultural labourers, share-croppers and tenant-cultivators. Assam Bengal Railway started construction of a railway track on the eastern side of Bengal in 1891. The Partition of the country in 1947 brought about a dislocation and new railway lines had to be laid in the 1950s in order to link the North-East with the rest of the country. The need of hardworking labour force prompted migration of the *adivasis* from central India. A section of tea garden labour force, particularly in Darjeeling Hills and Dooars, had migrated from Nepal and a section of them are considered the original Hill tribes, particularly the Lepchas. Since their presence in Terai and Dooars is not significant I have left them out of the scope of the present paper.

The migration of tribal work force almost came to a halt by 1940s when the tea gardens stopped expanding and as the land management system underwent major transformation after the abolition of the *zamindari* system in the 1950s. Absence of any major development project was another reason for the decline of migration. In the Dooars and Terai, the surplus labour force, ejected from the tea gardens, took hold of the fallow land or cleared forest land and took to settled cultivation. In this way, new tribal villages came up, alongside the existing villages where the migrant workforce who worked as construction labour or agricultural labourer had settled down. Lack of access to material resources or education (and skill) made them dependent on agriculture and tea almost exclusively.

Tribal economy, largely defined as subsistence economy, is based on agriculture in four districts of North Bengal, namely, Cooch Behar, North Dinajpur, South Dinajpur and Malda and on tea in Jalpaiguri and Darjeeling districts. Census data show that over the years the percentage share of cultivators (owner-cultivators) has declined sharply in these districts with corresponding rise in the number of agricultural labourers. Reading these two trends together one can draw an understanding of the massive land alienation the tribal population in the region has experienced. Loss of land has happened and continues despite government efforts to protect tribal land and despite the much acclaimed redistribution of land among the landless *adivasis*, as a part of land reform programmes undertaken during the Left Front rule (for detsails see, Roy, 2008: 41-42; Roy, 2009a).

Another trend in tribal economy has been a decline in significance of household industry over the years. In the districts the share of the 'main workers' engaged in household industries hovered around 0.5 to one per cent in 2001 (Roy, 2008: 42). The 'other workers' category, that includes jobs in the tea gardens, in the offices or other organised sector, did not grow to any significant scale. Interestingly, such growth is higher only in Darjeeling and Jalpaiguri districts where the *adivasi* work force is primarily engaged as tea garden workers; the growth of jobs in other districts has been less than 0.5 per cent per annum. Even in Jalpaiguri district, which accommodates most of the tea gardens, the growth of jobs has been only by 16 per cent in four decades, from 1961 to 2001.

The slow growth of jobs in 'other worker' category has to be understood in the light of stagnation in tea industry and the planters' refusal to recruit permanent workers. The strength of permanent work force in tea has declined in Jalpaiguri and Darjeeling districts although there has been some increase in the number of casual workers. It has been a feature of the tea gardens that the strength of male workers has declined while there has been a marginal increase in the number of female workers, both in the permanent and causal categories– a feature that can be termed as 'feminisation of workforce' (Roy, 2008: 46-48). The increase in work participation as 'other workers', although meager, is the only positive development the *adivasis* of North Bengal have achieved.

In my understanding, five factors are primarily responsible for the economic plight of the *adivasis* in the region: (a) meager and declining control over material and human resources, (b) incapacity to take advantages of the market opportunities, (c) inadequate state support, (d) ineffective state-initiated 'development schemes' and (e) exploitative penetration of the market forces and the outside groups, representing dominant communities. The increase of control over the material and human resources would have enhanced the 'capacity' of the tribal population to take greater advantage of the market opportunities and to thwart the penetration of the more powerful exploitative forces. But the state has only done some relief-works here and there and introduced provisions of reservation in education and government jobs, which have failed to enhance the capacity of the *adivasis* to arrest the falling quality of life. The low rate of literacy (while total ST literacy is 43.4 per cent, ST female literacy is only 29.15 per cent in West Bengal in 2001), high rate of dropout at the school level and very little spread of higher and technical education have hampered the process of human resource development over these years (See Roy, 2008: 26-27).

The penetration of the outsiders, from East Pakistan (and later Bangladesh), Bhutan, and Nepal, into the tribal belt in Terai and Dooars and the market forces have contributed to land alienation and economic marginalisation of the *adivasis*. The artificial 'crisis in tea industry' created by the tea garden owners, a process of actualisation of the work force and the threat of closure of the garden are widely read as strategies to deprive the tea workers of their rights and to weaken the trade union movement. The closure and abandonment of the tea gardens in the Dooars have brought miseries for the *adivasis*. In a recent study, I have found that the small tea gardens, which have come up in Jalpaiguri, Darjeeling Terai, and North Dinajpur districts, the brick kiln factories, expansion of highways, and land speculators have hugely contributed to the alienation of tribal land. The inheritance related division of family land is another factor that has contributed to growing decline of 'cultivator' category and the proportionate rise in the 'agricultural labourer' category (See Roy, 2012).

The tea gardens were brought under the panchayat system in 1998 but the panchayats have not been given enough space to work inside the gardens and implement development programmes for the garden dwellers, excepting the introduction of 100-days work programme (under NREGA) in the closed or abandoned tea gardens. There has been a long-standing demand from the panchayat bodies and the *adivasis* to open up the surplus fallow land under the control of the garden owners for undertaking development programmes. But the state government has not made the necessary legislation to make this possible. There is also a long standing demand from the *adivasi* garden workers that they should be given homestead land inside the garden and be given *patta* for such plots. The tea garden lands are owned by the state government but given to the garden owners on long-term lease.

A survey conducted by the state government reveals that only in 78 per cent of the 273 tea gardens in North Bengal there is arrangement for supply of safe drinking water. This forces the garden workers to drink waters from the natural streams, which, in turn, spreads water-borne diseases. According to Plantation Labour Act, 1951 it is mandatory for the garden authorities to provide free health services to all the workers. But the survey informs that there is no existence of health centres in 107 gardens, many health centres are run without doctors and there is no nurse in 116 garden health centers. The garden owners often refuse to construct new houses for the workers and repair the existing houses according to the provisions of the Plantation Labour Act, 1951. According to the tripartite agreement signed on 4th November, 2011, the garden owners were to revise the wage structure keeping parity with the rate of inflation, but the owners have not done anything on this leading to a fall in quality of life of the workers. The irony is that the garden owners flout the laws and agreements despite making huge profit from their business and the state government does not take any action against the law breakers (Sarkar, 2013: 9), while the trade unions prefer to remain silent.

The *adivasis* working in the tea gardens in Terai and Dooars regions for generations have long been guided by a false perception that the gardens will sustain them for generations. They could hardly perceive what the 'crisis' in tea industry would bring for them. They never prepared themselves by way of enhancing their control over human resources, to be able to tap the opportunities in the larger market, outside the garden. Thus, when gardens were closed or abandoned the workers, particularly the aged and those of ill-health face starvation death. The able bodied ones migrate to distant places in search of manual work and the women become the most likely candidates for human trafficking. When the crisis in the tea gardens deepens the protections and services provided in the Plantation Labour Act break down, taking a toll on the quality of life of the garden workers.

When the 'protector' state is retreating and the market on the rampage it is quite obvious that the powerless and voiceless people, who live on the margin, would find themselves more vulnerable. Being a part of the neo-liberal market the *adivasis*, with minimal control over material and human resources and 'culture capital', are entangled in a fierce survival battle as the dominant sections with much greater control over resources not only do not give them much economic and socio-political space but often intrude into whatever economic, social and cultural capital they control. With very little effort to human resource development initiative, the *adivasis* cannot reap the benefits offered by the policy of protective discrimination or the special development initiatives of the state. The corrupt yet inefficient bureaucracy and the *panchayat* functionaries come in the way to their reaping the benefits of development initiatives. The over-exploitative arrangement in tea gardens and loss of land perpetuate their marginalised existence in the region. The market uncertainty, the penetration of the forces of globalisation and crisis in the tea gardens make them even more vulnerable as a social category.

The irreversible process of marginalisation that the *adivasis* in the region are subjected to by the systemic forces is not just economic (land alienation, conversion to wage labour and extraction of surplus value, and by forcing them to find jobs in the informal sector, where exploitation is harsher, and by converting the tribal girls into easy prey by the human trafficking rackets and the capital that runs the flesh trade) it is at the same time cultural and political. Tribal boys and girls from the poverty-infested Terai and Dooars regions are 'trafficked' to the urban centers and metropolises, near and far, and are made to work as domestic help.

The cultural life of the tribal communities faces alienation of different forms. On the plea that these communities have been animists (nature worshippers) for generations the organised religious groups, both the Protestant and Catholic sects, lure them to Christianity. The Visva Hindu Parisad has joined the bandwagon by undertaking initiatives for reconverting them into Hinduism. The anthropologists have written about a long course of Hinduisation that the tribal communities have been through (Bose, 1941; Bhagabati 2012). Asked about their religion, all non-Christian tribes in the region would claim that they are Hindu, although the fact is that they have not found a place in the Hindu caste fold and the Hindu Brahmins (*purahits*) do not provide service to them. The tribal communities who regard them as Hindu have merely adopted some Hindu deities, namely, Kali, Laxmi, and so on, and offer them *puja* in their own animistic style. The churches of Catholic and Protestant denominations and the Bisva Hindu Parisad approach them as easy prey taking full advantage of their marginalised living. The missionaries often cite the economic plight of the *adivasis* who continue to claim to be Hindu and their non-recognition in the Hindu social order as one of the arguments as to why they should accept Christianity. The grand presence of the Church, the 'Westernised' and egalitarian religious activities, the support in the areas of education, health, and material support in times of crisis attract the hapless *adivasis* towards the Church and Christianity. The *adivasis* who get converted in the process often justify their action with logic since the benefits are tangible and difficult to deny. There is no denying that in the absence of adequate state support the *adivasis* find the Church as a major force that can bring about some economic and social wellbeing and mobility. Thus, if we term loss of faith as a form of culture loss one can perceive that the process will continue and would gain strength in the days to come (for details see Roy, 2009b).

Another form of culture loss is the loss of tribal language or dialect. The tribes of Central India and of other origins came to North Bengal with their respective language or dialect—the Santal, Oraon or the Munda or the other tribes, without an exception. In North Bengal the tribal population being linguistically mixed has adopted Sadri, a hybrid dialect as their lingua franca in order to be able to communicate among themselves. The use of Sadri as the dialect of inter-tribal communication is so widespread that it can be termed as the *adivasi* language in North Bengal, although while intra-tribal communication the members of a particular tribe still speak in their own tribal language. Again, while interacting with the members of the dominant Bengali community the *adivasis* are under compulsion to pick up the language of the former. The problem is more complex for the tribal children who do not get an opportunity to study in their mother tongue; they have to study in Nepali, Bengali, Hindi or English medium neither of which is their mother tongue. This is one of the reasons responsible for their poor examination performance and high rate of drop-out.

The strong penetration of the 'modern' culture industry, the television, cell phone, cinema have had a strong influence in the decline of their rich cultural forms—the folk songs, folk dance forms, the folk-music instruments and so on as they have now become addict to Hindi and Bhojpuri commercial cinema and film music which have overwhelming presence in their social and religious festivals and functions. The food-habit, dress, the belief systems are also in the process of change. The belief in witchcraft is still near universal but a section of the *adivasis*, the educated youth in particular, are now showing signs of disapproval of the practice of witch-hunting. While witch killing still widespread in the districts of North Bengal and has the support of the 'conscience collective' and witch lynching often takes the shape of a community festival there are instances of resistance from within, particularly from the side of the family members of the declared 'witch' to such killing and cases of police intervention. Among the other positive changes are: growing awareness about modern medicine, habit of visiting health centers, care for mother and child, and so on.

Scholars observe that while participating in the process of modernisation and development the tribal communities have experienced growing class inequality and gender-inequality, which were largely absent among the *adivasis* earlier. Only a small section of the *adivasis* has experienced upward economic mobility by enhancing its control over social and cultural capital (education and power in particular). The achievement in the field of education opens up the possibilities for access to white collar jobs through the provisions of protective discrimination, which results upward economic mobility. A few of them even make entry into the bureaucracy and well-paid paid jobs as school, college and university teachers. Such mobility is largely restricted to a very small minority of the *adivasis* of the younger generation in the region. A large majority of the tribal labour force, however, take up manual low-wage jobs in the absence of higher education or technical education. Those who achieve middle level education often struggle to secure ST certificates and often do not have access to information about availability of jobs or about reservation and other constitutional rights. The positions reserved for the ST candidates in higher education, in technical education and in government jobs often remain vacant in the absence of adequate number of applicants. Another new development among the tribal communities is widening gender gaps in different walks of life and increasing penetration of the elements of patriarchy. Being in touch with the members of the dominant communities the tribal women are now subjected to greater discrimination. The women members are made to shoulder the double their responsibilities as earners and as home maker. The *adivasi* men, though work as earners often do not extend their supporting hands to their wives in doing the domestic chores (For details see Xaxa, 2012; Roy, 2009c: 196-225).

The *adivasis* in Terai and Dooars have always responded to the organised political parties, their trade union wings and mass organisations with great deal of enthusiasm. They supported the freedom movement, the Communist movement in the post-independence period, the Naxalite movement in the late 1960s, and have been closely associated with the Left parties, the CPI, CPI (M), CPI (ML), the SUCI, the RSP and Forward Bloc, and the nationalist party like the Indian National Congress, besides the trade unions and the mass organisations of all these systemic forces. Being part of these organisations and taking advantage of seat reservation some from amongst the advanced section of the *adivasis* have become MPs, MLAs, and got elected in the different tiers of Local Self Governments. This representation in the political society has not been translated into any major development or elevation of quality of life of the *adivasis*. What have come to them in the hay days of Left regime can be termed as some reliefs that kept them at the subsistence level. Their condition deteriorated when the crisis (real or artificial) in the tea economy was made an excuse to close down or abandon the gardens. The state-sponsored reliefs, in the form of monthly allowance for the workers in closed gardens and engaging them in the 100-day work programme, were not good enough to keep them afloat.

This representation in the decision making bodies, which is often token rather than effective, quantitative rather than qualitative, has failed to negate a generally shared feeling of political isolation or even alienation among the *adivasis*. The leadership that is drawn from amongst the *adivasis* is often given local and insignificant positions. While the effective leadership comes from the non-*adivasi* higher level leaders the local leaders are made to function as active agents of the systemic forces and are allowed only a small space to operate. In the tea gardens, for example, the workers are nearly totally unionised as they seek membership of the leading trade unions in a particular garden. They take membership of the trade unions at the behest of the elderly male members of the family or community, pay the membership fees and respond to the occasional fund raising drives, take part in gate meetings and political rallies. They seek, in return, some kind of protection and security in life. Yet they remain largely indifferent to these trade unions and their outside leaders and to their efficacy in redressing their grievances and in securing their just rights. Their political consciousness does not go beyond remembering the name of the leaders and the symbol of the political party they are supposed to vote for; they even do not know the name of the trade union of which they are members. Being in the margin of the democratic process, where, over generations, they are made to remain 'loyal supporters' of the systemic institutions and organisations it is only logical for the *adivasis* to nurse a feeling of political alienation. Whatever space the *adivasi* leaders are given in the local self governments or in local party or trade union hierarchy they often let the opportunities pass by misusing the power and position for their selfish gains and not for empowering the community. The 'will to power', a search for a 'real' political self, however, remains alive at the community level which waits for the time and space to find expression.

Being a part of such a depressing social, economic and political reality, the *adivasis* in the region gradually lose confidence in the state and in the conventional organs of the civil society (trade unions and mass organisations) which they had trusted for so long as the protectors. The state-initiated development programmes do not make any noteworthy improvement in the quality of their living and the leaders of civil society organisation fail to do much since they essentially remain systemic organs, the organs of integration.

Placed under the systemic forces of alienation and marginalisation, the *adivasis* in the region and in other places the *adivasis* draw heavily from their rich tradition of rebellion and work for a platform of their own that would be close to their collective self and which would be platform for their self-articulation and expression. The *adivasi* responses to the state and the systemic forces are not uniform. While in Andhra Pradesh, Orissa, Jharkhand, Chhattisgarh and Midnapore district of West Bengal they follow the class-line mobilisation under the leadership of the Naxalite groups, which do not have any respect for the Indian Constitution or for the systemic forces, or for the mainstream political parties. In Terai and Dooars of North Bengal, on the other hand, they take the ethnic route to mobilise themselves. The search for an *adivasi* ethnic self has found articulation in the last few years in the form of the *adivasi* movement for autonomy under the provisions of the Sixth Schedule of the Indian Constitution, which is being spearheaded by the Akhil Bharatiya Adivasi Vikas Parishad (ABAVP).

The in-migration of more resourceful non-*adivasis* (Nepalese, Bengali refugees and Rajbanshis) into 'their territory' has additionally created a sense of insecurity in the collective psyche of the *adivasis* since they are outnumbered in their region and handed down a sense of insecurity relating to livelihood. Neither the state nor the expanding market has any mechanism to free the *adivasi* psyche of this sense of insecurity. It may be noted, in this context, that although the *adivasis* constitute a significant part of the population and the electorate in the blocks claimed in the proposed Sixth Schedule, they are not in majority in any of the blocks. The agricultural land and the business opportunities in the area are controlled almost exclusively by these non-*adivasi* migrants in the area. These migrants, because of their greater control over the resources and business-strategies often establish exploiter-exploited nexus with the *adivasis* who are largely confined to tea gardens and to small plots of cleared land. The demographic and ethnic heterogeneity factors have therefore weakened the demand for Sixth Schedule of the *adivasis*.

Although the *adivasis* in the region are out to build their movement on ethnic solidarity, the system forces are active to confuse them and spoil their solidarity by inflicting splits among the rank and file of the leadership and working out electoral alliances. The rebellious character of the movement and unity of the *adivasis* soon become the casualties of the strategies of the systemic forces. When the movement loses its sting the leaders look towards the mainstream political parties for support for their existence. It is in this context that the ongoing *adivasi* movement in Dooars and Terai, under the leadership of the ABAVP, has to be looked into.

Ethnicisation of the Adivasis in Dooars and Terai

The Akhil Bharatiya Adivasi Vikas Parishad (ABAVP) is a Delhi-based NGO 'which was formed for the social and cultural uplift of the *adivasis* in the country' sometime back (Bromwich, 2011: 27). Going by oral history, the organisation had its root in Adivasi Bikas Manch, which was founded in Delhi in 1966-67 by Kartik Oraon, an engineer by profession, and a Congress MP then. The NGO was active in the 1960s and thereafter in the tribal dominated areas of Bihar, presently Jharkhand. Mr Oraon visited the Tarai and Dooars regions of North Bengal to bring all the *adivasis* under the umbrella of the organisation. Although he did not meet with much success he could spread the message of a need for an *adivasi* identity and unity. The leaders of Jharkhand statehood movement visited the region on occasions in the 1980s to draw support for the movement. In recent past, Sibu Soren of Jharkhand Mukti Morcha (JMM) visited the area to spread his organisational network but without much success. Only in 2013, a breakaway faction of the ABAVP set up a unit of Jharkhand Mukti Morcha under the leadership of John Barla.[1] One common feature of these efforts is that they all had originated in Jharkhand with the aim to integrate the *adivasis* of North Bengal into their Jharkhand-based organisations. These efforts failed to cut much ice because the leaders were outsiders to this region and could not strike a common cord with the aspiration of the *adivasis* of the Tarai and Dooars regions of Darjeeling and Jalpaiguri districts of North Bengal.

The other important reason that blocked the tribal solidarity movement has been the strong association of the *adivasis* of the region with the locally dominant parties. The trade union wings of the Left parties, particularly the Communist Party of India (CPI), the Communist Party of India (Marxist), and the Revolutionary Socialist Party (RSP) and the Indian National Congress had spread their organisational network among the *adivasis*. The organised parties also penetrated into the tribal villages which fall outside the tea gardens through their frontal organisations. The early leaders, particularly of the Left parties, were strongly committed to the revolutionary ideology and worked for the organisation with missionary zeal. They sacrificed their life working for the organisation and mixed with the *adivasis* as their close kin. The first generation leaders were uncompromising and committed to the cause of the workers. Their missionary style of operation earned them a respectable place in the hearts of the workers. They could speak the language of the workers and could adjust with their lifestyle at ease.

The *adivasis* too, influenced by the 'class' ideology, extended wholehearted support to the trade unions and the mainstream left political parties. Alongside their 'natural' identification with the term *adivasi* the tribal population in the region was united by their common class position, depending heavily on the sale of their manual labour, as tea workers and as agricultural labourers. The left parties and their trade union wings retained the unquestionable support of the *adivasis* in the post-independence period, and particularly in post-1977 period because of their early initiative and also because the other all-India parties did not give them much challenge. The mainstream political parties made efforts to integrate the *adivasis* into their organisational fold by spreading wings of frontal organisations and by involving them in the democratic processes at the grassroots level. The redistribution of land among the landless, as a part of land reform programme of the Left Front government in the early 1980s consolidated the organisational base of the Left parties among the *adivasis*. In 1998, tea gardens, which were outside the *panchayat* system until then, were brought under the three-tier *panchayat* system. This was another opportunity to incorporate the *adivasis* into the democratic polity and in the organisational fold of the parties. The *adivasis* participated in the *panchayat* bodies with great enthusiasm and helped consolidation of the hold of the mainstream political parties on them. Not only most of the *panchayat* seats but all the Lok Sabha and Bidhan Sabha seats in the tribal dominated regions have been consistently won by the Left Parties, the CPI (M) and the Revolutionary Socialist Party in particular. As a result of these political processes a section from amongst the *adivasis* emerged as local level leaders; a few of them became MLAs, MPs, and even ministers in the state government. Spread of education and opportunities for organised sector employment helped the emergence of *adivasi* leaders. There were, thus, some early signs of formation of neo-elite among the *adivasis*.

However, an important slag in the process of class formation was that the average *adivasis* remained supporters and only supporters; they were far from becoming a 'class for itself'. The trade unions of the national political parties had their wings at the garden level and a few *adivasi* men workers were inducted into the leadership who in turn mobilised support for the party and the trade union. The average *adivasi* workers, women workers in particular, had no ideological training. The other important slag was that the *adivasis* carefully and distinctly nursed their tribal and *adivasi* identities, which might have come in the way to class formation. The domination of the non-tribals in the leadership of the trade unions and political parties also prevented an organic integration of the *adivasis* with these organisations. The insurmountable crises in the tea gardens created by the market and the owners and the repeated failure of the trade unions and political parties to overcome them have resulted into loss of faith in their efficacy. The trade unions and political parties remained hapless spectators to the deepening livelihood crises and other kinds of crises that resulted from the closure and sickness of the tea gardens. Sharp drops in the quality of the present generation leaders of the mainstream political parties and their indifferent mode of mixing with the workers also have brought about a gap between the two. The present generation leaders, who are also busy political leaders, now operate with bureaucratic attitude and they no longer live in the workers' quarters; they in fact maintain a distance from the workers. The proximity of the leaders with the owners and their ineffectiveness in realising the demands raised from time to time have also contributed to workers' loss of faith in the leaders. The leaders of the ABAVP and the JMM nurse a deep-rooted grudge against the leaders of the established political parties for failing to reciprocate the unqualified support for the *adivasis* in the region. They, in their assessment, have been used as a captive vote bank by the Left parties and the Congress. A lack of understanding of this structural strategy of captivation had to a large extent blocked the emergence of an *adivasi* organisation which would have been an articulation of political self of the *adivasis* in the region.

The leaders of the ABAVP have attributed the following factors for the emergence of the movement: (1) the threat to their territory and self posed by the aggressive and advancing Gorkha Janmukti Morcha (GJMM), (2) the fear of losing their hold over the territory to the non-*adivasi* settlers, (3) the loss of faith in the established political parties and trade unions, (4) the long perpetuating crisis in the tea gardens and their unsettling effect on the life of the *adivasi* tea workers, (5) the plight of *adivasi* workers in the Bodoland area of neighbouring Assam and the continued atrocities against the tribal women there, (6) their long subdued aspiration for a distinct *adivasi* identity, and (7) absence of any perceptible development in the existing power arrangement.

The mood of the adivasis has been captured in a recent article by Bhowmik (2011) who has identified four major factors that have contributed to the spread of the *adivasi* movement in the region: (i) domination of middleclass Bengalis in the leadership of the trade unions in the tea gardens where the workers are overwhelmingly *adivasis*, (ii) the GJMM's demand for inclusion of most of Dooars and Terai, where the *adivasis* have significant presence, into the territory of the proposed Gorkhaland, (iii) spread of the organisational base of the GJMM in the *adivasi* dominated areas in Terai and Dooars, and (iv) growing and shared anger over mal-treatment of fellow *adivasis* in the neighbouring Assam, where the *adivasis* are demanding for ST status. On the whole, Bhowmik argues: 'The *adivasis* in Dooars and Terai (have) started becoming aware of the need for unity because they had long been deprived of their rights and were marginalised from the leadership of their trade unions' (Bhowmik, 2011: 27).

The Organisational Efforts

The leaders of the movement inform that the ABAVP has a four-tier structure with a National Committee, State Committee, Regional Committee and Block Committees. The Terai-Dooars Committee is a regional committee of the ABAVP. Within the regional committee again there are block level and village level committees. The Terai-Dooars Committee is constituted of thirty one members who elect the President, Secretary and other office bearers of the Committee.

The effort to form ABAVP begun in early 2008 when a long march was organised from Sankosh to Naxalbari in which 200 tribal youths took part and a motor cycle rally was held in the month of April from Ghoshpukur to Sankosh to press the demand for autonomy and to protest the plight of the *adivasis* in the neighbouring state of Assam at the hands of the Bodos and the Assamese. The rallies covered the entire length of the area the ABAVP wants under the Sixth Schedule. Agitations followed opposing GJMM rallies in the area, protesting the different acts of atrocity and injustice against the *adivasis* by the police and administration and the members of non-*adivasi* communities.

The Parishad released a map comprising the tribal belts of the Dooars and the Terai demanding Sixth Schedule status, which it believes, would give the adivasis the satisfaction of having their own territory and an opportunity to develop the region, which a awfully backward. The ABAVP leaders submitted a memorandum in support of the Sixth Schedule to the Chief Minister and the Prime Minister on 25th July, 2009 and subsequently held several rallies to reiterate its demands including the one for non-inclusion of the region in proposed Gorkhaland.

It should be noted in this context that the GJMM's movement for a separate state has threatened to rob the tribal population in the region of their claim over the land and their identity. The Gorkha statehood movement is a strong sub-nationalist movement which is considered to be an imposition from the above over the minor ethnic communities, such as Lepchas and the *adivasis*, who are keen on retaining their respective ethnic and cultural identities. Apart from being distinct communities, with some sense of sharing similar objective conditions, the emotive bonds and political interests help ethnic community formation in the present case. The major shared objective conditions include similar position in the production relations, their common places of origin, history of migration, position in power relations, religious and traditional belief system and the sense of being *adivasis* including confrontation of the similar constraints of development.

The ABAVP fought the GJMM tooth and nail against the latter's efforts to spread its organisational network in the Dooars and Terai. The public rallies and agitations organised by the GJMM were physically opposed by the supporters of the ABAVP. The GJMM initially underestimated the strength of the ABAVP and confronted the latter with an attacking posture. But by the middle of 2010, the GJMM worked out a policy-shift to woo the *adivasis*. It started showing some respect to the *adivasi* leaders and recognised the existence and strength of the *adivasi* outfit. The GJMM tried to woo the *adivasi* youth by inducting them into the Gorkhaland Police (GLP) and floated a compromise proposal to the ABAVP. The name of the proposed state in Darjeeling Hills was also changed to 'Gorkha-Adivasi Pradesh' in an effort to woo the *adivasis* opposed to the idea of inclusion of Dooars and Terai in the map of the Gorkha state. The ABAVP leadership however showed no intention of joining the Morcha or in extending support for the so-called demand of Gorkha Adivasi Pradesh. They rather felt that 'it is a conspiracy to derail their movement and again create tension in the brew belts as they will not part with any portion of the Terai and the Dooars for the separate state' (*The Telegraph,* 1st June, 2010).

Besides pressing their right to land, autonomy and identity the ABAVP has demonstrated its keenness to raise the issues of civil rights as a part of their solidarity movement. They often raise issues like the rights of the tea garden workers, rights to proper education, development of infrastructure and their entitlements according to various government sponsored development schemes. The issues like non-development of the *adivasis*, closure of tea gardens, starvation, out-migration in search of income, women trafficking, and the spread of prostitution are often raised by the political and non-governmental organisations that are opposed to the Left Front in the state. In the anti-Left media, the Left-Front government in the state is held solely responsible for the non-development of the *adivasis* both in Southern and Northern districts. The leaders of the Left trade unions are labeled as corrupt, self-seekers and indifferent to the problems of the workers. The ABAVP has taken up some of these issues and raised the ante against the constituents of the Left Front and its trade unions.

Peeved at the silence of the State Government on its demand for Sixth Schedule status for Terai and the Dooars to ABAVP decided to take up the demand with the Centre. 'Considering the state's apathy to the Parishad demands, it is only autonomy that can save the region from backwardness', Mr Tirkey said (*The Telegraph*, 15th January, 2010). The organisation observed one-day strike in the Dooars on 27th January to protest against the nomenclature of a government-sponsored Adivasi festival and to press the demand for Sixth Schedule. It was argued that 'the fest has turned into a platform of the ruling CPI (M) and does not serve the purpose to portray the ethnic culture of the tribal population residing in this part of the state' (*The Telegraph*, 28th January, 2010).

In order to step up pressure on the administration, the ABAVP prepared for intensification of its agitation. It announced to organise a rally at Malbazar and called for another strike on 29th January, 2010. However, after the strike on 27th January the administration cancelled the fest citing security reasons. Following this, the outfit suspended its agitation programmes for two days and decided to organise a 'mega rally' at Malbazar on 29th January. The ABAVP also organised a public rally at Banarhat on 9th June, 2010 to mark the 110th death anniversary of the tribal icon Birsa Munda. The rally was attended by nearly 30,000 Parishad supporters from the Dooars and Terai.

The movement organised by the ABAVP has not always been peaceful. There have been incidents of conflict between the ABAVP supporters and the supporters of other political organisations and the management of tea estates. It is worth noting here that the *adivasis* in Terai and Doors regions are a heterogeneous lot; there are about 30 tribes each of which is distinct in terms of name, language, social structure and rituals. They nurse a sense of hierarchy and a feeling of difference in terms of religious faith. Yet, a common geographical root, migration history, common socio-economic standing, and common sufferings have united the tribals under the term *adivasi*. The leaders of the movement understand the value of *adivasi* unity and they are out to exploit some cultural symbols to this end. In their effort to revive some of their otherwise insignificant festivals they have demanded holiday on the day of Karam festival (on 20 September every year) and Sarhul festival.[2] The leaders are hopeful that their demand will be met by the State government and this will go a long way to consolidate the *adivasi* unity.

Medium of instruction in schools and colleges has been identified as one of the major problems of education of *adivasi* children in the region. Every *adivasi* community has a language and because of this heterogeneity they use Sadri as their *ligua franca*. Despite being a symbol of *adivasi* unity Sadri does not have a script, nor is it used as a medium of instruction in schools. The ABAVP therefore has demanded opening of Hindi medium schools and colleges in the region.[3]

Participation in Democratic Process

Democratic elections in a pluralist polity provide opportunities to political parties to test their relative strength or the scale of public support they command. Although the use of undemocratic means, particularly by the ruling party/parties is common elections to local bodies are fought with unusual enthusiasm which see voter turnout ranging between 80 and 90 per cent. Elections also bring to light some of the hidden agenda of the political organisations and the kind of chauvinistic politics they intend to indulge in while compromising on their declared ideology or objective.

The ABAVP contested the by-election to Kalchini State Assembly seat (ST) in 2009 and lost the seat by a slander margin to the GJMM candidate. It polled more than 30,056 votes against 36,091 votes secured by the GJMM candidate. The Revolutionary Socialist Party (RSP) and Congress candidates were relegated to third and fourth positions. In the 2006 election, the RSP had won the seat securing 52,748 votes defeating the Congress candidate who got 47,759 votes. One can thus notice significant erosion in the support-base of the mainstream parties. Many of the *adivasi* members in the three-tier *panchayat* bodies who represented the mainstream parties have now switched their allegiance to the ABAVP. The organisation has tested huge success in the 2008 election to local bodies as well; its candidates have won a good number of *panchayat Samiti* and *gram panchayat* seats, at the cost of Congress, CPI (M) and RSP. It may be noted here that many local-level *adivasi* leaders of the mainstream political parties have joined the ABAVP which helped the latter gain strength. Most of the leaders of the ABAVP had association with the CPI (M) and the RSP or the Indian National Congress.

With the intensification of Gorkhaland agitation and growing strength of ABAVP, a large number of the tea workers in Dooars and Terai, who were earlier members of trade union wings of the National Trade Unions like INTUC, CITU and AITUC, have now switched their allegiance to the trade union wings of the GJMM and ABAVP. While GJMM has strong support base particularly among the Nepali-speaking workers, the ABAVP has taken control of the *adivasis* workers. The disillusionment of the workers with the national trade unions has prompted this sudden shift of allegiance. ABAVP has been able to form its own trade union wing, namely, Progressive Tea Workers' Union (Terai-Dooars) (PTWU) in all the 200 plus tea gardens in the Dooars and Terai. In 2009, it had submitted a membership list claiming recognition of PTWU to the labour department of Government of West Bengal.

The tribal outfits went into local body poll in 2013 under changed circumstances. In the period since last local body election in 2008 the Trinamul Congress had replaced the Left Front as the ruling party in the state, the united ABAVP was now a divided house with a large chunk of its followers under the leadership of John Barla and some other top leaders had formed a regional branch of Jharkhand Mukti Morcha, led by Sibu Soren. The JMM had forged an alliance with the Gorkha Jana Mukti Morcha (GJMM), and the Trinamul Congress with all its might and resources was busy wooing the tribal outfits for an electoral alliance. Jalpaiguri district, the home of more than 6.5 lakh tribal people (nearly 19 per cent of the total population of the district), went into panchayat polls on 9th July, 2013. It was the only district in West Bengal where the LF retained its control over all the three tiers of the Local Self Governments. Of the 37 zilla parishad seats LF won 27; of the remaining 10 seats Trinamul and Congress had four each, one each was won by Gorkha Jan Mukti Morcha and the Jharkhand Mukti Morcha. In late November 2013, two Congress members joined the TMC, helping the latter getting recognised as the main opposition party in the district board. Out of 13 panchayat samities the LF own six, followed by TMC two and Congress one. In remaining four, no political party secured a clear majority. Of the 146 gram panchayats the LF won 58, TMC 14 and Congress 32. In the tribal and Nepali dominated areas in Dooars, the GMM-GJMM alliance won a good number of *gram* panchayats. Of the total panchayat samiti seats in the district, LF won 216 seats, TMC 118, Congress 53, JMM 22 and GJMM secured 13 seats. Of the total GP seats, LF secured 1010 seats, TMC 742, Congress 296, BJP 32, JMM 108 and independents have won158 seats. Many of the independents are ABAVP candidates, who fought election with an understanding with the Indian national Congress.

The tea garden areas in the district are tribal dominated where the JMM and the ABAVP have overwhelming support. But in this election, in some tea garden areas, the parties in the Left Front, CPI (M) the RSP in particular, have regained some ground they had lost to the *adivasi* ethnic outfit, ABAVP, which was a united force in the last panchayat election in 2008 and in the subsequent state assembly election. Three tea gardens—New Land, Kumargram and Sankosh together constitute NKS gram panchayat, where the LF secured 41.44 per cent votes (as against 36.76 per cent polled in last Assembly election). In the neighbouring Turturi gram panchayat in the last Assembly election (2011), ABAVP and GJMM together secured 56 per cent of votes and the LF got 22.37 per cent. But in 2013 election, the LF secured 32 per cent of votes, a rise of about 10 per cent at the cost of the ABAVP and GJMM, which together got 44 per cent. Lataguri GP is another example where the Left Front constituents won seven out of ten seats, which indicates presence of Left support among the *adivasis* and the Rajbanshis.

In Kumargram, Alipurduar 1, Alipurduar 2, Matherihat, Nagrakata, Metelli, Malbazar blocks of Dooars, the Left Front regained its support among the *adivasis* and led in zilla parishad seats. Only Kalchini block, where the GJMM had a strong present (as it won the Assembly seat) the LF could not make much dent. In Birpara-Madarihat block, the two zilla parshad seats have been won by the LF. Most interestingly, both the seats in tribal dominated Nagrakata block have been own by the tribal candidates, Dilhumar Oraon and Birashmoni Ekka of the LF. The LF leaders attributed this success to overwhelming tribal support which they had lost to the ethnic outfits in 2011 Assembly poll (*Ganasakti,* 31st July, 2013: 3).

The JMM forged an alliance with the Grokha Janmukti Morcha on the issue of inclusion of Dooars in the GTA, a proposal that was opposed by the ABAVP and all the major political parties. The alliance secured majority in 13 panchayats in the Dooars, winning altogether 250 gram panchayat seats. In panchayat samities, the Morcha-JMM won 28 of the total 422 seats in Dooars. The highest number of seats secured by the alliance was in Madarihat, where 10 of their candidates won out of 26 seats. In Nagrakata and Madarihat panchayat samities, where no party got majority, the alliance did relatively well as it would be the deciding factor in forming the board. The alliance secured two zilla parisad seats, one each in Metelli and Madarihat, both in Dooars. Banarhat 2 panchayat is a case where the ethnic outfits have eroded the Left support base drastically. In 2008 election, of the 17 GP seats the CPI (M) had eight, RSP four, and the Congress had five seats. But in this election out of 20 seats, the JMM has won eight, GJMM two, TMC six, and Congress four. The TMC worked out defection in the rank and file of the ABAVP, while the GMM and GJMM fought in alliance. The Congress had an electoral understanding with the ABAVP, which is not a registered political party. In Madarihat gram panchayat, which has a mixed population of different ethnic groups, the TMC has made a dent. Out of 16 seats, the TMC has won ten, CPM three, RSP one and JMM two (*Uttarbanga Sambad,* 31st July, 2003: 3).

Birpara-1 GP, which has tea gardens and a substantial tribal population, is another case where the tribal outfit did not do well. Out of 23 seats RSP has won seven, CPI (M) four, GJMM seven, TMC three and the Congress two. RSP and CPI (M) together have got eleven seats, two short of the majority. Jaigaon-1 gram panchayat is Nepali dominated, where the JMM-GJMM alliance has secured ten, the LF four and the remaining five seats have been won by the Congress. Jaigaon two GP is hung; out of 21 seats, Congress has won six, LF six, TMC five, JMM-GJMM alliance three and independent one (*Uttarbanga Sambad,* 31st July, 2003: 3). Nagrakata, block is almost totally tribal dominated. The panchayat samiti was controlled by the CPI (M) in the last five years. In this election, no party or alliance secured majority in the panchayat samiti. Out of 14 seats, the CPI (M) won four, TMC, Congress and JMM won three seats each and one seat is won by an independent candidate supported by Progressive Trade Union of the ABAVP (*Uttarbanga Sambad,* 31st July, 2003: 4).

In its effort to gain a foothold among the *adivasis* in Dooars the TMC tore apart the possibility of an alliance with the 'willing' *adivasi* outfits, the JMM and the ABAVP. But it was ambitious and in a haste to spread its influence among the *adivasis*. It worked out defection among the local level leaders of the ABAVP, JMM and GJMM and fielded them as candidates. The TMC had approached both the Morcha and the JMM for a tie up to prevent division of anti Left votes. Several rounds of discussions were held but nothing worked as Trinamul, in an aggressive manner, brought in leaders from the Morcha and even close aides of Barla into the party. The strategy did not work. Trinamul, fighting the election alone, secured only seven panchayats, could not secure a single *panchyat* in the tea belt of Malbazar, Metelli and Kalchini, where the Morcha-JMM alliance bagged panchyats in six of the seven blocks in this region. The Trinamul was preoccupied with the notion that frequent visits by Mamata Banerjee, its supreme leader, in the region would help them win elections. What the party did not realise is the absence of tribal and Gorkha leaders in their rank. Despite winning 27 panchayat samiti seats in Dooars, Trinamul could not secure majority in any of the panchayat samities. In the zillla parisad Trinamul won four seats but none from the Dooars (*The Telegraph*, 'Dooars dividends for Morcha', 31st July, 2013: 1).

The Congress did not field candidates in *panchayat samiti* and *gram panchayat* seats at Malbazar, Dhupguri and Nagrakata blocks, all reserved for the STs and went for an electoral understanding with the ABAVP. This political gesture of the Congress is for passing on an oblique message to the tribal leaders that in case they find it uneasy to all with Trinamul, the Congress is all set to welcome them and field their candidates in the vacant seats (*The Telegraph*, 12th June, 2013, Siliguri: 8).

The Left parties the CPI (M), the Revolutionary Socialist Party (RSP), CPI and Forward Block maintained their organisational presence among the *adivasis* and fielded candidates in alliance in most of the seats reserved for the STs in the Dooars region. Multi-factional splits among the *adivasis* in panchayat polls and in other elections to the democratic bodies and their association with many trade unions, mainstream as well as ethnic, had a severe toll on the *adivasi* unity and on the future of *adivasi* ethnic movement for setting up an autonomous council.

The election results demonstrate that despite the overwhelming presence of the resurgent Progressive Tea Workers' Union, an affiliate of the ABAVP, the presence of the mainstream trade unions has not been completely wiped out; trade unions of the Indian National Congress, CPI (M) and RSP still maintain some following among the *adivasi* tea workers in the region. By working out defection in the rank and file of the Congress leadership the Trinamul Congress was trying to make a dent among the *adivasis* of the region. The split in the ABAVP and the formation of a JMM unit in the region and desperate attempts of the mainstream political parties to maintain their support base have been the major spoiler of *adivasi* unity.

Areas of Success

Even though there are serious doubts about the prospect of achieving territorial autonomy under the Sixth Schedule by the ABAVP, the movement, for the first two years of its existence until mid-2010, was united and was able to put enormous pressure on the mainstream political parties, their trade unions and the state (including local administration) to take issues of *adivasi* development far more seriously. A stock-taking of the gains of the movement, particularly in the first two years (2008-2010, would substantiate this point:

It is largely because of the *adivasi* movement that the GJMM was now prepared to restructure its proposed boundary to include only those parts of Dooars and Terai which have Nepali domination; instead of statehood it was now prepared to accept an interim arrangement of autonomy and further it dropped the demand for inclusion of entire Terai and Dooars within the map of the proposed interim arrangement (*The Telegraph*, 31st January, 2010).

The ABAVP had succeeded in exerting enough pressure on the state and district administration to take their organisation seriously and to agree to frequent meetings and dialogues even on the smaller issues raised by the outfit.

The fear of *adivasi* consolidation in the region had put the Left parties and the Left-Front Government under pressure. Leaders of these parties and their ministers now stressed on proper implementation of development programmes to retain support base among the *adivasis*.

The ABAVP's demands for enhancing the daily wage of the workers to Rs.250 had forced the Coordination Committee of the Tea Plantation Workers, which include all the major trade unions, affiliated to mainstream political parties, to demand an equal hike in wages.

The mainstream trade unions were put on alert by the movements, which was gaining popularity among the *adivasi* garden workers. Under pressure the mainstream trade unions had taken initiatives to resolve the long pending PF-related problems. About 102 garden owners in Terai and Dooars were reported defaulter in depositing the owners' share of workers' provident fund to the tune of Rs 7 crores

The movement had given an effective voice to the otherwise voiceless *adivasis*, who now appeared learning to articulate their demands and rights in an organised manner and more forcefully. The pressure was felt by the established political parties and their workers' wings. The garden authorities and the state administration too felt the pressure to pull up their socks and take the issues raised by the ethnic outfit more seriously. The government now recognised the fact that the development related issues of the *adivasis* have long been neglected and therefore there is an urgent need to step up developmental initiatives in the areas of *adivasi* concentration.

However, the gains of the movement were short-lived. Soon, with the change of government in the state, and even before that, the signs of disunity among the adivasis surfaced.

Fissures within and the Surrender

The ABAVP has not been able to wipe out dissent from within. Differences among the leaders on issues and interests and several rounds of splits in the organisation, defection of the leaders to Trinamul Congress, and so on, have taken a serious toll on the *adivasi* unity. A breakaway faction of the ABAVP, mostly from its Nagrakata unit, formed Progressive Peoples' Party (PPP) on 25th July, 2010 under the leadership of Kiran Kalindi. The split took place on the question of support to the GJMM which offered the ABAVP in mid-2010 to be a part of the proposed state of Gorkha-Adivasi Pradesh (*The Telegraph,* 8th September., 2010). The ABAVP leaders complained that its Nagrakata office has been captured by the PPP and following this Rajesh Lakra, the Secretary of the

Terai-Dooars Committee, resigned from his post. Three more office bearers of the Terai-Dooars Committee followed Lakra. They complained about undemocratic style of functioning of the unit and alleged that norms of the Parishad were being violated by some leaders heading the outfit. The state leadership of the ABAVP expelled Kiran Kalindi and Rajesh Lakra from the organisation while reacting to their dissent.

Although it is not a political party the ABAVP, following its declared policy, participates in the electoral politics in order to mobilise the *adivasis* under its banner. At the same time, it resorts to 'strategic' understanding with the national political parties and sometimes fall prey to the manipulative strategies of the latter. The mainstream national parties resort to various tacit and dubious strategies to garner support of the regional and ethnic political groups and formations. In the state assembly election held in May 2011 the ABAVP fielded candidates in Malbazar, Nagrakata, Madarihat, Kumargram and Kalchini constituencies, which are reserved for the scheduled tribes and fought with bow and arrow symbol. In the Terai, in Matigarah-Naxalbari (SC) and Phansidewa (ST) constituencies the ABAVP extended support to Congress candidates. Sibu Soren and a host of tribal leaders of the Jharkhand Mukti Morcha toured Dooars and held election meetings in support of the ABAVP candidates. The election results, however, were not very encouraging for the ABAVP as the *adivasis* continued to vote for the mainstream political parties, the INC and the Left parties. In most constituencies in the Dooars, the ABAVP candidates returned a distant third. The extension of support to the Congress candidates in the Terai constituencies was a 'local arrangement' as the State committee censored the local leaders for the 'local level and tacit' understanding with the Congress. The state level leaders suspected it to be a 'deal' in exchange of cash ('Parishad Sacn on Terai Leader', *The Telegraph,* 20th April, 2011: 6) and promised action against the local leaders involved in the 'deal'.

In the state assembly election held in May-June, 2011, the Trinamul Congress-Indian National Congress alliance came to power with a thumping victory. The TMC, which controls state power now, has been active in working out some form of understanding with the outfit so that it can have a foot-hold among the *adivasis*, who have historically been either with the Left or the INC. The other political force that takes interest in co-opting the *adivasis* into its fold is the Gorkha Jan Mukti Morcha (GJMM).

Late in October 2011, again the GJMM succeeded in roping in the top leaders of the Dooars-Terai Committee of the ABAVP whereby the latter agreed to an understanding of formation of GATA (Gorkhaland-Adivasi Territorial Administration) in place of GTA (Gorkhaland Territorial Administration), which has been formed through an agreement between the State government and the leadership of the GJMM after the Trinamul-led government came to power). On 30th October, the top leadership of the GJMM and the ABAVP held a joint press conference at Mungpoo where, in a joint declaration, they proclaimed to form

GATA while bringing the 'entire Dooars and Terai under the jurisdiction of the proposed GTA'. In the new arrangement the whole of Dooars and Terai, which have substantial tribal population, would merge with the GATA. Both Bimal Gurung, the president of the GJMM, and John Bala, the president of the Terai-Dooars Committee of the ABAVP, justified the move in the name of 'development' of both the communities and the entire region. Barla justified the move arguing that the prospect of formation of an autonomous tribal district under the Sixth Schedule, which has been the main demand the ABAVP movement, is bleak and the *adivasis* of the region would benefit by joining the proposed GATA. Citing his recent discussion with the Chief Minister Mamata Banerjee, Barla said: 'The chief minister, while promising an effective administration in the hills, did not give us any assurance. In fact, Mamata Banerjee told us that there was no need for any separate arrangement for Dooars and Terai. That is why, for the sake of development in the region, we decided to go into an agreement with the Morcha' (*The Telegraph*, 7th November., 2011: 12). He further said: 'We have convinced our local leadership that if the Terai and Dooars were included in the hill set-up, we would have a sizeable representation in it and could work for our own development'. He added saying 'the Morcha would try and convince Mamata about the need for a Gorkhaland Adivasi Territorial Administration' (*The Telegraph*, 7th November., 2011: 12). The chief minister, who seemed to have instigated the Gorkha-Adivasi alliance and a break-up in the adivasi leadership, perhaps wanted an entry of her party in the region, through an electoral alliance.

Following the joint declaration to form GATA the top leaders of the Terai-Dooars Committee of the ABAVP held a number of meetings and conferences to convince the *adivasis* in the region about how they would gain 'from joining a proposed hill set-up because of their numerical strength'. John Barla, Tejkumar Toppo, and other top leaders held a closed-door meeting with office bearers of the ABAVP's block, zonal and regional committees and members of the ABAVP at Malbazar on 6th November, 2011 and then organised a public meeting at Nagrakata on 15th November to put across to the *adivasis* as how they would gain from the move.

The leadership of the state committee of the ABAVP did not approve of the joint declaration made by the Dooars leaders of the outfit and the GJMM. Birsa Tirkey, the state president of the ABAVP, served show-cause notices on John Barla, Tejkumar Toppo and on three other influential leaders, namely, Nicotin Minz, Joseph Hembram and Sukra Munda on 2nd November, 2011 for not taking the consent of the State Committee before signing the agreement with the Morcha. The five were given a week's time to reply. The five leaders led by John Barla and Tejkumar Toppo then took the issue to their followers and tried to mobilise support for their stand. The leaders in reply to show-cause notice justified the step they had taken and asked the state leaders to 'realise the ground realities' in the Terai and Dooars, and outlined how the people of the Terai and Dooars would benefit by joining the hill set-up. Tejkumar Toppo, the general secretary of the Parishad, one of the showcased leaders, said: 'If we join the GJMM and for the Gorkhaland and Adivasi Territorial Administration, a lot of benefits would accrue to us. This is what the state leadership must understand and appreciate. However, we will admit that it was a mistake on our part to have signed the agreement with the Morcha without informing the state leadership' (Sinha, 2011: 6).

Birsa Tirkey, the state president of the Parishad, stuck to his guns, criticised not only the method of dissidence but dismissed the argument that joining hands with the GTA and the Gorkhas would benefit the *adivasis* of the region. He criticised the efforts of the dissident leaders to split the ABAVP and harm the *adivasi* unity saying 'they should not have called the meeting (6th November., Malbazar meeting) under the Parishad banner' and asserted that the dissident leaders would soon be isolated from the *adivasis* for their treachery (Sinha, 2011: 6).

The ABAVP chief claimed during his visit to Dooars on 14th November, that the tribal people in Terai and Dooars were against the inclusion of the regions in the GTA. Birsa Tirkey's claim came a day after Parisad supporters confronted him at Malbazar for serving show-cause notices on the five regional leaders who had batted for the GATA. The chief of the state committee said: 'I have realised during the tour that people of our community are not interested in the GTA. It is only a handful of Parishad leaders who are mooting the alliance with the GJMM. The majority of the *adivasis* are not with them' (*The Telegraph*, Siliguri, 15 November., 2011: 6). The state president also argued that since the Terai and Dooars were covered under the Centre's Integrated Tribal Development Project, the region could not be included in any set up like the GTA. The state committee has already submitted its stand on the territorial jurisdiction of the GTA and opposed its inclusion before Justice Sen Commission, which was looking after the demand of the GJMM.[4] The efforts of the state committee to sort out the differences with the dissident leaders failed and finally in late December 2011 John Barla was removed from the post of President of the Terai-Dooars Committee of the ABAVP while the suspension period for other leaders was extended.

The developments thus confirm that the ethnic outfit is vulnerable to the cooption strategies of the larger political forces and that the latter would every now and then try to destabilise the movement and its source of strength, *adivasi* unity. It appears that ABAVP is yet to form a solid unit organisationally and ideologically. The commitment of the leaders and workers to the altruistic cause is still questionable. Their ideological, moral and economic vulnerability is not difficult to notice. There are developments that suggest that the leaders individually are being lured with lucrative doles to sabotage the organisation and join hands with them. The formation of the PPP is a clear illustration of the point. The break-away leaders seem to be frustrated at not being able to make any headway with their demand for autonomy.

By the time *panchayat* election came in 2013, the ABAVP was further split with the formation of the regional unit of the Jharkhand Mukti Morcha, which went into an electoral alliance with the GJMM. The fundamental issue of ABAVP movement, for formation of a tribal council in the Dooars and Terai, lost its sting since the JMM unit openly advocated inclusion of the region into GTA after renaming it GATA. The Trinamul Congress exploited the vulnerability of the *adivasi* ethnic outfits and effected defection in the leadership of both ABAVP and GJM. The fragility of *adivasi* unity found reflection in the 2013 local body election as the confused *adivasi* voters voted for all the political parties. The Left parties, too, regained some ground it had lost to the *adivasi* ethnic outfit in the elections held since 2008. The maneuvering strategy of the Trinamul Congress remained alive even after 2013 *panchayat* election, as on 5 December, 2013, it managed to rope in Sukra Munda, the chairman of the Progressive Tea Workers' Union (PTWU), and who had earlier defected to JMM with John Barla in 2012 (*The Telegraph*, 6 December, 2013).

The experience so far clearly indicates that an ethnic movement like the one led by the ABAVP may find it extremely difficult to sustain itself for long, particularly when the state and all the systemic integrationist forces are out to derail it. When their demands fail to draw any attention of the state and central governments, the leaders and supporters of the movement lose heart and soon they tend to fall into grip depression. They then fall easy prey to the maneuvering tactics of the organs of the government and the state (e.g., the trade unions, political parties, *panchayats*, and district administration) and often they are lured by the welfare programmes ('biopower', to use Foucault's terminology), which matter a lot for their survival. It is also evident that the tribal leaders, individually or in groups, are 'willing' to make chauvinistic compromises with the larger political forces while betraying the interest of the fellow marginalised *adivasis* and often at the cost of the ethnic outfit.

The systemic forces of integration have all the ammunitions in their armory to split and co-opt the leaders of the autonomous movements. The efforts of the GJM and the Trinamul Congress have met with much success; while the former forged an alliance with John Barla led JMM the latter lured many of the tribal leaders into its fold by distributing 'doles' of different kinds. The GJMM MLA Wilson Chapramari has already joined the Triamul Congress and the party offered MP seat in the forthcoming (2014) parliamentary election to the sitting Nagrakata Congress MLA Joseph Munda as a 'dole' to join the party. The surrender of the leaders of the tribal autonomy movement to the maneuvering 'governmentality' (strategies of governance and integration used by the state over its populations—Michel Foucault) of the Trinamul Congress-led state government seemed nearing completion by end-December 2013. The mainstream *adivasi* outfit ABAVP felicitated Mamata Banerjee, the

Chief Minister of West Bengal, in a function at Nagrakata on 12th February, 2014 for the two 'historic decisions, namely, (1) the formation of the Tribal Advisory Council, and (2) the formation of a separate tribal welfare department. The state leadership, in presence of the all-India president of the ABAVP Somji Bhai Damor, conferred the highest *adivasi* honour *Singi Dai Veerangana* on the Chief Minister. This was the first positive step towards a political alliance between the Trinamul Congress and the tribal organisations. Defending the decision Birsa Tirkey said that the decisions of the state government are 'historic' and 'of paramount significance' and applauded the state government for its 'strict stance on the Gorkhaland issue' (*The Telegraph* 26th December, 2013). Accepting the title, the CM made some promises: (1) installation of drinking water project in Madarihat, Mateli, Kalchini, Birpara and Malbazar, (2) issuance of ST certificate within one month of application, (3) inclusion of Hindi as a subject at the undergraduate level in NBU, (4) a campus of the University at Raiganj, (5) filling up of jobs reserved for STs within two years, (6) addressing the issues of land-grab (*The Telegraph,* 13th February, 2014). That Birsa Tirkey was trying to cover-up his outfit's betrayal of the *adivasi* cause was soon clear as on 11th March, 2014, he declared the ABAVP's support for the Trinamul in Jalpaiguri and Alipurduar seats in the Lok Sabha election held on 17th April, 2014. An ethnic movement with a lot of promise thus slept into the lap of an aggressive integrationist regional political party (*The Telegraph,* 12th March, 2014: XXNL).

Conclusion

The integrationist package, that liberal democracy and the free market combination is, is ridden with 'crises' which end up alienating the communities and groups living on the margins. The ethnic movement in the Terai and Dooars of North Bengal spearheaded by the Akhil Bharatiya Adivasi Vikas Parishad strove to unite a group of culturally distinct tribes highlighting their collective experience of similar systemic exploitation, oppression and exclusion. The prime objective of the movement at least initially was to project a united self of the otherwise distinct tribes in the name of their common roots and shared symbols and their claim over a territory they have made their home for nearly one and a half century. Another objective was to expose the hollowness of the integrationist organs of the liberal state and to counter the forces that are out to threaten their security and claim over the region.

Being a part of the neo-liberal market, the *adivasis* in North Bengal, with minimal control over material and human resources and culture capital, are engaged in a fierce survival battle as the dominant sections with a greater control over resources have left little economic and socio-political space for them to cultivate. The state, armed with its welfare package, does occasional repair works here and there, but ends up extending support to the liberal market and the economically dominant sections thus alienating the *adivasis* who live on the margin. Despite the Plantation Labour Act, 1951, and periodic tripartite meetings the state has failed to protect the rights of the workers and improve the quality of their life against the atrocities and exploitation of the owning class. With very little control over human resources the *adivasis* often fail to access the benefits of the policy of protective discrimination or the special development initiatives undertaken by the state periodically. The corrupt yet inefficient bureaucracy and the *panchayat* functionaries come in their way to reaping the benefits of development initiatives. The over-exploitative arrangement in tea gardens and loss of land (because of division of holding among the heirs and alienation by the manipulative and resourceful neighbours) in areas outside gardens perpetuate their marginalised existence in the region. The market uncertainty, the penetration of the forces of globalisation and crisis in the tea gardens make them even more vulnerable as a social category. Being a part of such a depressing reality the *adivasis* in the region are lose confidence in the ability of the state and other systemic organs to give them much needed protection.

The economic marginalisation and livelihood threats that face the tribal communities in the region and which are in-built in the liberal democratic order prepare the ground for tribal dissent. The inability of the pre-existing civil societies such as trade unions, mass organisations and political parties—the systemic organs of integration—to create enough social and political space also prompts the *adivasis* to form their own civil societies in ethnic line, asserting tribal identity. However, the fundamental question is whether the alternative civil societies put up by the tribes will work as anti-systemic organs or would settle with a 'negotiated and compromised space' in the existing politico-economic frame.

Besides systemic marginalisation a new threat in the form of the Gorkha Janmukti Morcha looms large on the *adivasis* in Dooars and Terai regions. The expanding influence of the Gorkha statehood movement in Dooars and Terai among the ethnic Nepali speaking population and the demand of inclusion of these *adivasi* dominated areas into the proposed Gorkha state pose a serious threat to the *adivasi* attachment and right to the area where they have lived for generations. The shared perception of losing their land and a common experience of marginalisation in the economic, social and political spheres together have prepared the ground for the formation of the tribal ethnic movement. Between 2008 and 2010, the resurgent ABAVP expanded its influence among the *adivasis* in the Dooars and Terai regions which seemed to be a clear indication of the decline of the influence of welfare state and its ideological apparatuses like the political parties and their trade union wings. The ethnic outfit was also able to consolidate its political base in the region by unifying the tribals against the 'other' – the GJMM and the integrationist forces of the 'order'.

In its first two years, the *adivasi* movement appeared well scripted: (1) it took care in avoiding the violent course, (2) took the ethnic route to mobilisation consciously exploiting cultural symbols , (3) formed a strong trade union wing to protect the interest of the tea garden workers, (4) participated in democratic and electoral processes, (5) pursued the development issues of ethnic interest–issues relating to land, education, employment, and so on—with the state administration, and (6) even put up to physical resistance to the attacks by the GJMM and used its muscle power for strategic counter offensive. The demand for autonomy under Sixth Schedule seemed to have caught the collective imagination of the otherwise marginalised and alienated *adivasi* communities of the region. The movement seemed to be heading towards an effective civil society movement of the *adivasis* because of its flexibility in framing demands and strategies, because of the consolidation of the ethnic tribal communities by one *adivasi* identity, because of its ability to create pressure on the state and its organs to pursue the development programmes with greater care and seriousness, and because of its ability to put up organisational challenge to the established political parties and trade unions.

However, after the initial phase of advance the ethnic movement of the *adivasis* ran into rough weather for a number of problems. The 'parochial' ideology of the movement, which tends to bypass the class issue, failed to keep the leaders and the common *adivasis* united for long. Lack of experience on the part of leadership and its shortsightedness led to dissidence and splits in the organisation. The movement never seemed to be taking a revolutionary course; it aimed to find a comfortable space for its collective *adivasi* self within the existing liberal-democratic order. Even in realising its moderate and 'just' objectives the movement has faced stiff challenges both from within and without. From within, the movement lacks ideological solidity and unity of purpose and its leaders, driven by narrow and selfish interests, are always 'willing' to compromise with the systemic forces and the mainstream political parties. From without, the hegemonic forces loom large to destroy a movement that could have given, had it been successful, a voice to the voiceless and alienated *adivasis* of the region. The movement has already experienced several rounds of splits among its top leaders and followers because of differences on whether to stick to demand of the creation of an autonomous tribal council under the Sixth Schedule of the Indian Constitution or to be a part of the Gorkhaland Territorial Administration (GTA). Recent defection of tribal leaders to the ruling Trinamul Congress and extension of support to the Trinamul Congress candidates in 2014 Lok Sabha poll in the area are being read as steps in self deception. Disgusted at 'chauvinistic' acts of the leaders the ordinary adivasis seem to be reacting by siding with the Left parties, as they did in 2013 local body elections, and their trade unions. The leadership's alliance with the ruling party for otherwise insignificant measures of the state government can be explained only in terms of chauvinistic politics of the leadership and be read as a move in betrayal of the adivasi cause.

Notes

1. I tried to grasp the course of the movement and have a feel of the *adivasi* mind-set that prompted the movement by talking to some of the leaders of the movement, namely, John Barla, the then President of the Terai-Dooars Committee of the ABAVP, who later became the President of the Doors unit of Jharkhand Mukti Morcha, and some local leaders of the organisation, namely, Jerom Lakra and Peter Minj of Athalbari in Jalpaiguri district.
2. Karam and Sarhul are considered holy trees by the *adivasis* of Chotanagpur; they offer *puja* to these trees in continuation of their tradition of nature worship. After coming to power in 2011, Mamata Banerjee declared the day a holiday.
3. In a letter to the Editor, Ganasakti (9th February, 2010) Parag Mitra regrets that although the Left-Front Government has secured recognition of Santhali, helped inclusion of the language in the Eighth Schedule of the Constitution and encouraged the introduction of Alchiki in schools, the ABAVP is demanding introduction of Hindi medium schools and colleges and not showing any interest in Santhali or Alchiki. He regrets that when the small languages are losing out with the encroachment of global language (English in particular), there is no effort on the part of the smaller communities to protect their own language and culture. Mitra further opposes the aggressive ethnic mobilisation by the ABAVP on the ground that the area has a mixed population and the ethnic movement will result disharmony among the communities and will affect the unity of the poor and middleclass inhabitants of the region. Mitra, it seems, has missed the point that the Santhals are an insignificant minority in the Dooars and Terai and Santhali is not used even as a spoken language by *adivasi* communities in the region; they speak Sadri.
4. After signing the agreement on formation of the GTA in 2011 the state government set up one man Sen Commission to look into the demand of inclusion of nearly 198 additional *mouzas* into the territory of the GTA. The Sen Commission gave its report in 2013 recommending inclusion of only five addition *mouzas*, which upset the Gorkha leaders.

References

Bhawmik, Sharit, 2011. 'Wages and Ethnic Conflicts in Bengal's Tea Industry', *Economic and Political Weekly*, August 6, pp. 26-29.

Bhagabati, A., 2012. *Issues of Social Transformation, Ethnicity, and Identity Assertion Movements in North-East India: An Anthropological Overview*. Jhargram: Indian Confederation and Academy of Anthropologists.

Bose, N.K., 1941. *'Hindu Method of Tribal Absorption', Science and Culture 7 (1), pp. 188-94.*

Foucault, Michel, 1991. 'Governmentality', in G. Burchell, C. Gordon and P. Miller (eds.) *The Foucault Effect: Studies in Governmentality*. London: Harvester Wheatsheaf, pp. 87-104.

Ganasakti 31th July, 2013, Siliguri.

Habermas, Jurgen, 1992. 'Further Reflection on the Public Sphere' in C. Calhoun (ed.) *Habermas and the Public Sphere*. Cambridge: MIT Press.

Mitra, Parag, 'Letter to the Editor' *Ganasakti*, Siliguri, 9th February, 2010.

Roy, Sanjay K., 2008. *Work Participation of Tribal Women and Marginalisation: The Case of Tribes in North Bengal.* Kolkata: Levant Books.

Roy, Sanjay K., 2009a. 'North Bengal Tribes in Development Perspective' in *Journal Anthropological Society*, 44, pp. 5-27.

Roy, Sanjay K., 2009b. *Christians of North Bengal: A Community or Communities? (North Dinajpur District Report),* Unpublished project report, Department of Sociology, North Bengal University.

Roy, Sanjay K., 2009c. 'Areas of Freedom and Subjugation in the Life of the Tribal Women', in Anita Bagchi and Sanjay K. Roy (eds.) *Changing Fasces of Indian Women*. Kolkata: Levant Books, pp. 196-225.

Roy, Sanjay K., 2011. *Alienation of Tribal Land and its Implications for Ethnic Movements of Tribes in North Bengal.* Unpublished project report, Department of Sociology, North Bengal University.

Sarkar, Jyoti, 2013. 'Gramin Karmasuchir Suphaler Asai Voter Dike Takie Cha Boloyer Manush', *Uttarbanga Sambad*, Siliguri, 23rd June, 2013, Siliguri: 9.

Sinha, Avijit, 2011. 'Tribal 5 to stand by deal with Morcha', *The Telegraph*, Siliguri, 8th November., 2011: 6.

Xaxa, Virginius, 2012. 'Tribes and Development: Some Observations' in Biswajit Ghosh (ed.) *Interrogating Development: Discourses on Development in India Today*. New Delhi: Rawat Publications: 307-323.

The Telegraph, Siliguri, 15th January, 2010.

The Telegraph, Siliguri, 28th January, 2010.

The Telegraph, Siliguri, 1st June, 2010.

The Telegraph, Siliguri, 8 September., 2010.

The Telegraph, Siliguri, 20th April, 2011: 6.

The Telegraph, Siliguri, 15th Nov., 2011: 6.

The Telegraph, Siliguri, 15th Nov., 2011: 12.

The Telegraph, Siliguri, 'Dooars dividends for Morcha', 31 July, 2013: 1.

The Telegraph, Siliguri, 12th June, 2013: 8.

The Telegraph, 6th December, 2013, Siliguri.

Uttarbanga Sambad, 31st July, 2003: 3, Siliguri.

Uttarbanga Sambad, 31st July, 2003: 4, Siliguri.

The Telegraph, 12th March, 2014, Siliguri.

SECTION–III

ETHNICITY IN NORTH-EAST INDIA

12

Indigenised Ethnicity, In-Group-Out-Group Syndrome and Governance Issue in Northeast India

N.K. Das

The article examines how the foundations of ethnic unrest in north-eastern India were planted in colonial era, through introduction of various repulsive laws, division of hills and plains by installing an Inner-Line, and promoting and 'importing' a huge non-indigenous workforce, to protect economic interests of the colonisers. The article discusses the issues of indigenised ethnicity, growing minority syndrome and governance breakdown which have triggered the ethnic unrest perpetually in post-colonial northeast India. The article uses an ethno-historical approach to elucidate, how a range of colonial 'exclusionary' strategies and continuity of outmoded 'divide and rule' policies in post-colonial era marginalised the communities, and reinforced the sentiments and perceptions of insider-outsider/minority-majority which ignited the ethnic unrest, resulting in autonomy movements and armed militancy. We also briefly review efforts of the state and the civil society organisations in bringing peace by applying multiple approaches, including by empowering the indigenous tribes with constitutional legislations, devolution of power at grassroots level and facilitation of democratic institutions, which often failed on account of leadership rivalries within tribes and the hegemonic style of functioning of dominant tribes.

In physiographic terms, Northeast India is divided into the Eastern Himalaya, the North-eastern hills, and the Brahmaputra and Barak valleys/

plains. Northeast India, comprising the states of Arunachal Pradesh, Assam, Manipur, Meghalaya, Mizoram, Nagaland, Tripura, and Sikkim, encompasses vast hilly regions, which account for 70 per cent of territory. The states of Nagaland, Arunachal Pradesh, Mizoram, Meghalaya and Sikkim are all located in the hills, while half of Tripura, 1/5th of Assam and 9/10th of Manipur are hilly areas. Northeast India forms the international border, touching countries such as Burma/Myanmar, Bhutan, Bangladesh, Tibetan region of People's Republic of China and Nepal. This international border is also a product of colonial regime. The people of the Northeast region identify themselves as hill tribes, the plains tribes and the non-tribal populations of the plains. Most of the hill tribes in Manipur, Meghalaya, Mizoram, Nagaland and Tripura are now Christian while a substantial proportion of those living in the plains of Assam, Manipur and Tripura are Hindu; a small segment pursuing Islam. The population of Northeast region is 38.50 million as per 2001 Census. At an early stage, the colonial administration had undertaken an ethnographic survey in 1920s (Hutton; Mills). A more cohesive empirical survey by professional anthropologists was accomplished in 1980s (Singh, 1992, Das, *et al.,* 1994). Unfortunately the ethnographies of colonial administrators often suffered from Oriental value-pattern. Ethno-history of Northeast region suggests enormous ethnic-linguistic linkages with South East Asia. Having immigrated and settled in northeast region, the Mongoloid groups crystallised into distinct 'tribes' (Bhagabati, 1988: 1-2; Das, 1960, 1970). Colonial regime had put an end to linkages of Mongoloid ethnic groups of northeast with their counterparts in Southeast Asia. Diverse ecologies encouraged different polity– formations, such as 'tribe', 'chiefdom' and 'state' (Das, 1987, 1993). One such immigrant community, the Tai-Ahom, occupied upper Assam and established a vast Assam kingdom which existed for over six centuries. The ruling Meitei dynasty of Manipur ruled the state almost uninterrupted for over ten centuries. The kingdoms of Kachari, Ahom, Jaintia, Koch, Tripuri, and Meitei were basically 'tribal-states', whose ruling families, adopted Hinduism. Assam plains witnessed the spread of Sarania dharma of Shankar Dev, which engrossed the tribespeople also. The hills tribes, mostly of Mongoloid origin, can be grouped into four major groups: the Kuki-Chin-Mizos, Nagas, Khasi-Jintia-Garos and tribes of Arunachal Pradesh.

Colonial Exclusionary Stratagem, 'Civilising' Mission and Indigenised Ethnicity

Colonial policy of separating the north-eastern hills from valleys not only led to early intensification of in-group identity consciousness but also reinforced the cause of early ethnicity which came to be expressed through ethnic mobilisations undertaken around generic identities such as Naga, Mizo, and Kuki and aggressive regionalisation of ethnic demands for self-governance. There are many instances of early protests which defined the earliest narrative of indigenised ethnicity, a minority syndrome and authentic anti-British retort, right from 1930s till 1940s. It was the Bengal Eastern Frontier Regulation, 1873, which allowed the government to establish an Inner-Line (between hills and plains) and thereby prohibiting any subject to cross that line. Within inner-line the tribes were left to manage their own affairs through their own headmen and chiefs. A grand plan of 'social exclusion' was thus laid, mainly because these policies had led to a permanent segregation between hills and plains. Regrettably, such isolationist policies persist in the post-Independence period under the mistaken motive of 'protecting' the tribes against exploitation by 'outsiders' (Sahni, 2002; Das, 2007, 2009). The Inner Line Regulation kept the Indian culture and religion effectively on the other side of the fence; the Christian missionaries were inducted for proselytisation in hills areas. The greatest benefit from the Regulation of 1873, according to Jafa (1999), was launch of Christian mission's policy for 'civilising the savages', creating an impregnable Christian fortress safe from the prying eyes of the neighbouring Hindus and Muslims (Jafa, 1999). The British promoted a separate identity, both religious and social, in most of the indirectly ruled areas which ran counter to the growth of nationalism in the directly ruled areas of the country. In view of growing anger and persistent resistance alongside rising indigeneity consciousness, the government commissioned the Simon Commission (Indian Statutory Commission, 1930) to review administrative conditions. After prolonged interactions with indigenous representatives and tribal chiefs, the Commission proposed to introduce the Government of India Act, 1935 (to administer the backward tracts by regrouping as excluded and partially excluded areas. The British administration categorised hill areas/hills districts within Assam as 'Non-Regulated Areas', 'Backward Tract' and eventually as 'Partially Excluded Areas' and 'Excluded Areas'. Consequent upon the visit of the Statutory Commission, apprehension of a minority syndrome had further hastened among the tribespeople. Those who asserted their resentment initially were the Khasi, Ahom, Naga, Mizo, Bodo-Kachari, Miri and Deuri. On the eve of transfer of power, the hills people of northeast became restive as the local tribal elite had variously questioned the right of new Indian nation-state to have control over the hills areas, even as a new tiny state East Pakistan had emerged in their vicinity. They became apprehensive about their destinies, as the fear of plainspeople subjugating the hills areas had created anxiety (Das, 1982, 2009). Anxiety arose mainly because the post-colonial Indian (Provincial Constitutional) Order, 1947, by and large, retained the essentials of the repressive Government of India Act, 1935, including Inner Line Regulation, which existed in the Hills (NEFA/Arunachal Pradesh, Mizoram and Nagaland).

At this stage, the Indian government enacted the Sixth Schedule (1950) of the Indian Constitution, aiming at providing utmost 'autonomy' towards self-governance to tribespeople. This led to launch of several Autonomous District Councils in tribal areas. However, soon it was realised that the autonomous councils were unable to protect in true spirit the economic resources, the land, custom, tradition and identity of tribespeople. It created multiple power centres and state-control often derailed realistic initiatives of the Autonomous District Councils. The failure of Sixth Schedule model, led to rethinking on part of hills tribes who decided to fight for a separate Hill State within Assam. In December 1952, it was resolved to form the Assam Hills Tribal Union (later renamed as the Eastern India Tribal Union (EITU) in October 1953). EITU was critical about proposal of Assam Administration to impose Assamese language and culture on the hills peoples. During a meeting on 28th April, 1960, hill-leaders vehemently opposed the mono-language decision of Assam. This led to birth of the All Party Hill Leaders Conference (APHLC), which spearheaded the Hill-State Movement.

The discourse of indigeneity self-esteem and minority symptoms had rapidly surfaced in 1950s mainly on account of several prejudiced policies such as the official language policy in educational institutions, through imposition of Assamese language and script. It triggered several agitations and minor communities opposed the language policy. Superimposing the majority language on minority indigenous tribes of Assam, in hills as well as plains, was seen as huge obstacle. The Mizos were first to react to such shift. Many plains tribes in Assam had been disturbed and alarmed by such hegemonic stances of dominant Assamese community. Thus, grew a nascent tendency of revulsion against Assamese linguistic-cultural domination throughout the Brahmaputra valley, amongst the minority tribes. This situation led to feeling of elimination and social-exclusion on part of tribes such as the Bodos, the Ahoms, the Karbis and many others. Fearing forced introduction of non-tribal language and alien script on indigenous communities many Assam tribes had felt forsaken. The Bodos were the first among the plains-tribe to oppose the language policy and they launched a strong agitation in 1952. The Bodos were supported by the Bodo Sahitya Sabha and the Plains Tribes Council of Assam (PTCA). As a result they succeeded in making the Bodo language the medium of instruction (up to the secondary level). This led to movements by other minor tribes, such as the Mishing. The Mishing Agom Kebang (Mishing Sahitya Sabha) and several other Missing organisations worked consistently and succeeded in 1980s to have Mishing language as a subject of study in primary schools. The Mishings were ultimately allowed to use Roman script, and their text books came to be printed in the Roman Script, so also some newspapers and journals (Miri, 1993: 71).

Another burning issue in most parts of northeast has been the issue of land alienation. Alienation was possible as tribespeople did not have the documents related to individual rights over lands. The changes made in the land laws in Assam in 1948 facilitated tribal land alienation. As a result, the number of tribal blocks from which land cannot be alienated to non-tribes has declined from 35 in the 1950s to 25 in 2005 (Shim Ray, 2006: 17-18).

Land alienation has been the basis of most ethnic conflicts, for example, those in Bodoland and Kari Angling areas. Land alienation causes shortage of resources and competition for the remaining scarce resources. In that situation many immigrants try to create 'myths' explaining their indigeneity falsely to declare itself the original indigenous community of a given area, such as in Bodo and Kari and North Catcher areas. On the other side, there are evidences to show that, immigrants of Bangladeshi and Bihari origin have been encroaching on tribal and other land. Since the land is essential to basic survival it explains why most killings in Kari Angling are those of the Bihar is in post-colonial era (Fernandez, 2007).

Émigré question has its origin in the colonial era. How dangerous the issue was may be glanced in the following statement of the colonial era Census Report of 1931:

> Probably the most important event in the (Assam) province during the last 25 years - an event, which seems likely to alter permanently the whole future of Assam and to destroy more surely—the whole structure of Assamese culture and civilisation—has been the invasion of hordes of land-hungry Bengali immigrants, mostly Muslims, from the districts of Eastern Bengal and in particular Mymensingh (Maitra and Maitra, 1995).

The factors that influenced the immigration in the past were search for arable lands for settled paddy cultivation supported by hard labour that was put by the immigrants from then East Bengal. Immediately after independence, the partition brought lakhs of East Pakistani refugees, including Muslims, into Assam and Tripura. Their immigration continued even after 1950. Apart from the official figure of registered immigrants who were granted rehabilitation facilities, a large number of refugees came on their own and found their own mode of rehabilitation without official assistance or registration (Bhattacharyya, 1988: 14). That this Bangladeshi Hindu influx continued after 1956 and even beyond 1971 can be seen from the fact that the tribal proportion in Tripura had declined from about 60 per cent in 1951 (Chattopadyay, 1990: 101) to 30 per cent in 2001 (Banthia, 2001: xlvi). Infiltration of millions of emigrants (foreigners) kept disturbing the demographic pattern, ethnic composition and economic opportunities of the Northeast. The local people felt the huge crisis (Goswami, 1984: 39; Singh, 1987: 163). In course of time 'migrant communities' could gain more and more control over primary sources of livelihood like land and over secondary sources like government jobs (Singh, 1987: 141, Das, 1987). The British had attempted to enhance the land revenue and augment the exchequer by exploitation of the natural resources and by encouraging tea-plantation but they found that the shortage of manpower in Assam was the greatest obstacle to the fulfillment of their plans (Singh, 1987: 140). Since Assam had no labour force, *Adivasi* labourers were brought from Jharkhand, Odisha and Bengal. Immigration became a social factor in Assam ever since the development of the tea gardens around 1850. After 1891 those workers were joined by Muslims from East Bengal and also from the beginning of the 20th century, by Nepali grazers. A good number of Gorkhas were part of the British army and many of these Gorkha-Nepalis settled down in Assam.

The year 1979 saw Assam explode into a massive agitation against illegal immigration, with an agenda of compelling the government to identify and expel illegal immigrants and prevent new immigration. The agitation leaders formed a political party, *Asom Gana Parishad*, which came to power after the Assembly elections of 1985 (Jethmalani, 2012). In November 1998, the Governor of Assam, S.K. Sinha presented an official report to the President of India entitled *Illegal Migration into Assam*. The Report warned:

> As a result of population movement from Bangladesh, the specter looms large of indigenous people of Assam being reduced to a minority in their home state. Their cultural survival will be in jeopardy, their political control will be weakened and their employment opportunities will be undermined... It will be then a matter of time when a demand for their merger with Bangladesh may be made. The rapid growth of international Islamic fundamentalism may provide the driving force for the demand *(Report on Illegal Migration into Assam,* 33, 17-18.).

Indian government of that period is reported to have asked Assam Chief Minister to go easy on deportations and even stop them, even as the problem was so critical that Assam's demography and culture was going to be permanently changed (Hazarika, 2000: 60). There has been a disturbing growth of Islamic militancy in the Northeast. Islamic fundamentalism, militant groups seeking links to international terrorist groups, and mushrooming of Islamic schools whipping up radical students are all combined (Linter, 2002; Das, 1994). More recently, on 6th September, 2012, replying to an un-starred question in Lok Sabha (Indian Parliament) the Union Minister, Salman Khurshid said there are reports of 'illegal infiltration' and 'immigration of Bangladeshi nationals', who manage to 'infiltrate into the country despite checks and control' at the International border (indiatimes.com).

Assam Agitation, Assam Accord and ULFA

There are millions of illegal immigrants in Assam, and the Indian government has failed in its duty to prevent this illegal migration (Dev and Lahiri, 1985). The concerns of the Assamese people have been not only to expel foreigners, but also to protect the Assamese language and culture and preserve Assamese dominance in the state's political arena. It would be an over simplification to characterise the conflict in Assam solely as a matter of Indians versus non-Indians. Although the *casus belli* for the agitation might be Indian nationalism, it is Assamese sub-nationalism that is its driving force (Misra, 1988; Gosselink, 1994). The failure of Assamese politicians to compel the national government to promote and protect Assamese interests led eventually to the rise of grassroots organisations devoted to maintaining the status and position of the Assamese in Assam (Das Gupta, 1988). The first popular movement on the problem of 'Illegal immigration' was launched by All Assam Student Union (AASU). In 1979, with illegal immigration at an all-time high, the AASU began agitating for the government to evict all illegal aliens from Assam. The AASU's main demands were (1) the detection of foreign nationals on the basis of the 1951 National Register of Citizens, (2) the disenfranchisement of foreigners by removing their names from Assam's electoral rolls, and (3) the deportation of foreign nationals. When the Assamese 'movement against foreigners' was launched it was labeled variously as secessionist, anti-Muslim, and anti-Bengali (Das, 1982: ix). The Assamese involved in the movement have long denied these characterisations. They insist that their struggle has been to 'protect' Assam from non-Indians and is not a religious, ethnic, or separatist movement. Rather, it is 'a *national* movement against the continued presence of foreigners in Assam', and is designed to succeed where both the Indian government and the Indian Constitution have failed (Gosselink, 1994).

Illegal immigrants continued to cross into Assam from Bangladesh and tensions continued to build leading to sporadic violence and communal clashes. These conflicts claimed the lives of hundreds of people from 1981 to 1983. The first real step towards a solution to the ethnic conflict in Assam was the 1985 Assam Accord ('Accord'), which was brought about by the new national leadership of Rajiv Gandhi. The Accord called for (1) the expulsion of all immigrants who had entered Assam illegally after March 24, 1971; and (2) a ten-year disenfranchisement of illegal immigrants who had entered the state between 1966 and 1971. Those who came to Assam before 1966 were to be granted Indian citizenship. When elections were held a few months later, the Assam Gana Parishad, a political party formed mainly of activists from the Assam movement, won a majority in Assam's Legislative Assembly. With an Assamese nationalist party in control of the state assembly, the central government was faced again with the possibility of ethnic tensions and violence in Assam, the Indian Parliament therefore alleged to have delayed the implementation of the Accord. This, in turn, led to renewed agitation by the AASU. This soaring frustration led to the emergence of the United Liberation Front of Assam (ULFA), a secessionist organisation, which continues to operate even today, though one faction of the outfit has come over-ground to start peace parley with Indian government. In the meantime no concrete administrative action could be initiated as per clauses of the Assam Accord. Resultantly, the 2001 census showed an excess of 4,000,000 persons over and above the natural growth of the population of 1971, around 1.7 millions of them Bengali-speaking Muslims, presumably of Bangladesh origin, and 2.3 millions of Bihari or Nepali origin (Fernandes, 2005: 3238). Studies show that several

Bihari families have their *pattas* at Lanka in the non-tribal Nagaon district of Assam for the land they own in the neighbouring Karbi Anglong district, which comes under the Sixth Schedule of the Constitution that is meant for the hill tribes and bans land alienation to non-tribes (Fernandes and Barbora, 2002: 79; Das, 1987). Such an arrangement could not have been done without corruption in the administration (Das, 1987).

Sixth Schedule: Self-governance and Hegemony of 'Dominant' Tribes

The Constitution Drafting Committee of free India set up a sub-committee (North East Frontier Tribal and Excluded Areas Committee) with Gopinath Bordoloi, then Premier of Assam, as its Chairman. The sub-committee recommended autonomous district councils to safeguard the hill tribes of Assam in respect of their land, social customs and usages, language and culture. It was ensured that Autonomous District Councils (ADCs) will enjoy Legislative, Administrative and Judicial powers under the Sixth Schedule. No law of the Centre or the State in respect of the legislative powers could be extended to those autonomous areas without their prior approval. The district councils are also empowered to constitute Village councils and also Village courts. The non-Sixth Schedule States in the North-East where 73rd and 74th amendments (Panchayati Raj Institutions) have been implemented are Assam (barring Karbi Anglong Autonomous District Council and NC Hills Autonomous District Council), Manipur, Tripura (barring Tripura Tribal Areas Autonomous District Council), Arunachal Pradesh and Sikkim. While the ADCs have the advantage of legislative powers the Panchayats do not have them. The councils, unlike Panchayats, do not have provision for reservation for women, and powers such as social forestry management, though the new Forest Rights Act, 2006, which is applicable in entire India, is yet to be implemented by the state governments of the region. The Autonomous District Councils (ADCs) comprise of 30 members for a term of five years. The Governor of the state is empowered to nominate not more than four members to the Council while the others are elected on the basis of adult suffrage. The Chief Executive Member (CEM), the Chairman and the deputy Chairman of the Council (equivalent of Speaker and Deputy Speaker) are elected from the members and the CEM selects the other executive members. Autonomous District Councils were formed in the tribal districts of Assam, except in the Naga Hills District. The first set of autonomous district councils came to operate right from 1952. There was further extension of the provision in the Mizoram and in the Tribal areas of Tripura later on. In due course, separate Autonomous District Councils were formed in the Jowai and North Cachar Hills Districts. Nagas had opposed any such "restricted" design of self-governance.

Autonomous District Councils are responsible for looking after the social, economic and minor criminal and civil matters of the tribal people. Councils are empowered to make laws with respect to land, forest, water course, shifting cultivation, establishment of village and town and its administration, appointment of, or succession to, chiefs or headmen, inheritance of property, marriage and divorce and other matters relating to social customs. Unfortunately, the model of Sixth Schedule Autonomous Councils ended up creating multiple power centers instead of bringing in a genuine process of democratisation or autonomy in the region. The introduction of the sub-federal entity in the shape of Sixth Schedule was meant to protect the rights and particular ways of life of tribespeople. However, the domination of the 'majority' tribes in the district councils created further fissures. Thus, the Dimasas came out openly against the N.C. Hills Autonomous Council and they took up arms demanding creation of a separate 'home-land' for themselves as they found themselves helpless in safeguarding their culture and identity under the provision of the Sixth Schedule within the State of Assam. Local competition over the land and other resources, including claims over homelands are in the core of most of the ethnic conflicts in the Northeast. Hence, numerous administrative arrangements were implemented such as self-ruled Autonomous Councils and mini-ethnic-states. However, such constitutional-federal institutions could not settle all disorders. Enticement of power and wealth enjoyed by the dominant tribes and their elite in autonomous councils often created irregularity in equitable distribution of development schemes to all regions. Such biased priorities gradually left smaller and peripheral tribes neglected. Many smaller tribes, often forced in bifurcated diverse administrative/political zones, thus came to experience the relentless repression of worst kind. Below we shall revisit the theme of exploitation of minor tribes within the autonomous councils of hill-states, by citing case studies.

Majority-Minority Syndrome, Inter-Ethnic Clash and Self-Rule Demands

In the long politico-historical narrative of the region we encounter numerous tribes suffering from minority-disabilities such as enforced linguistic-cultural assimilation, 'social-exclusion' and marginalisation. Exploring the backdrop we find that it has been the Assamese cluster which shaped the domineering majority vis-à-vis communities like Bodo, Khasi, Naga, Mizo, Kuki etcetera, who felt suppression from the former, right from the beginning of the identity politics which grew in colonial era.

(1) ***Bodo Ethnicity and Bodo Peasants vs. Muslim Peasants:*** The Bodo dissent needs to be seen as the struggle of Assam's most prominent ethnic "minority' and the indigenous populace of the region, aspiring to protect its cultural identity as also economic resources such as land, which is also endangered. The Bodos first encountered the cultural pressure and linguistic suppression of the Assamese society and then they confronted the illegal encroachment of their land by invading immigrants, right from colonial era, from within and across borders (mostly Muslims). It is natural therefore that ever since the agitation for a separate Bodoland began; the prime target of the

Bodo leadership has been the Assamese middle class and its hegemonic ambitions (Misra, 2012). Misra endorses that the Assamese over-zealousness in protecting their own language and identity eventually resulted in alienating the plains tribal communities of which the Bodos are a major constituent (Misra, 2012). The Bodo movement may be portrayed as the longest ethnic movement in the plains of Assam. The first two phases of the Bodo movement were of cultural-solidarity-reformist nature (1947-1967) focusing on consolidation of the Bodo ethnic-identity vis-à-vis the Assamese community (1967-1987). An even earlier phase of the Brahma movement (1907 onwards, crystallising in 1947-1967), Bodo 'Sanskritisation movement', led by the Mech-Bodos, had wide impact. A solid base of cultural awakenings had been laid in colonial era already. As a result of this we observe formation of the Bodo Sahitya Sabha in 1952, which placed the first ethnic demand in the shape of recognition of Bodo language as the medium of instruction at secondary level. Since then Bodo movement passed through many ups and downs. In the early 1960's the Plains Tribal Council of Assam (PTCA), a political formation representing Bodos and other plains tribes of Assam realised that tribal belts and blocks were gradually being acquired by rich peasants and immigrants through illegal means. This perception of marginality led to fostering of extreme ethnicity (1967 onwards) wherein a new section of Bodo elite emerged which demanded a greater share in political power (Singh, 1982; Das, 1989, 2011). By 1980s the Bodo movement matured considerably and witnessed several splits, including launch of the Bodo insurgency. Under the leadership of the All Bodo Students Union which had the support of the militant United Tribal Nationalist Liberation Front (UTNLF), the movement acquired an increasing violent turn. Following the accord of 1993, there was retrospection and thus it was observed that the so-called Bodo–Accord was an exercise in futility. At this stage, the Bodo militancy took on new wings with the formation of organisations like the Bodo Liberation Tigers (BLT) and the National Democratic Front of Bodoland (NDFB). The Bodo Accord creating a Bodoland Autonomous Council (BAC) was a non-starter, as the territorial boundary issue remained unresolved. After much negotiations ultimately, the militants gave up the demand for a separate Bodoland state and reconciled for a greater autonomy under Bodo Territorial Council (BTC) on 10th February, 2003. It was accomplished within the Sixth Schedule. BTC, as an autonomous self-governing body, aimed at fulfilling all economic, educational and linguistic–cultural aspirations of the Bodos; and specially to speed up the infrastructure development in BTC area.

Creation of the Bodo Territorial Council was not favoured by the several 'minority' ethnic communities of the region who viewed the BTC with greater fear and anger. The unrest among the non-Bodos of the region is not a sudden outburst. Right from the 1990s, non-Bodo minority communities have organised themselves under the Non-Bodo Protection Forum (NBPF) which included representatives from the All Bodoland Minority Students Union (ABMSU), the All Assam Koch-Rajbangsi Students Union, Bengali Students Federation, the All Assam Gorkha Students Union, and All Assam Tea Tribes Students Union. Amongst these components, the ABMSU, representing the Muslim settlers was an influential outfit. Another forceful outfit which came to operate was the Adivasi Cobra Force, the Santhal militant wing. Among those who resented the BTC were also such plains Assam tribes such as the Mising, the Rabha and the Tiwa (who have been part of respective autonomous councils). As the ADC concept had already proved to be ineffective, these tribes were attracted by the greater power and authority provided to the BTC. Hence, they now demanded the elevation of the status of their Councils to that of Territorial Council. It is presumed that the Sonowal Kachari and the Deori, with respective autonomous councils (created in 2005), may follow suit. There is no doubt that Assam has been generous in granting statutory Tribal Councils (outside the Sixth Schedule) to numerous tribes such as Tiwas, Rava-Hasongs, Sonowal Kacharis, Mishings, Deoris, Thengal Kacharis and the tribals of Barak valley. Resultantly remaining 'minor-tribes' too are demanding similar status. All of them want to be included in the Sixth Schedule of the Constitution. Having been excluded from basic policy of the BTC, a Bodo hegemonic council, in a multi-ethnic setup, several 'minority' ethnic communities of the region formed the Sanmilita Jana Gosthiya Sangram Samity (SJSS), an amalgam of 18 non-Bodo groups, to oppose and to protest against the biased accord. SJSS argued that the Bodos are rewarded an ethnic council through the Bodo Territorial Council but the Bodo population in the area was around 20 per cent. It alleged that the government has imposed an 'ex-parte settlement' on the 80 per cent non-Bodo population in the BTC area. The 'treaty' considerably led to the volatile ethnic polarisation in the region (Barbora, 2005). Consequently, a further amendment was added to the Sixth Schedule with electoral reservations for respective communities (the Bodo community allotted 30 of the 46 seats in the BTC, five seats given to non-tribal communities and another five open seats). In the context of tribal development an important setback is that the BTAD has not implemented the Forest Rights Act, 2006 that would have reaffirmed the community rights of the Bodos (Saxena et al., 2010).

The cross-border immigration from Bangladesh has been an irritating issue in the region; 'colonisation' of Bodo lands by the invading Muslim groups has historically led to several Bodo-Muslim clashes. According to Bodo leaders, there has been large scale influx of illegal immigrants, mostly Muslims, to the Bodo areas right from colonial era. Threat from illegal encroachers had indeed been realised from early 1940s. Indeed, by the 1940s the Barpeta region (Lower Assam) had become a stronghold of immigrant Muslims (they rose from one per cent in 1911 to nearly 49 per cent in 1941 census). In view of looming threat, the government amended the Assam Land Revenue Regulations, 1886, and created reserved tribal belts with the aim of protecting the tribal people from encroachments of non-tribes, mainly immigrants (Misra, 2012). The moot point is that during the colonial period and afterwards, the Bodo and other Assamese tribal communities were averse to acquiring permanent tenure over land. As the flow on migration increased in the immediate years before and after Independence, tribal land was increasingly acquired by non-tribal immigrants who secured permanent tenure. Therefore, it was a losing battle for the Bodos who were pitted against the migrant farmers who started raising cash crops (Misra, 2012). The Bangladesh war added to the changing demographic scenario, with several lakhs of immigrants, mostly Bengali Muslims, settling in the Brahmaputra Valley. It is apparent that when the Assam Movement against foreign nationals erupted in 1979, the land issue proved to be the central one (Misra, 2012).

The earlier immigration of Muslim peasants settling along the fertile alluvial riverside tracts of Assam, mainly between 1905 and 1933, was primarily aimed at supply of raw jute for the jute mills of Bengal. A combination of factors accelerated this migration. Apart from the high demand for jute from the Bengal jute factories, it was the flow of credit from the Assamese and Marwari traders that accelerated the process of jute cultivation. The migrant Muslim peasants settled down over vast alluvial riverine tracts, as they were conducive for cultivation and processing of jute. The low-lying lands also supported the cultivation of the Boro variety of paddy which could be grown along with jute. As the 20th century progressed and the jute-dependent economy became unprofitable, Muslim peasants slowly diversified their choice of crops (Saikia, 2012). The Muslim peasantry had been conscious to retain their landholding with valid documents from the beginning. Thus they used many fraudulent means to get documents in their names. The absence of formal documents pertaining to land tenure, which became obligatory in the modern democratic nation state, turned the Bodo peasantry into encroachers/illegal settlers in State-controlled forestland. Without modern tenure rights, the Bodo peasantry remained economically insolvent when compared to the Bengali-Muslim 'settlers', who turned into paddy agriculturists, having procured valid documents. It is stated that it was the Dewanias, a class of middlemen, who negotiated between the petty revenue bureaucracy and Muslim peasants to confirm landownership (Saikia, 2012). Need to meet ever increasing demand prompted Muslims to go in for purchasing lands from the Bodo peasants (Saikia, 2012). Thus, ultimately the Bodos found themselves in a crude localised politico-territorial crisis due to the restrictions imposed on them by the regulations of the nation state, over land and forest, which they owned once. The previously nomadic/migrating Bodos got trapped in a comparatively smaller geographical space, where they are indulged in multi-pronged conflicts involving Bodos and Muslims on the one hand and Bodos and non-Bodo tribe/non-tribes on the other. More recently the BTAD area witnessed the Bodo-Muslim clash over land. Bodo-Muslim clash is often portrayed as a

Hindu-Muslim communal clash, which is not realistic. Fact remains that while the greater part is followers of the Brahma sect (Hinduism) about 12 per cent of the Bodos are Christians and a large section pursues the traditional tribal Bathou religion.

(2) *Minority Syndrome and Dissent among the Karbis:* The Karbis, who were declared as a 'primitive' tribe, had led a miserable life, resulting from gradual linguistic and cultural subjugation, on the one hand and on the other through the encroachment of their territories by the emigrants. The Karbis traditionally practice Jhum (slash and burn cultivation) in the hills of Assam. However, with the penetration of the market economy, many of the traditional institutions and way of life have been damaged, bringing about unending sufferings on the people. In 1984, this author had conducted economic survey of 250 Karbi families (Das, 1987:175-183) in selected villages of Lumbajong and Howraghat blocks such as Rongkangthir, Chutianala, Sarthe Ronghang, and Siding Teren and so on. First major observation was that the indigenous Karbis remained obsessed with olden nomadic value system and did not venture into agriculture practice like many plains tribes of Assam. Most Karbi villages, close to the hills areas, were not permanent settlements, although some signs of permanency were emerging. Some villages still had their living founders. One major effort of the administration was then to encourage the people to settle down permanently. Some model villages were created with modern 'huts' which were never accepted by them. On account of non-fixity of tenure rights the Karbi cultivators had least attachment towards land. One reason for economic degradation was the irrational expenditure during *pujas*, mainly towards country-liquor-rice-beer and animal sacrifice. Another economic constraint was the land mortgaging or the tendency to lease in their land for fixed produce to the non-Karbis, through *paikas* system, which had been abolished later. We saw that families with sufficient number of adult workers also resorted to such mortgaging. The reason partly was the hedonistic approach in life and partly the abhorrence to settled wet-agriculture, which required a consistent labour supply. Walter Fernandez has also studied the economic dimension of the troubles and predicaments of the Karbis. The formation of ethnic states such as Meghalaya and Mizoram in succession triggered the demand for the formation of the Karbi Autonomous State Demand Committee (ASDC). The Karbis had formed Karbi National Council, which demanded in 1986 an autonomous district. Later the Karbi Students Association and the ASDC spearheaded the movement for creation of a separate Karbi state. The ASDC-led movement culminated in the Memorandum of Understanding (MoU) signed in Delhi on 1st April, 1995 between the Assam government and the leaders of the ASDC. Consequent upon the signing of the MoU, the nomenclature of the two autonomous district councils was changed to autonomous councils. Ten years after signing the MoU, the same sets of leaders are now disillusioned with the autonomous councils and have demanded creation of separate state comprising the geographical areas of Karbi-Anglong and North Cachar Hills.

(3) ***Indigeneity Factor and Plight of Minority Zeliangrong, Mara and Others:*** The term 'Zeliangrong' is used by Zemi, Liangmei and Rongmei tribes to identify themselves as a single cultural group. They live scattered in Manipur, Nagaland and Assam. The Puimei of Manipur is also part of this alignment. The Zeliangrongs resent that they have been forcibly distributed into contiguous regions of Manipur, Nagaland and Assam for centuries, by colonial arrangement of 'divide and rule' policy. However, their common legend of origin, a mutually intelligible language, common kinship terms, common patrilineal norms and a widespread clan organisation unite all the Zeliangrong people as a single and cohesive ethnic cultural entity, as we discovered in our survey conducted in three states. In Manipur, Tamenglang district may be described as the core socio-cultural area of entire Zeliangrong. In our interview Rani Gaidinliu had informed us that she and her people fought British colonisers to protect the Zeliangrong tribes spread in three states. Her followers had resented the spread of Christianity in the area where her cult followers inhabited. While fighting with the British she went underground but was caught and put in prison. In post-colonial era, she was honoured with the title of the 'freedom fighter' but during her lifetime she did not succeed in getting a common administrative platform for all Zeliangrong tribes, even though some recommendations were available to justify the recognition of scattered tribes under a single nomenclature (Das, 1988, 1994, 2007). The contemporary leaders of the Zeliangrong have continued to fight for such recognition and for sanction of special economic package for them so that they may protect their language and culture. The segments of Zeliangrong have also been alert to injustices becoming visible in their respective territories ('Zeliangrongs Warn of Mass Social Unrest, Civil War', 3 October 2012, northeasttoday.in).

Pillai (2006) has discussed the issues of the *ethnicity, autonomy and governance in context of the Maras, who are also called as* Lakher and exposed the inherent weakness of the provisions of autonomous councils, mainly in Mizoram. What he observed may be summarised and reproduced here to see the internal contradictions. In 1952, the Lushai Hills District of the Assam State became the Autonomous Mizo Hills District under a District Council. In 1953, the Pawi-Lakher tribes were also grouped into Pawi-Lakher Regional Council under the Sixth Schedule of the Constitution. Both these Councils, in theory, were granted a fair degree of autonomy regarding land and forest management, taxes, agricultural practices, village administration and customary law. But in reality, the authority of the Governor, the District Commissioner and his administration overlay this autonomy. Hence, the Pawi-Lakher Regional Council was unable to function effectively due this authority distribution and also on account of the ethnic power struggles. The Mara, a minority tribe, unilaterally opted out of the Regional Council in 1963 and consequently set up a self-styled Interim District Council, which functioned up to 1972, even as political turmoil and insurgency raged in the Mizo Hills. In 1972, the Maras, Lais and Chakmas were given an Autonomous District Council (ADC) each, while the Mizo District Council became a Union Territory (UT). The three ADCs for the Pawis, Lakhers and Chakmas functioned within the UT. In 1987, Mizoram was granted statehood. However, the statehood and the local autonomy could not solve the problem of ethnic conflict. The Maras then demanded UT status. Pillai observes that if such a demand is not efficaciously handled, it could inevitably lead to further demands for statehood, secession or a trans-border merger. Mizoram walks a thin dividing line between peace and separatist movements. Several tribes are giving call for a Greater Mizoram from the 1980s. Ethnicity unites people (Maras) as well as divides (Mara-Lai) or marginalises (Mizo-Mara) sub-ethnicities. Minorities, depending on their size and location, react differently to the major communities. While some smaller groups (Lamkhangs, Monsangs, Fanais) voluntarily get assimilated, some in the periphery tend to opt for secession when they feel threatened by assimilation and neglect (Pillai, 2006).

Declining Insurgencies and Changing Ideologies

Northeastern India has a protracted record of violent autonomy movements, militancy and insurgency. Naga insurgency, unleashed in the 1950s, is the oldest unresolved armed conflict in the world. It is regarded as the mother of all insurgencies of northeast India. Insurgency first erupted in 1956 in Naga Hills and then in 1966 in Mizoram. In the late 1970s, the insurgency spread to rest of the Northeast. It is amazing that just a decade ago as many as 90 militant/ insurgent groups operated in India's northeast. In Assam alone, there are as many as 12 armed ethnic groups, including an ISI-backed Muslim group, which is active against the state (Jafa, 1999). Presently insurgency in Mizoram has been totally eradicated. In Tripura too the insurgents maintain low profile. In Manipur the insurgency is active but it has taken on more of a criminal nature and lacks unity of purpose. Due to a large number of Naga tribes in Manipur, the unrest in Manipur is greatly affected by the uprising in Nagaland. In Nagaland, the ceasefire agreements signed with the two NSCN groups in 1997 and 2000 remain in force. The use of Bangladeshi and Bhutanese territory by insurgents operating in India's Northeast is regarded as a grave security concern (Sahni, 2002). Assam witnessed two major violent insurgencies such as United Liberation Front of Asom (ULFA) and Bodo and several smaller violent movements. The fostering of ULFA is said to be the side-effect of the Assam agitation (led by the All Assam Students' Union) against illegal influx from Bangladesh. Assam agitation, started in 1979, was basically a peaceful movement. A 1985 settlement, known as Assam Accord, brought student activists to power in Assam. The AGP government formed by the student leaders was largely ineffectual and no deportation of the foreign nationals could be seriously initiated. Hence, by 1990 emerged the ULFA to fill the vacuum thus created. ULFA's objective was to 'liberate Assam through armed national liberation struggle from the clutches of the illegal occupation of India' and to 'establish a sovereign independent Assam'. ULFA pledged to oust the illegal migrants from Bangladesh. ULFA argues that Assam has been victim of dual-colonisation, at first by colonial rulers and subsequently by modern Indian state. Reports indicate that at least 200 ULFA activists received training in Pakistan and Afghanistan. Bangladesh authorities arrested its leader Anup Chetia on 21th December, 1997 (Khan, 2007, 'Profile of the Terrorist Insurgency in North East India', asiantribune.com). Assam witnessed the second insurgency unleashed by major insurgent outfits of the Bodos, which ultimately agreed to shun violence and endorsed a peace deal. Among smaller insurgent outfits mention may be made of the Karbi uprising, fighting for Hemprek Kangthim, meaning 'self-rule/self-determination' of the indigenous Karbis. The Karbi led United People's Democratic Solidarity (formed in March 1999 with the merger of two terrorist outfits Karbi National Volunteers (KNV) and Karbi People's Front (KPF) had been active till recently. Sahni (2002) has observed that the culture of violence propagated by the ULFA and the Bodo outfits seems to have set a pattern for a number of copycat insurgent groups. At one point in recent past Assam faced 34 insurgent groups including the ULFA, National Democratic Front of Bodoland (NDFB), Bodo Liberation Tigers (BLT), United People's Democratic Solidarity (UPDS), Dima Halim Daoga (DHD) and Muslim United Liberation Tigers of Assam (MULTA). The NDFB operates in the Bodo-areas of the State and the UPDS dominates the Karbi-Anglong and North Cachar districts. Most of the other groups listed are currently dormant. The Kamatapur Liberation Organisation (KLO) was formed in 1995 by the Koch-Rajbangsi tribes with the objective of carving out a separate Kamatapur State, comprising six north Bengal districts and Goalpara, Dhubri, Bongaigaon and Kokrajhar districts in lower Assam. KLO operates in tandem with the ULFA (Sahni, 2002).

Insurgency in the State of Tripura has its roots in dislocation and dislodgement of the indigenous tribes of the state. Tripura is the only State in India's Northeast that has been transformed, in recent history, from a predominantly indigenous territory to a predominantly non-tribal state. Both in pre-Independence and post-Independence eras, Tripura witnessed regular inflow of emigrants, and land alienation of tribals was rampant. The tribespeople thus became a minority in their own homeland. Tribal leaders of Tripura, right from 1974, voiced demands of reservation, restoration of tribal land and specially the restoration of indigenous Kok-Borok language as one of the official languages, and lastly the Autonomous District Council. The insurgent groups in Tripura had emerged towards the end of the 1970s, as ethnic tensions between the Bengali immigrants and the indigenous tribes, who were outnumbered and reduced to minority status, became alert for safeguarding tribal rights and cultures (Mukherjee and Singh, 1982). Several insurgent outfits came to be formed such as the National Liberation Front of Tripura (in 1989). The All Tripura Tiger Force was formed by the local aboriginal tribes in 1990. The failure of democratic politics to correct the imbalance and rising tribal discontent, led to the emergence of the *Tripura Upajati Juba Samiti* (TUJS) in June 1967. TUJS was primarily a political front that raised four demands such as formation of the autonomous district councils for tribals; extension of inner-line regulations to Tripura; introduction of Kokborok in the Roman script as the medium of instruction for tribal students in the State; and restoration of alienated tribal lands. By 1970, however, the feeling that only armed action could secure relief for the tribals was growing and the TUJS raised a force of armed volunteers, the Tripur Sena (Tripura Army). A brand of virulent ethnic politics flourished and a Bengali organisation, Amra Bangali (We are Bengalis) came into being to counter the TUJS campaign. In May 1990, the All Tripura Tribal Force came into being, allegedly with the support of the Left parties and in the wake of deep political polarisation and allegations of rigging in the State Assembly elections (vide Sahni, 2002). A significant Bengali militant group, the United Bengali Liberation Front (UBLF) came into existence in October 1999. The unyielding polarisation between the tribal population and the non-tribes has been exacerbated, at once, by electoral politics and by extremist atrocities. Tribal terrorists specifically target the non-tribal population, whom they call 'settler refugees'. Terrorist outfits in Tripura also strengthened their existing network with Pakistan's ISI and with other groups in the region. The year 2000 also witnessed a violent conflict between the cadres of NLFT and the Bru National Liberation Front (BNLF), a Reang-dominated outfit based in Mizoram. The differences of opinion inside the NLFT between the Christians and the Hindus led to its further break up on February 18, 2001, with Nayanbasi Jamatiya forming a separate faction of the Jamatiya community. There have been several peace initiatives in place since then and the state is relatively peaceful.

Ironically, after the Mizo Accord, which saw surrender by the major Mizo tribe, several of Mizoram's minority tribes such as Hmar, Chakmas, Brus, Pawis, Lais and the Riangs came to indulge in insurgencies after having failed to secure a comfortable solution of their grievances. The 'Hmar People's Convention-Democracy', an armed insurgency group formed in 1995, claimed to create an independent Hmar Tribal State. It is the offspring of the Hmar People's Convention (HPC), which had entered into agreement with the Government of Mizoram in 1994 resulting in the formation of Sinlung Hills Development Council (SHDC) in North Mizoram. The Bru National Liberation Front was formed in 1997 to protect the rights and dignity of the Riangs. There was an initial settlement in 2006. In the meantime, the organisations such as the Zomi Reunification Organisation (ZORO) and Hmar Peoples Convention

(HPC) continue to pursue acts of potential violence. Certain minority tribes, such as the Pavis and Lakhers, also allege neglect and discrimination, even though their problems with the Mizos is said to have been addressed (Sahni 2002). Manipur has a long tradition of insurgency. The most prominent of the Manipuri insurgent groups are People's Liberation Army (PLA) and United National Liberation Front (UNLF). Insurgent groups in Manipur may be broadly classified into hill-based (Naga, Kuki) and valley based (mostly 'majority' Meiteis). While the former demand autonomy through hill- tribal state to preserve their tribal cultures, the latter have based their demands for independence from historical outlook claiming that Manipur (as an independent state had its geographical area extending to Kabaw valley of modern Myanmar) earlier and was never a part of India. Manipur has experienced militancy and insurgency right from the 1960s. Manipur was merged fully with the Indian Union on 15th October, 1949, but it became a separate State only in 1972, after a long and frequently violent agitation. The circumstances of the merger and the delay in granting statehood caused discontent among the Meiteis. The emergence of an insurgency is formally traced to the constitution of the United National Liberation Front (UNLF) on 24th November, 1964, under the leadership of Samarendra Singh. The insurgents also began to raise their voice against Mayangs (outsiders) settled in Manipur, and the People's Republican Army (PRA) was set up in the early 1990s to target this group. Like in most of northeast, about 90 per cent of the hill-based insurgents and a few of the valley-based insurgents have now conceded to what is called Suspension of Operation (SoO).

Ceasefire, Peace Parleys and Human Rights Activism

There has been a steady erosion of the popular support towards the insurgencies in the region. Rather there is growing public pressure for a peaceful resolution of all agitations. In recent decades the region has witnessed a good number of settlements and 'cease-fire' agreements between militant groups and the government. There was a time when greater numbers of militants were active and so was military operations against the armed insurgents. All such operations did not result in cessation of insurgency. Rather it is the dialogue for peace with militant leaders that has brought some respite to the region. Dialogue with the Mizo National Front (MNF) culminated in the Mizo Peace Accord, which ended the 20-year-long uprising in Mizoram in 1986. The 3rd December, 2003 en masse surrender of the cadres of the Bodo Liberation Tigers (BLT) and subsequent formation of the Bodoland Territorial Council (BTC) solved a decade long insurgency in the areas inhabited by the Bodos in Assam. Not all peace efforts met with the success. Thus, the peace deals such as the Shillong Accord (1975) with the Naga National Council (NNC), the 1988 agreement with the Tripura National Volunteers (TNV), the Bodoland Autonomous Council (BAC) agreement of 1993 with the Bodo hardliners in Assam could not do well since new factions, dissatisfied with the terms of the 'Accords' resumed hostilities under new leaderships. Right now, a peace parleys with Naga leaders is continuing (Das, 2011).

In order to establish peace and facilitating peace parleys between the government and the insurgents, several civil society organisations have played crucial roles in northeast India. At the same time human rights activists of the region have been very forceful and judicious in raising the issues of numerous human rights violations, mainly the highhandedness of the military establishments in some areas of northeast where the human rights violations are reported. The rights groups in northeast India have vehemently resisted the operations under draconian Armed Forces (Special Powers) Act, 1958 and they have urged the government to repeal it. The AFSPA, 1958, was brought in as a short-term measure to allow deployment of the army to counter militant activities in the Naga Hills. Nevertheless, AFSPA has been in place for the last five decades and has been extended to entire Northeast region now. The AFSPA, 1958 (as amended in 1972) confers special powers upon members of the Armed Forces in the disturbed areas in the states of northeast. The Act gives no definition of 'disturbed area'. The declaration of any area as 'disturbed' under Section 3 of the Act is the prerogative of the Governor of the state, or the Administrator of the Union Territory, or the Central Government. According to the Human Rights Watch Report (August 2008), 'The AFSPA Act violates provisions of international human rights law, including the right to life, the right to be protected from arbitrary arrest and detention and the right to be free from torture and cruel, inhuman, or degrading treatment. It also denies the victims of the abuses the right to a remedy.' A fact-finding commission, appointed by the government in 2004, complained that the 'AFSPA has become a symbol of oppression, an object of hate and an instrument of discrimination and highhandedness'. The Naga Hoho, the Naga Mothers' Association (NMA), Naga People's Movement for Human Rights (NPMHR), the Naga Vigil, a Human Rights Group, and the Church have all been active in Naga inhabited areas, including some areas in Burma. The NPMHR has been leading the movement to highlight human-rights abuses by the security forces and is working to bring about peace in political sphere. NMPHR opposes anti-democratic legislations such as the AFSPA which gives the Indian Armed Forces the power to shoot to kill on mere suspicion; to search, enter and arrest without warrant; that a gathering of five people and more can be declared as an unlawful assembly; and that the soldiers under this act are protected against any legal proceedings. The Naga Vigil, a Human Rights Group, was founded in 1989 and its area of concern includes the area commonly referred to as 'Free' or 'Eastern' Nagaland, presently under the political map of Myanmar (Burma). NPMHR believes that the suppression of the rights of the Naga people will only weaken India's own democratic framework (Das, 2011).

The Assam Human rights Commission was constituted on 19th March, 1996. The Human Rights situation in Assam deteriorated rapidly after the Indian Army was deployed in November 1990 to fight against secessionist insurgents. The common villagers were intimidated and terrorised to divulge information about insurgents. Manipur has a good record of human rights activities. Human Rights Alert (HRA), an Imphal-based NGO consisting of human-rights activists, journalists, lawyers, academicians, and community workers, has highlighted human-rights abuses by security forces. HRA coordinates its activities with Amnesty International, London; the International Service for Human Rights, Geneva; and the International Human Rights Internship Program, Washington DC the Civil Liberties and Human Rights Organisation (CLAHRO), founded in 1983, consists mainly of lawyers. It takes up cases involving human-rights violations in the law courts. Peace initiatives have been taken up by various organisations in Tripura, but most of them are linked to political parties. There is hardly any NGO movement in the state. The NGOs that exist operate as welfare and development organisations and have not made any attempt to initiate conflict-resolution activities. More powerful and enduring has been the work of the organisations linked to the Communist Party, mainly the Students Federation and the All-India Democratic Youth Federation. The Tripura Adimjati Sevak Sangh (TASS) and the Borok Human Rights Group (BHRG) launch occasional agitations and organise seminars, workshops and conferences on conflict and resolution (Sahni, 2002.). The Meghalaya People's Human Rights Council (MPHRC) took a major step by alerting the UN Human Rights Council to the persistent and deteriorating human rights situation of the indigenous peoples living in Northeast India who are 'experiencing the worst kind' of human trafficking and 'other racial discrimination' which is part of a decades-old neglect by the Government of India (www-assam.org). Among the active civil society organisations mention may be made of Mothers Associations in Manipur and Nagaland. These Mother's organisations have been active in enforcing the 'prohibition' of alcoholic drinks.

The most significant contributions of the Civil Society Groups in Northeast have been in eroding armed militancy and helping in conflict-resolution process. There is also a long tradition of involvement of the Church leaders in peace process. The churches in Nagaland have played crucial role in this respect. The churches had played significant roles in the finalisation of the Mizo Accord. In Nagaland, the Naga Hoho, the Church, the Naga Mothers' Association (NMA) have been instrumental in establishing ceasefire between the NSCN-IM and the Indian government since 1997. Among several church organisations, it is the Baptist Church in Nagaland, which has been involved in the peace process since the beginning of the conflict. Baptist Church was successful when it organised the Atlanta peace meeting at the end of which the NSCN leadership accepted initiatives to start a dialogue with the government of India. In the resolution of the Bodo insurgency, organisations like the Bodo Sahitya Sabha (BSS) and the All Bodo Students Union (ABSU) have made crucial contributions. In Manipur, the Meira Paibis (Women Torch bearers) have made significant attempts for the establishment of peace. In Meghalaya, the role of the Church in bringing the ANVC 'over-ground' has been significant. In Assam, the Assam Sahitya Sabha had made several attempts at establishing peace. In Tripura, effective counter-insurgency measures have brought down the level of insurgent activities. In Meghalaya, peace talk was offered to Hynniewtrep National Liberation Council (HNLC) in October 2008 but was rejected by the militant outfit. Arunachal Pradesh was brought under the unified command structure in December 2008 to deal with the low-profile insurgency problem of the state. Arunachal has no local militant outfit but is used by other militant outfits of the northeastern region as a transit route to Myanmar (Peace process overview, 2011, cdpsindia.org). The Naga Hoho, representing several smaller units of the Hoho belonging to several Naga tribes, has also been very active to find an acceptable solution to protracted Naga issue. Describing the Naga situation Das (2011) observed:

> … the traditional political institutions of the Naga tribes have been highly democratic and germs of the civil society concept can be seen in the customary practices and relations of the ethnic institutions. The civil society organisations, in modern times, could succeed because the basic social norms and jural structures of the people had the inherent capacity to embrace them. Therefore mobilising public opinion in Nagaland and Manipur for right causes was easier. Informal traditional 'chiefs'/headmen/elders and the government recognised 'gaon-buras' could thus be mobilised to play crucial role. In essence it was the need for peace which led to establishing the Naga Mothers Association, and rejuvenating the Naga Students' Federation, Naga people's Movement for Human Rights and the Naga Hoho. Several human rights bodies too have initiated peace efforts. Undeniably these civil society organisations, in association with Church leaders, have played significant role in laying the foundation for peace. They have been successful in reaching out to communities, both Naga and other ethnic tribes, and promoting dialogue and understanding between contesting communities, which the political outfits engaged in talks could not do. The Naga Hoho, incorporating all minor Naga tribal councils, thus successfully launched a 'reconciliation campaign'. The Naga Hoho, which believes that the settlement of the Naga problem is not possible without the unity of all Naga tribes, has initiated the reconciliation campaign to help end the clashes between the different extremist groups operating in vast areas and to bring together all underground factions, for the larger cause of rebuilding the Naga

society and ending the years of bloodbath, through a peaceful negotiation with authorities (Das, 2011).

There are several obstacles to peace in the region. It is widely alleged that negotiations for peace is futile as long as the governance issue is not attended. Levels of corruption in governments in the States of the Northeast are higher and the quality of governance is abysmal.

Conclusion

The people of vast valley and hills areas in Northeast remained in turmoil, right from the colonial era, mainly on account of unscrupulous policies and ill-defined administrative strategies, as we discussed. The 'poor governance', 'lack of economic development', 'mushrooming of outsiders and dislodgement of indigenous people', 'failure of democratic institutions as also rampant corruption' and the 'majority hegemony' had gradually fostered a sense of alienation and social exclusion, particularly among the vast minority communities. These factors had aggravated disadvantages and sufferings, as we discussed with empirical evidences, drawn from hills and plains. We observed that identity politics of the region is basically an outcome of conditions of exclusion, marginalisation, displacement and dislodgement of different groups in Northeast India. These exclusions often conceptualised in binary terms such as majority-minority, locals-outsiders, hills-plains, are linked to the local people's anxiety for regional development and the preservation of their language and culture.

Special provisions for self-governance and autonomy are provided for people of the Northeast within the Constitution of India, particularly through such acts as the Sixth Schedule, North Eastern Council (NEC), and Department of North Eastern Region (DONER). Centrally controlled DONER and the NEC need to be more pragmatic in their approach and effectively tackle the problems of unemployment, underemployment, and economic backwardness of the region more effectively. Northeast India is a vital and strategically vulnerable border region, consisting of linguistically and religiously diverse populations, who have been historically cordoned off by 'the Inner line'. In the decades following independence, over 100 groups emerged to fight with various objects of regional or tribal autonomy. Analysis of the roots of the ethnic conflict in Northeast India may be highlighted briefly in the following points:

(a) Indian independence, partition, an influx of émigrés into the region and a fear of linguistic-cultural subjugation has led to a so-called 'sense of narcissistic self-awareness among Northeast minorities. Also implicated as contributory factors are economic negligence and the failures of various political institutions.

(b) Many ethnic movements of the region have worked within the constitutional framework, while others have opted for an extra-constitutional or secessionist path.

(c) New evidences suggests that most militant groups, gradually and through outside support, turned into the terrorist entities and thus no longer work towards their original objectives or follow their proclaimed ideologies. For example, Assam's United Liberation Front of Asom (ULFA) has gone back on its original anti-Bangladeshi position.

(d) Security forces continue to operate in the area, at both state and paramilitary levels. Even though there have been human rights violations, but alert civil society organisations and women activists are raising the pertinent questions to establish justice. There have been several successful peace initiatives, and many insurgents now follow 'ceasefire'.

(e) Given the poor governance experienced by the region, it should be unsurprising that locals feel alienation and social exclusion from an Indian mainstream which has neglected them.

Despite best initiatives, poor governance and rampant corruption remain in place. Hence the entire region is seen clamoring for self-rule, bureaucratic transparency and greater autonomy. There is thus urgent need to resolve the persisting troubles and predicaments of the indigenous people by involving them meaningfully on a priority basis. A few propositions which this author had presented earlier seem pertinent even today (Das, 2009, vide www.gsdrc.org). They are as follows: The Department of the North-Eastern Region (DONER) and the North-Eastern Council should work to combat unemployment, underemployment and the overall economic backwardness of the region. The representatives of the people should ensure that implementation takes place in all earnest. Numerous financial packages and grants have been directed to Northeast, including those from international agencies such as the World Bank and the Asian Development Bank. Such provisions in future should be regulated and designed so as to assuage ethnic misgivings. The right procedures adopted will ensure institutional adjustments to win over hostile ethnic groups and extending special safeguards to the region. Government at the national and regional levels should see that they continue. The indigenous/native people's concerns for variously perceived threats to their distinct ethnic identities and their anxiety for preservation of culture and language and their desire for development cannot be seen as dysfunctional in democratic society. Their aspirations need to be valued as basics for distributive justice, to which no post-colonial nation state can neglect.

References

Banthia 2001. *Census of India*, Registrar General and Census Commissioner. 2001: xlvi: Provisional Population Totals, Paper 1 of 2001. Delhi: Controller of Publications.

Barbora, Sanjay, 2005. *Quiet History, Unquiet Peoples: The "Tribal Question" in Assam*. Guwahati: Anwesha Publications.

Baruah, Sanjib, 2005. *Durable Disorder: Understanding the Politics of Northeast India*. New Delhi, Oxford University Press.

Bertil, Linter, 2002. 'Bangladesh: A Cocoon of Terror', *Far Eastern Economic Review*, Hong Kong, April 4.

Bhagabati, A.C., 1988. 'Tribal transformation in Assam and North East India: An appraisal of emerging ideological dimensions', *Presidential Address*, Section of Anthropology and Archaeology, Seventy-fifth Indian Science Congress, Pune.

Bhattacharyya, Gayatri, 1988. *Refugee Rehabilitation and its Impact on Tripura's Economy.* Guwahati: Omsons Publications.

Bhattacharyya, Harihar, Partha Sarkar, Angshuman Kar (eds.), 2009. *The Politics of Social Exclusion in India: Democracy at the Crossroads*. London: Routledge.

Bhattacharya, Hiranya Kumar, 2001.*The Silent Invasion: Assam versus Infiltration.* Guwahati/Delhi: Spectrum Publications.

Bhaumik, Subir, 2003. 'Tripura's Gumti Dam Must Go', *The Ecologist Asia* 11 (No. 1, January-March), pp. 84-89.

Chattopadhyay, Dilip Kumar, 1990. *History of the Assamese Movement since 1947*. Calcutta: Minerva.

Das, A.K., 1982. *Assam' Agony: A Socio-economic and Political Analysis*. New Delhi: Lancers Publishers.

Das, B.M., 1960. *Ethnic Affinities of the Rabhas*. Guwahati: Guwahati University.

Das, B.M. (ed.), 1970. *Anthropometry of the Tribal Groups of Assam, India,* Field Research Projects. Miami, Florida.

Das N.K., 1982. 'Naga movement', in K.S. Singh (ed.) *Tribal Movements in India,* Volume I. Delhi: Manohar Publication.

Das, N.K., 1987 (1989). *Ethnic Identity, Ethnicity and Social Stratification in Northeast India.* New Delhi: Inter-India Publications.

Das, N.K., 1993. *Kinship, Politics and Law in Naga Society*, Memoir No. 96, Kolkata: Anthropological Survey of India.

Das, N.K., 1994. 'Ethno-Historical Processes and Ethnicity in Northeast India', *Journal of Indian Anthropological Society,* 29(1-2), pp. 3-35.

Das, N.K., 1996. 'Rani Gaidinliu', *Journal of the Anthropological Survey of India*, 45, pp. 111-118.

Das, N.K., 2005. 'Self-governance, tribal institutions and state; case studies from Northeast India'. *IASSI Quarterly*, Vol. 24. No.1, pp. 35-60.

Das, N.K., 2007. 'Ethnicity, Nationalism and Regionalism in North –East India', in R.K. Bhadra and Mita Bhadra (eds.) *Ethnicity, Movement and Social Structure: Contested Cultural identity*. Jaipur: Rawat Publication: 133-169.

Das, N.K., 2009a. 'Identity Politics and Social Exclusion in India's North-East: The Case for Redistributive Justice', *Bangladesh e-Journal of Sociology*, Vol. 6, No. 1.

Das, N. K., 2009b. 'Identity Politics and Social Exclusion in India's North-East: The Case for Redistributive Justice', Harihar Bhattacharyya, Partha Sarkar, and Angshuman Kar (eds.), 2009. *The Politics of Social Exclusion in India: Democracy at the Crossroads*. London: Routledge.

Das, N.K., 2011. 'Social Exclusion, Misgovernance and Autonomy Movements in Northeast India', *Humankind*, Vol. 7.

Das, N.K., 2012. 'Social exclusion in northeast India: self-governance issue, development politics and autonomy movements', *International Journal of Social and Economic Research, 2011*, Vol. 1, Issue-1 (Online published on 3st1 January 2012).

Das, N.K., 2011. 'Naga Peace Parleys: Sociological Reflections and a Plea for Pragmatism', *Economic and Political Weekly*, Vol. xivi, No. 25.

Das, Nava Kishor, 2009. 'Identity Politics and Social Exclusion in India's Northeast: A Critique of Nation-building', *Berichte und Kommentare 1 Anthropos*, 104.

Das, N.K. and C.L. Imchen, 1994. 'Nagaland', in K.S. Singh (ed.) *People of India*. Calcutta: ASI /Seagull Books.

Das, N.K. and P. Gupta, 1982. 'The Ahom Movement', in K.S. Singh (ed.) *Tribal Movements in India*, Vol.1, Delhi: Manohar.

Das Gupta, Jyotirindra, 1988. 'Ethnicity, Democracy, and Development in India: Assam in a General Perspective', in Atul Kohli (ed.) *India's Democracy: An Analysis of Changing State-Society Relations.* Princeton: Princeton University Press.

Deb Barma, Sukhendu, 2009. 'Refugee Rehabilitation and Land Alienation in Tripura' in Walter Fernandes and Sanjay Barbora (eds.) *Land, People and Politics Contest over Tribal Land in Northeast India.* Guwahati: North Eastern Social Research Centre and IWGIA, pp. 88-112.

Dev, Bimal J. and Dilip K. Lahiri, 1985. *Assam Muslims: Politics and Cohesion*. Delhi: Mittal Publications.

Fernandes, Walter, 2007. 'Hawks Descend on Assam', *Himal South Asian,* February 1.

Fernandes, Walter, 2005. 'Reservations and Social Change: The Case of the Northeast', in Stephanie Tawa Lama-Rewal (ed.) *Electoral Reservations, Political Representation and Social Change in India A Comparative Perspective.* Delhi: Manohar Book Centre and Centre de Sciences Humaines, pp. 83-104.

Fernandes, Walter and Sanjay Barbora (eds.). 2002: *Land, People and Politics Contest over Tribal Land in Northeast India.* Guwahati: North Eastern Social Research Centre and IWGIA.

Goswami, P.C., 1984. 'Foreign Immigration into Assam', in B. L. Abbi (ed.) *NE Problems and Prospects of Development.* Chandigarh: Center for Research in Rural and Industrial Development.

Ganguly, J.B., 1984. Marketing in North-East India: problems of rural markets. Guwahati: Omsons.

Gosselink, Robert G., 1994. 'Minority Rights and Ethnic Conflict in Assam, India', *Boston College Third World Law Journal*, Vol. 14, Issue-1.

Gohain, Hiren, 2007. 'A Question of Identity: Adivasi militancy', *Economic and Political Weekly, 8rd* December, 2007.

Haokip, Rebecca C., 2008. 'Kuki-Paite Conflict in the Churchandpur District of Manipur', in Lazar Jeyaseelan (ed.). *Conflict Mapping and Peace Processes in Northeast India.* Guwahati: North Eastern Social Research Centre, pp. 185-208.

Hazarika, Sanjoy, 2000: *Rites of Passage: Border Crossings, Imagine Homelands, India's East and Bangladesh*. New Delhi: Penguin Books.

Hutton, J.H., 1921. *The Angami Nagas, With Some Notes on Neighbouring Tribes*. London: Macmillan.

Hutton, J.H., 1929. *The Sema Nagas*. London: Oxford University Press

Jafa, V.S., 1999. 'Counter-Insurgency: The use and abuse of military force', *Faultlines,* November 1999.

Mackenzie, Alexander, 1884. *History of the Relations of the Government with the Hill Tribes of the North-East Frontier of Bengal*. Calcutta: Government of India Press.

Maitra, Ramtanu and Susan Maitra, 1995. 'Northeast India: Target of British apartheid', www.larouchepub.com. October 13, 1995.

Misra, Udayon, 1988. *Northeast India: Quest for Identity*. Guwahati: Omsons Publications.

Misra, Udayon, 2012. 'Bodoland: The Burden of History', *Economic and Political Weekly*, Vol. XLVII No. 37.

Mills, J.P., *The Lhota Nagas*. London: Macmillan and Co.

Mills, J.P., 1926. *The Ao Nagas*. London: Macmillan and Co.

Miri, Mrinal (ed.), 1993. *Tribal India: Continuity and Change*. Shimla: Indian Institute of Advanced Study.

Mukherjee, Bhabanand and K.S. Singh, 1982. 'Tribal Movements in Tripura', in K.S. Singh (ed.) *Tribal Movements in India,* (Volume I). New Delhi: Manohar Publications.

Nath, Bhupen Kumar and Dilip C. Nath, 2012. 'The Change of Religion and Language Composition in the State of Assam in Northeast India: A Statistical Analysis Since 1951 to 2001', *International Journal of Scientific and Research Publications*, Vol. 2, Issue-5, May 2012.

Pillai, Sushil K., 2006., 'Ethnicity, Autonomy and Governance - The Maras: A Case Study', *South Asia Terrorism Portal* (SATP.org) 25th July, 2006.

Sahni, Ajai, 2002. 'Survey of Conflicts and Resolution in India's Northeast, Faultlines: Writings on Conflict and Resolution', Vol. 12, May, 2002; *satp.org/satporgtp*.

Saikia, Arupjyoti, 2012. 'The Historical Geography of the Assam Violence', *Economic and Political Weekly*, Vol. xivii, No. 41.

Saxena, N.C. *et. al.,* 2010. *Manthan: Report, National Committee on Forest Rights Act 2010,* MOEF.

Shimray, U. A., 2006. *Tribal Land Alienation in North East India: Laws and Land Relations.* Guwahati: North Eastern Social Research Centre and Indigenous Women's Forum of Northeast India.

Singh, B.P., 1987. The Problem of Change: A Study of North-East India. New Delhi: Oxford University Press.

Singh K.S., (ed.), 1982. *Tribal Movements in India* (Vol. 1). Delhi: Manohar.

Singh, K.S., 1992. 'People of India: An Introduction' in K.S. Singh (ed.) *People of India National Series*. Kolkata: Anthropological Survey of India. (2002) Revised Edition. New Delhi: Oxford University Press and ASI.

Singh, K.S., 1994. 'Scheduled Tribes'. *People of India, National Series*. New Delhi: Oxford University Press and ASI.

Singh, K.S., 1996. *People of India: Identity, Ecology, Social Organisation, Economy, Linkages and Development Process: A Quantitative Profile*. New Delhi: Oxford University Press and ASI.

Sinha, S.K., 1998. *Report on Illegal Migration into Assam*. Submitted to the President of India.

Verghese, B.G., 2010. 'Towards a Naga settlement Need to embrace emerging opportunities', *The tribune online edition / The tribune online edition*, Thursday, 11th March, 2010, Chandigarh.

Website Sources

asiantribune.com (Isha Khan, 2007, Profile of the Terrorist Insurgency in North East India).

northeast-today.in, Bangladeshis in Meghalaya Makes Garo Community a Minority, June 01, 2012.

northeasttoday.in Hmars (Zeliangrongs Warn of Mass Social Unrest, Civil War, 3 October, 2012).

www. nnwpsg , Frontier Nagaland demand, October 31st, 2011).

www-northeastindiadiary-bogspot.com, Sriram Ananthanarayanan, (2008).

www-assam.org. The human rights and civil society.

www. indiatimes.com.

www. Wikipedia.com.

www. gsdrc.org.

www. cdpsindia.org/ne_peace.asp.

www. nnwpsg.

www.satp.org/satporgtp/publication/faultlines/volume10/Article2.htm).

twitter.com,www.sunday-guardian.com/.../assams-tragedy-has-roots-in-history-2 -Jethmalani, Ram, 2012.

The Statesman, 18th July, 2002.

13

Political Aspiration and Autonomous Council Movement: A Study of the Rabha of Assam Valley

Surajit Kumar Pal

Movements by different ethnic groups for gaining political space and for maintaining separate identities as well as for resource management for survival are a common phenomenon in contemporary India. Such movements result from governance failure and pursuance of Western model of development where the common are denied of their legitimate share of resources, which in turn threatens their existence as a cultural group. The forces of modernisation and globalisation or Westernisation often adversely impact the social, economic and political institutions of different vulnerable communities, particularly the tribal communities living in different parts of the country, including those living in the region called North-East India.

The North East India, strategically an important part of India, comprising Assam, Arunachal Pradesh, Manipur, Meghalaya, Mizoram, Nagaland and Tripura is popularly perceived as seven sisters. In recent time, Sikkim has got the status of an integral part of the Northeast for its cultural diversity and backwardness.[1] The region encompasses rich ethnic, cultural and linguistic diversities which are unique in nature that cannot be comparable with other parts of India, inhabited by a large number of ethnic groups of tribal and caste background who articulate a sense of identity in ethnic, cultural and linguistic terms; competing over to have their own homeland, territory and sharing of resources for survival. The competitive attitude of each and every community for maintaining own entity in a geo-political boundary leads them to adopt conflict and violence against each other and also against the state. The coercive and repressive attitude of the state often brews intolerance among different communities that make them to remain isolated from mainstream (the term bears a significant meaning nowadays in the arena of strengthening the foundation of a nation) culture and polity. Against this backdrop, a tribal group of Lower Assam, named Rabha, gets a special attention in this junction who aspire for an autonomous council through which their ethnic entity is being safeguarded to great extent.

The Rabha, a prominent plains tribe having agricultural economy, are predominantly found in Goalpara, Dhubri, Kokrajhar, Kamrup and Darrang districts of Lower Assam. Until recently, they were a full-fledged matrilineal tribe, but now have accepted patrilineality.[2] They are divided into a number of sub-categories, namely, *Rongdani*, *Maitori*, *Pati*, *Kocha*, *Dahuri*, *Totla* and others of which first four sub-groups are mainly concentrated in the districts mentioned above, having arbitrary territorial boundaries of each group maintaining some kind of linguistic difference though such kind of difference is minimal in the arena of inter-group interactions. However, the social intercourse, especially in the sphere of marriage alliances among the *Rongdani*, *Maitori* and *Pati,* are quite common as they are found to live in the south bank of the Brahmaputra river. This means, they are primarily distributed in a contiguous geographical locations stretching from Kamrup and Goalpara districts of Assam that goes up to the bordering areas of East and West Garo Hills of Meghalaya. These three sub-groups are in majority in the entire Rabha population of the concerned state. The *Kocha* sub-group is primarily concentrated in the north bank of the Brahmaputra, spreading from the Parbatjowar tract of present-day Kokrajhar district to the parts of Eastern Duars, up to Bhutan border and also a few villages of Dhubri district. While the *Totla* and *Dahuri* are predominantly found in the erstwhile district of Darang which has again been split into Darang, Sonitpur and Mangaldoi districts and also sporadically distributed in Goalpara district.

Earlier, every sub-group was largely endogamous, but in post-independence era such sub-group-endogamy is not rigidly followed due to the forces of modernisation, globalisation, spread of communication network and education. The degree of interactions among all the sub-groups in different spheres has increased manifold over the years, which has led them to come closer in projecting as one of the strong and dignified plains tribes of Assam. This closeness provides ample scope in strengthening the unity of all sections that helps them to fight for establishing a separate territorial council of their own, similar to the ones achieved by the Bodo-Kachari and other tribal groups of Assam in recent times. Although the pace of unity move received momentum in post-independence phase, its beginning was in the early 20th century.[3] During that time the geographical area of the Brahmaputra Valley, also called the Assam Valley, was covered with dense forests and wild denizens that enriched the biodiversity of the area. And this ecological condition as well as the nomadic nature of livelihoods of the people was one of the prominent barriers of their unity. Hence, a brief historiography of the then Rabha society needs to be examined which bears relevance in the context of their emerging aspiration for a separate political entity for safeguarding their survival interests.

Beginning of 20th Century and the Rabha Society

In their movement for autonomous council, the Rabhas have passed through many phases. Prior to first decade of 20th century they had no centralised political structure. In the past, every section used to roam from place to place in group under a chief, who was supreme in authority of such group and used to do slash-burn type of agriculture. It is not known how they got transformed into a full-fledged settled agrarian community. It is very difficult to reconstruct the history of their transformation to a settled agrarian community as no recorded history is available.

Prior to 1916, the Rabhas had no formal apex body to govern their society. They were regulated mainly by the village councils. The village councils were headed by the village headmen popularly called *Tangams* or *Mandals* (or the *Gaonbudas*). They used to be assisted by their deputy, *Siana* or *Mukhial*, and the village elders who were the supreme authorities of villages. Before 19th century, there was no unity among the Rabha sub-groups living in different parts of Assam valley. Even in 19th century, the area was quite isolated and difficult to access. This situation compelled them to remain secluded from outside world. That continued till the first decade of 20th century (Sarkar, 1976). They came in contact with the world outside when there were some improvement in the infrastructural facilities like road communication and opening of some primary schools in certain pockets of their territory (Sarkar, 1976).

The youths who were empowered to some extent felt the need of unity of all sub-groups for having a platform for collective action their development. However, their efforts were often thwarted by the elders who were so powerful in traditional village councils. This perturbed the youth, who wanted to reform the old system of village governance, in the initial phase and blocked hindered the emergence of a strong, powerful and progressive community. There is no denying that the old arrangement of village governance failed to bring any fruitful unity and constricted interaction among the members of different Rabha sub-groups.

Traditional village councils never thought of the unity of the Rabhas as a community. The councils were rather responsible for brewing disunity in society. Over time, the influence of the village headmen and village elders waned and this left even the local communities in disarray. At this juncture, a young leadership emerged which wanted to bring about a new form of social control by replacing the age-old social norms and customs. The new leadership realised the importance of modern education, which they thought, would accelerate the pace of change in society. They also felt, once the Rabhas are empowered with modern education they would understand the significance of unity and would be conscious about the modes of exploitation and deprivation they are subjected to by the non-tribal neighbours. Some student leaders with progressive outlook came forward to establish one platform for greater Rabha unity and safeguarding the interests of the Rabhas. But their initial efforts did not achieve much success due to various reasons (Sarkar, 1976).

The early decades of 20th century are very significant in terms of the emergence of various socio-religious movements.[4] These have had positive role in reforming the Rabha society. During these reform movements, they had given up various age-old socio-cultural norms and customs which were considered major impediment to their socio-economic uplift. The reform movements spearheaded by the youths played a positive role in social awakening and in cleansing various evil practices from their society. The young leadership to a great extent succeeded in bringing about certain degree of unity at community level.

In 1916, when the first Rabha students' convention was organised at Rangjuli in Dudhnoi Police Station of Goalpara district, an initiative was taken to thoroughly review the state of affairs of the Rabha society. In this convention, some important resolutions were adopted with reference to literacy and education, unity among all sections of Rabhas and social reform, all of which were preconditions for empowerment of Rabhas. This was the turning point in the history of Rabha society (Sarkar, 1986). This convention provided a platform to the students and youths of different sections in addressing various issues that had crippled the progress of their society. From the very beginning the young leaders were emphasising on unity of their community.

Birth of Rabha Organisations and Process of Unification

After 1916, when the new leadership took control of Rabha ethnic movement a kind of social awakening started to emerge in Rabha society. As a part of this process the students and youths of different sections collectively organised three conferences at Madang (1919), Krishnai (1920) and Rangjuli (1925). The first two of the conferences were organised by the students' body and the other one was by the *Darhay Rabha Jatiya Dal* (DRJD). These three conferences enlightened the Rabhas on issues relating to their social, economic and political life. The Rangjuli conference of the DRJD dealt primarily with the redressal of various social offences committed against the Rabhas. But this body never took up the question of economic upliftment of the community. However, this conference bears special significance as it took a bold resolution to organise a mass convention of the Rabhas living in different districts of Assam, in a grand scale. In this context, the role of Gobardhan Sarkar (Rabha) deserves special mention.[5] Gobardhan Sarkar was instrumental in motivating the leadership of the DRJD to organise a conference of all Rabhas. Following his call, the student body came forward to extend its support in organising the proposed conference jointly with DRJD. In 1926, a joint conference of these two organisations was held at Rangjuli. In this conference the birth of the *Assam Rabha Sanmilan* (ARS) and the *Assam Rabha Chhatra Sanmilan* (ARCS) formally took place (Sarkar 1976). This was a turning point in the evolution of the Rabha ethnic movement.

Unfortunately, these two organisations were not free of crises. Such crises were largely responsible for premature death of the Assam Rabha Chhatra Sanmilan (ARCS). The Assam Rabha Sanmilan was active for some more years to make way to a new ethnic outfit called the Rabha National Council (RNC) or the Rabha Jatiya Parishad (RJP), which formally came into existence in Dhupdhara conference held in 1970 under the banner of the All Assam Rabha Sangha (AARS). The organisations like the ARS and the ARCS were also instrumental in forming the RNC. This RNC played significant part in uniting the Rabhas on social, economic, educational, cultural and political issues.

Chart 1. Evolution of Rabha National Council (RNC)

Assam Rabha Chhatra Sanmilan (1926) and

↓

Assam Rabha Chhatra Sanmilan (1926) and

↓

Assam Rabha Jubak Sangha or ARYS (1941)

↓

Assam Rabha Jatiya Seba Sangha or ARJSS (1948)

↓

All Assam Rabha Jatiya Sanmilan or AARJS (1956)

↓

All Assam Rabha Sangha or AARS (1963)

↓

All Rabha National Council (ARNC) or Nikhil Rabha Jatiya Parishad (NRJP)(1970)

The goal of the RNC was nourished by various other socio-political organisations, which contributed a lot in generating social, cultural, economic and political awareness among the Rabhas. The RNC passed through different stages with different names. They are: Assam Rabha Chhatra Sanmilan or ARCS (1926), Assam Rabha Sanmilan or ARS (1926), Assam Rabha Yubak Sangha or ARYS (1941), Assam Rabha Jatiya Seba Sangha or ARJSS (1948), All Assam Rabha Jatiya Sanmilan or AARJS (1956), All Assam Rabha Sangha or

AARS (1963), All Rabha National Council (ARNC) or Nikhil Rabha Jatiya Parishad (NRJP–1970). All these were the frontal organisations which ultimately came together to form RNC, the apex body of the whole Rabha society. After 1970, there were efforts to spread the activities of the RNC in the neighbouring states of Meghalaya and West Bengal. Records reveal that between 1926 and 2012 a total of 34 conferences have been organised under the banner of aforementioned organisations in different parts of Assam and its neighbouring states. The organisational evolution of the RNC is shown in Chart-1.

RNC and its Organisational Set Up and Roles

In pre-independence era, the RNC was not well organised and its operational capabilities were constrained by unqualified and weak leadership.[6] During those days, its primary concern was social reform which it tried to achieve by amending the customary laws. It gave a call to all Rabhas to give up the evil social practices which had crippled the forward movement of their society. The student leaders of those days extended their support to its leadership in this task and their contributions can never be belittled. Unlike today organising conferences was a difficult task at that time. Quite often, finance and other factors stood in the way of its activities. Moreover, it had no permanent office to coordinate its activities.

In post-independence phase, especially after 1960s, its leadership was taken over by a group of qualified and educated persons who shouldered the responsibility of strengthening RNC's organisational set up by opening of various branches from grass-roots to the apex level in different places of Assam, Meghalaya and West Bengal, with its central headquarter at Guwahati.[7] The RNC now has a three-tier body consisted of (1) Area Committee (2) State Committee and (3) Central Committee. Area committee functions at district level. A district is divided into a number of areas, each has an *anchalik* committee. In Goalpara district, for example, there are five to six area committees. They are Mechpara Purbanchal Rabha Samaj (MPRS), Mechpara Madhyanchal Rabha Samaj (MMRS), Pub Ajagar Rabha Samaj (PARS), Dudhnoi Purbanchal Rabha Sanmilan (DPRS), and Dudhnoi Paschimanchal Rabha Sanmilan (DARS) and so on. Prior to their inclusion under the jurisdiction of RNC, all these *anchalik* (area) committees were functioning independently in respective areas. The *anchalik* bodies came into being after independence in order to reform the Rabha society at the area level. Each Anchalik Rabha Samaj operates with four-tier set-up, namely, (i) *song* (village), (ii) *mandal*, (iii) *jamat* and (iv) *sanmilan*. All these tiers are democratically constituted.

The *song* (village) level *samaj* is headed by the village headman, *mandal;* three to four villages are headed by a head *mandal.* The other two tiers, which are larger in size, and are run by democratically elected members, are constituted of the president, secretary, treasurer and executive members, who enjoy powers as vested on them by the *samaj*. The *anchalik samajes* or *sanmilans* are the constituent parts of the RNC and are governed by its constitution. Each *anchalik* committee is constituted of 15 members out of whom the president, vice-president, secretary, treasurer are elected. The next tier is the state committee and it is composed of 21 members among whom there are the president, vice–president, secretary, assistant secretary, treasurer, organising secretary and 15 executive members. The similar pattern is followed in the composition of the central committee. The central committee, the supreme authority of the Rabhas, is empowered to deal with social, cultural, economic and political affairs of the society.

Over the years, the RNC took up the issues like economic betterment, social reform, educational development, and so on. The Rabha, an agrarian community, now suffers from a crisis called land alienation. A majority of them are sharecroppers. The share of crop, thus procured, sustains them for only a few months a year. For the remaining months they work as wage labour and do other odd jobs which are available sparingly. In the past they used to collect edible roots and tubers from the forests and also hunt wild games, abundantly available in their immediate environment that were very useful for their sustenance in lean season. But now they are deprived of all these alternative sources of livelihood because of massive deforestation.

It appears, from the proceedings and other publications of RNC, that land question always occupied the central place in the discussion of all the conferences and many resolutions have been passed. In 1948 conference of the ARJSS, the land problem was thoroughly discussed and the Assam Government was urged upon to distribute *khas* land among the landless Rabhas. Since then they have been demanding land for the landless in every Rabha forum. In 1956, the All Assam Rabha Jatiya Sanmilan (AARJS) adopted two important resolutions for the benefit of landless and other poor cultivators living in then Mechpara Zamindari estate area. They proclaimed: (1) transparency should be maintained strictly during the allotment of *khas* land to the landless cultivators against their applications and no manipulation be allowed by the estate employees; (2) exemption of 50 per cent revenue to the cultivators whose crops were damaged by natural calamities like drought and flood. After the enactment of Zamindari Abolition Act 1956, *khas* land available in the areas of Mechpara and Bijni Zamindari Estates was distributed to many landless cultivators of Rabha, Garo and Bodo-Kachari communities. But that was inadequate considering the number of poor and landless cultivators. 'Land' is still a vexed question in all the social movements of the Rabhas.

Way to Creation of Tribal Belts and Blocks

Continuing land alienation and deforestation have seriously affected the quality of life of the Rabhas in general. This forced the RNC leadership in raising a demand for creation of tribal belts and blocks, which, they thought, would help protect their community identity as well as livelihood opportunities and save them from the exploitation by the non-tribal neighbours. Before articulating the demand for autonomy the leadership assessed the ground realities in different Rabha inhabited areas. It would be relevant here to take stock of the reasons and concerns that led the Rabhas to raise the demand for autonomy.

(a) Migration from Outside: The erstwhile Zamindari estates, namely, Mechpara and Bijni of old Goalpara district, bordering Bangladesh, had been predominantly inhabited by the tribal communities. The Rabhas were numerically dominant among these tribes. There was continuous immigration of 'economic refugees' from Bangladesh, locally known as the Bhatia Muslims.[8] It was a land hungry population settled in the vicinity of their territorial boundary and in *char* lands of the Brahmaputra.[9] These settlers had seriously threatened to dislodge the tribals from their habitat and take over their economic, social and political space. Due to its geographical location and porous borders continuous inflow of the Bangladeshi Muslims to Indian Territory has led to considerable demographic imbalance in the tribal areas inhabited by the Rabha, Bodo-Kachari, and others, in Lower Assam.[10]

Also, during the *zamindari* regime a large number of Hindus belonging to different castes had also settled within the *zamindari* areas. They have taken a large share of the livelihood opportunities on which the tribals had monopoly earlier. These settlers have also caused severe damages to the forest resources which, in turn, have inflicted the ecological imbalance to the region and livelihood concerns to the tribals who were dependent on forest resources. The recent spurt of violence between the indigenous people and the immigrant Muslims bears the testimony of the seriousness of the issue of migration for the tribals. The print media in its recent reports has aptly articulated the issue of migration. They all argue that the threat to life caused by unabated inflow of the immigrant Bhatia Muslims in the vicinity as well as inside their territory has left thousands of indigenous tribes men homeless, and caused destruction of life and properties (*The Hindu*, 31.7.2012, 30.4.2013; *The New Indian Express*, 14.2.2013; *The Times of India*, 28.7.2012; *The Telegraph*, 31.8.2012). Such an ethnic strife between the Rabhas and the Muslims is not new in the Rabha areas. Ethnic conflict first erupted in 1983 which claimed a few Rabha persons killed and their houses were burnt on the occasion of *panchayat* election.

(b) Land Alienation: Alienation of land from the tribal cultivators of the Brahmaputra valley has left them impoverished. The land of the Rabha cultivator has been illegally captured by the non-tribal settlers over the years. A large number of land-grabbing cases have been reported in many Rabha villages of Mechpara area. The most affected among the villages are Shildanga, Chahari Hatishila, Chatabari, Medhipara, Pandoba, Darni, Nalanga, Baladmari, and so on. In these villages, a sizeable number of Rabha cultivators have become landless. Besides Mechpara area, other Rabha dominated areas in Goalpara, Kamrup, Dhubri and Darrang districts have also been victims of illegal land-grabbing. Restoration of lost land to the tribal owners is a difficult proposition not only for the Rabhas but also for the members of other tribal communities in the Brahmaputra Valley. The issue of land alienation thus is a major cause of recurrent tension and conflict between the indigenous tribal communities and the immigrant Muslims.

(c) Deforestation: The territory, inhabited by the Rabhas and other tribal communities, was once surrounded by dense forest, wildlife and other resources which were valuable sources of their livelihood. These resources were plundered by the unscrupulous traders and timber merchants, who were mostly the non-tribal settlers, leaving the Rabhas and other tribal populations impoverished. Loss of land and forest resources forced the tribals to look for alternative means of livelihood. As a consequence, a large number of landless, marginal and small cultivators are now seen doing share-cropping. As a part of their survival strategy, the tribals also work as wage labour and do other odd jobs. In the past they used to collect edible roots and tubers from the forests and also hunt wild games which were abundantly available in the forest. But now, they are deprived of all these resources because of massive deforestation, encroachment of non-tribals into forest land.[11]

(d) Eviction of Tribal Cultivators from Reserve and Protected Forests: It reveals from various documents, memoranda, leaflets, minutes and records of various Rabha organisations that in 1970s and 1980s a large number of landless, marginal and small categories of Rabha, Garo and Bodo-Kachari cultivators were evicted from the reserve forests of Goalpara, Darrang, Kamrup districts. Even the Rabhas who had settled earlier in the villages during the Zamindari period in the reserve forests of south Goalpara were evicted by the Forest Department on the plea of restoring the forest lands for silviculture and regeneration.[12] The cultivators' plea for *pattas* (ownership or occupancy right) on land made at the time of acquiring the Zamindari estates the Forest Department did not spare them from eviction. This has affected the livelihood options of the tribals living in the area and left them marginalised. Even the lands under the possession of the tribals have not been recorded by the authorities despite their repeated appeal to the government. The RNC and other frontal organisations took up the matter with the land revenue department of the government for its early settlement and also demanded a halt to the eviction operation. The matter, still unresolved, continues to generate unrest among affected cultivators.

(e) Indebtedness: Indebtedness is a paramount cause of land alienation in Rabha and other tribal societies. The landless and marginal farmers are the worst sufferers of economic slavery and indebtedness as reflected in some studies (Bordoloi, 1986; Pal, 2001). The Rabhas living in villages adjacent to Guwahati city have become the victims of indebtedness and land alienation. The Share-croppers' and Rayatari Acts were not enforced in these villages. The unscrupulous *mahajans* (moneylenders), land sharks and brokers took this advantage and grabbed lands of the poor cultivators who were ultimately evicted from their own land. The issue was taken up with the government for speedy redressal. But the matter was so complex that the Government of Assam failed to take any step in favour of the landless people despite RNC's constant pressure. Ultimately, the poor cultivators migrated elsewhere in search of alternative means of livelihood. Along with the expansion of Guwahati city many villages, once inhabited by the Rabhas, have now changed hands to the non-tribal city dwellers.

In Chotamatia area of Dudhnai police station and in many villages under Lakhipur police station area, a large number Rabha marginal and small cultivators got into a debt-trap and in the process lost their land. To save them from the grip of the moneylenders (*mahajans),* the RNC leadership took up this matter with the state government. They also pleaded for distribution of *patta* (ownership) of *khas* land among the victims of usury.

The above-mentioned factors and the RNC's repeated representations and demonstrations have compelled the Government of Assam to take a decision to create 'Tribal Belts and Blocks' in some parts of the affected areas in order to curb the illegal land deal with the non-tribals. But this arrangement failed to stop the transfer of tribal land as the impoverished Rabhas continued to 'sell' their land for their sustenance. Restoration of tribal land to their original owners has become a thorny issue which is too complicated to find a resolution.

Besides, other vexed issues like implementation of Share croppers Act, land reform, and land settlement of job quota come to the fore. The Rabhas demand a hike in their quota of jobs reserved in the Assam State services; they demand that the quota for STs be enhanced from 10 per cent to 15 per cent as their population has substantially increased over years. Out of 15 per cent quota for the STs the Rabhas demand a share of five per cent, which should be exclusively reserved for them since they are economically and educationally more backward compared to other plains tribes in the state. However, finding no amelioration to their condition and in the face of continued marginalisation the Rabha leaders have started to mobilise their fellow community members to fight for a rightful place in the social and political order of the state.

Phase of Political Mobilisation

The mainstream political parties always wanted to keep the Rabha, Garo, Bodo-Kachari and other backward masses of Goalpara, Dhubri, Kamrup districts in their folds to reap electoral gains in the democratic system. The Communist Party of India (CPI) established a strong base among them. Its peasant wing, the Krishak Sabha, played a key role in organising the poor tribal cultivators on agrarian and land related issues. The Krishak Sabha always pursued the issue of granting *patta* on *khas* land, eviction of landless cultivators from the forest land, enactment of Adhiari (share-croppers) and Rayatari Act, right to live in forest land, ruthless destruction of forest by unscrupulous contractors, timber merchants, and so on. Shri Sarat Chandra Rabha, a prominent member of the Assam State Committee of the CPI played a significant role in mobilising the tribals on these issues. He himself was once chosen as the president of the RNC for his outstanding leadership.

Right to live on forest land is one of the basic rights to the tribals of the country. The Rabhas are no exception to this, as they have been living in the forest areas since time immemorial. The Krishak Sabha of the CPI has been active in organising mass demonstrations against ruthless destruction of forest in the district and sub-divisional headquarters from time to time. During mass demonstration they submitted the following to the state authorities. These include: (1) permit for coup should be banned, (2) stringent action should be taken against the corrupt forest officials and contractors who are responsible for ruthless destruction of forest, (3) banning of license to the owners of all private saw mills and nationalisation of all such mills (4) diversion of 15 per cent of the total revenue earned by the concerned reserve forest authorities to the village *panchayats* located within its periphery for welfare of the villagers, (5) settlement right to the landless and marginal farmers who practice agriculture in the denuded areas of the reserve as well as protected forests and conferment of land right to all of them, (6) granting of procurement right to the people living in the fringe as well as within the reserve forest areas so that they can collect firewood, thatching grass and leaves, timber for building hut and also for making agricultural implements as they enjoyed in the past under the Goalpara Tenancy Act, 1929. By mobilising the Rabhas masses on all these long-pending issues the Krishak Sabha has successfully motivated them to go for collective action for the development of their community.

The RNC's outlook to the Rabha ethnic movement has changed under certain socio-political and historical compulsions in the recent past. Like other tribal organisations of Assam they have become politically conscious to mobilise their own people for a political end. But unlike other tribal outfits the leadership of the RNC was strong enough to lead a mass ethnic movement of the Rabhas. Its activities were confined mainly to holding conferences from time to time and adopting resolutions. But since 1980 their leadership has changed significantly; there are now many new educated youth who are qualified and dynamic to take the Rabha ethnic movement to a new height. The new leadership adopted several resolutions to give the movement a political shape. The birth of the All Rabha Sahitya Sabha (ARSS) in 1973 and the All Rabha Students' Union (ARSU) in 1980 has been a turning point of the movement.[13, 14] The ARSS and the ARSU have motivated the youth to be a part of the movement, and they ultimately turned aggressive.

Both the organisations have taken up the language issue for mobilising the Rabha masses. The argument is that Rabha being a minority language is getting lost under the overwhelming domination of Assamese language.

In order to save the language from extinction, it has to be introduced in schools as the medium of education. Generally, language issue has been a rallying point in most ethnic movements in the North-East. The Rabha leaders were quick to realise this. Responding to the aspiration young generation articulated by both ARSS and ARSU the RNC leadership came forward to give moral support to the language movement. The language movement thus has become an integral part of Rabha ethnic movement.

Emergence of language movement was not sudden. For long the Rabhas had been realising that their language was fast disappearing under the influence of the dominant mainstream Assamese language. It is a fact that the Pati section living in Boko area of Kamrup district and the Totla Rabha of Udalguri, Darrang and Baska districts have forgot their mother tongue and adopted the Assamese as their language for all practical purposes. Such a scenario led the ARSS and the ARSU leaderships to take up language issue for arresting further extinction of their language and culture. The leadership thought, the introduction of Rabha language as medium of instruction in the primary school level help protect their culture and ethnic identity.

For the sustained persuasion of ARSS, ARSU and the RNC for several years the Government of Assam agreed to introduce the Rabha language as medium of instruction in the primarily level. The Rabha language has been introduced in the primary level in 1988 as per the notification of the Government of Assam issued in February 1987. In the beginning it was introduced in 70 primary schools spread in the Rabha dominated areas. The successful language movement has united all the Rabha sub-groups and has given them a broad Rabha identity. Following the foot-steps of Bodo-Kacharis the Rabhas gradually transformed their movement into a political movement for their own 'Rabha-Hasong' homeland.

Movement for Rabha-Hasong Homeland

The leadership of the Rabha movement must have been observing the autonomy movements of their neighbouring tribal communities. Empowered with information, awareness and new ethnic consciousness, gained through a long course of social reform movement and language movement, the young leadership of the Rabhas decided to launch a movement for their own home land. The sense of insecurity was the main reason that pushed the Rabahs for the home land movement. The demand for creation of a Rabha-Hasong homeland, if actualised, would arrest their further marginalisation and would secure their cultural identity. That would also resole the long-standing tribe-non-tribe conflict in the region. The RNC's conservative approach was an impediment to the progress of such an ambitious movement.

The young leadership of ARSU, ARSS, RNC and the leaders of other regional Rabha organisations attended a general convention at Salpara, near Krishnai in July, 1992 to form a the 'Rabha Hasong Demand Committee'

(RHDC).[15] The objective was also to launch a movement for the creation of the 'Rabha Hasong Autonomous Council' (RHAC) in the line of Bodoland movement. The leadership of this new political outfit was mainly in the hands of college and university educated youth. So in 1992, the Rabha Hasong autonomous movement started and that continued till the period of signing of Rabha Accord in March 1995.

(a) The Movement and its Consequences: The Rabha Hasong autonomous movement began first in Dudhnoi, a prominent place of Goalpara district which is also considered one of the epicenters of all tribal movements. In the beginning, it was a peaceful mass agitation programme throughout lower Assam. In this mass agitation, the common Rabha people began to take part spontaneously. The Government of Assam decided to crush the movement by applying force; it wasted no time in arresting and imprisoning the leaders. However, the movement gained strength following the emergence of various other Rabha organisations, namely, Rabha National Volunteer Force (RNVF), Rabha Women's Organisation and Rabha Teachers' Forum. The Rabha men, women and children from different parts of the state joined hands in support of the movement. The movement took programs like blockade of National and State highways, closure of educational institutions, market centers, *gherao* of government officials and picketing in front of government establishments, *dharnas* and so on. Sometimes the programmes turned violent and many of the supporters sustained bullet injuries.

(b) Signing of 'Rabha Accord' and its Aftermath: The Rabha ethnic movement, which continued until February 1995, forced the Government of Assam to accept the demand for the Rabha Hasong Autonomous Council (RHAC) in principle. Following this, a 'Memorandum of Settlement' (Rabha Accord) was signed between the Rabha leaders and the Government of Assam in presence of the then Chief Minister, Hiteswar Saikia, in Guwahati on 10th March, 1995. The accord is officially known as the 'Rabha Accord, 1995' (see the memorandum of the Rabha Hasong Coordination Committee – RHCC, 2000). With the signing of 'Rabha Accord', a phase of struggle of the Rabhas ended.

The 'Rabha-Hasong Autonomous Council Bill (1995)' was tabled in the Assam Legislative Assembly and was passed in 1995. The aim was to establish an administrative council for the Rabhas in the line of 'Bodo Autonomous Council of Assam'. An ad hoc committee was given the responsibility to run the RHAC until a new elected body was formed. The first oath taking ceremony for the members of the interim body was held on 20th July, 1995 at Dudhnoi of Goalpara district. The RHAC accord facilitated the formation of the autonomous council covering an area of 3161 sq kms in the south bank of the Brahmaputra river, this had 856 revenue and forest villages with 60 per cent tribal population and a total population of 3,74,132. Also included within this area were the existing tribal belts and blocks. The border of the RHAC starts from Rani (west

Guwahati) to Joyramkuchi, Lakhipur revenue circle which falls under the districts of Kamrup and Goalpara (Anonymous, 2000: 2-3).

In the beginning, the council started functioning with 300 villages. But the State Government took no initiative in handing over the remaining villages to the council and that created resentment among the Rabhas. To resolve this problem, the Rabha-Hasong Co-ordination Committee (RHCC) submitted memoranda to the Governor and other executive authorities of Assam several times to expedite the implementation of the accord with the inclusion of remaining 556 villages. The demands included transfer of administrative, financial and legislative powers to the council and amendment of the RHAC Act, 1995. The State Government, however, did not concede the demands for over one and half decades from the date of signing the accord. This led to frustration and anger among the Rabhas.

(c) Present Crisis: Non-transfer of powers to the council, as promised in the accord, has been the bone of contention between the State government and the council. Without any executive powers and funds for different heads the council was unable to undertake any major development initiative. This interim arrangement continued for two consecutive terms. But it failed to bring about any visible improvement in the quality of life of the people living in the said council area. At the time of signing the accord it was promised that the council would be formed with 'areas having more than 50 per cent tribal population', but in the RHAC Act the language was changed to 'areas having 50 per cent Rabha population'. This led to confusion in terms of its jurisdiction over revenue villages and in administering the council. The Rabha leaders are arguing that there are several other flaws in the Act that need to be amended for making the council effective. The election to the council, which is not yet been held, is another bone of contention between the state government and the Rabha leaders. The ineffective council and the growing frustration among the Rabhas in the council area is an important reason behind the recent spurt of violence between the Muslim settlers and the tribal inhabitants in the region (Anonymous, 2013: 7-11).

The RHAC has filed litigation in the Gauhati High Court against the state government for violating the promises made in the accord and in the RHAC Act. Several issues like demarcation of the council boundary, notification for remaining 556 revenue and forest villages, inclusion of the villages of the adjoining areas, introduction of Rabha language in the primary level from 70 to 300 schools, allocation of 38 departments with defined administrative, legislative and financial powers and immediate election to RHAC however remain unsettled. It is, therefore, uncertain as to what would be the ultimate fate of the Council. Apart from the ARSU and its allied organisations the leaders of other national Rabha organisations and the Rabha and non-Rabha intellectuals of the council area are creating pressures on the state government to resolve the long pending issues.

However, by creating the RHAC the Rabhas have achieved certain goals. They are now an organised population and quite conscious of their identity and rights. They now appreciate the value of education, their own language and culture and understand the value of a united ethnic movement. The hegemonic state, with all its manipulative powers, appears to be in a mood to subvert the efforts of the RHAC in fulfilling its ethnic aspirations.

Conclusion

Formation of the Rabha Hasong Autonomous Council (RHAC) is a significant political development in the case of marginalised Rabhas in lower Assam. Its functioning largely depends on the activities of different frontal organisations like ARSU, ARWC, SSDC, ARSS, and RNC and the efficacy of the policies and development initiatives of the Government of Assam. The formation of the RHAC created hopes among the Rabhas since they thought it would resolve their long-standing problems like deprivation, discrimination, the issues relating to their language and culture. They thought, RHAC would be an important political apparatus for their advancement as well as restoration of their identity as a distinct community. But, due to non transfer of adequate power and money by the State Government the possibility of making the autonomous council an effective organ of development is fading. The on-going legal battle between the council and the state government has further complicated the prospect of a successful autonomous council. In case the council experiment fails the Rabhas would, in all likelihood, take recourse to another phase of ethnic movement.

Notes

[Acknowledgement: The paper is based on my fieldwork in different Rabha areas of Goalpara, Dhubri, Kokrajhar and Kamrup districts of Lower Assam in different phases between 2000 and 2012. I am extremely thankful Dr Jayanta Kumar Sarkar for his suggestions and critical comments on an earlier draft of the paper].

1. Sikkim has become the eighth constituent part of the Northeast annexed to the North Eastern Council (NEC) for its speedy development as its geographical location is quite proximity to this part of India. (See *The Hindu*, 'Editorial', 21.07.2000:12).
2. The Rabha of Assam, Mehalaya and West Bengal are now a patrilineal tribe which has given up almost all major matrilineal features from their social organisation. The members of the present generation are quite conscious about their own dignity; the authority of wife's maternal uncle is no more relevant. Ownership and management of properties are now mainly done by the husband. Husband's authority in all respects is considered supreme.

3. The move for unity of all the Rabha sections started with the formation of the All Rabha Sahitya Sabha (ARSS) in a conference held at Ghaksa village of Kashiabari area of then Kokrajhar subdivision of undivided Goalpara district in 1973, which is now a full-fledged district.
4. The Rabha society became enlightened spiritually and culturally by the waves of various religious forces since the beginning of 20th century. The Rabhas have been Hinduism, Brahmoism and Christianity in different historical periods, particularly from early decades of 20th century, which continued until 1980s. These religious forces as well as various religious movements were responsible for reforming their society, bringing new set of norms and customs to their social system. And with the process of various socio- religious movements social awakening began to start among the youths of the Rabha society during that time (See Chakravarti, 1966; Sarkar, 1982; Pam, 1986: 1-5; Pam, 1986: 43 – 50).
5. Shri Gobardhan Chandra Sarkar (Rabha) was a prominent personality of Rabha society. He witnessed various changes in his society that have been recorded in his handwritten memoir (in Assamese) entitled '*Background history of origin of the Rabha National Council*' (RNC). In such memoir, he noted down the activities of various Rabha organisations that contributed a lot in moulding the RNC to its present shape. He motivated his contemporary friends and students community of that time to be active in bringing about changes in the community and for the unification drive of different Rabha sections.
6. Educational qualifications of the RNC leaders in pre-independence era were mainly limited to primary level or up to the minor passed (then class VI standard) and economy was primarily subsistence agriculture. A large majority of them were landless. They had little exposure to outside world as they were confined to their locality. This prevented them from taking any grand move towards uniting the Rabha masses for a greater cause of their identity and survival. Only after 1970, educated youths started the RNC; under their leadership the RNC started movement for territorial autonomy for the Rabhas.
7. Between mid 1970 and early 1980s, some college educated youths came forward to take over the leadership of RNC, whose economic background was comparatively better than their predecessors; many were doing Govt. jobs and other white-collar professions. For them, agriculture was subsidiary occupation. The youth leadership was instrumental to mould the RNC's activities that proceeded towards movement for territorial autonomy in 1990s, for which various constituent Rabha organisations were involved.

8. In local dialect *Bhatia* (*bhati*–down, + *ya* = *Bhatia)* means 'a population hailing from a low-lying country where the land mass often gets flooded due to tidal wave of sea, river, rain, storms and other sorts of natural calamities'. The Bhatias are, by and large, Muslim by religion. Here this geographically low-lying country is primarily meant to indicate neighbouring present-day Bangladesh from where influx of Bengali Muslims has taken place since pre-independence era which has created demographic imbalance in different districts of Lower Assam. This is cited as one of the reasons for an upsurge of ethnic movements in Assam.
9. A strip of sandy land rising out of the bed of a river or sea above the water level. In Brahamaputra huge *char* area is found in Goalpara district of Assam which is inhabited mainly by the immigrant Muslims.
10. Till now lakhs of land hungry immigrants from Bangladesh (mostly the Muslims) have settled in the plains areas of the Brahmaputra Valley including the *char* areas. That has changed the demographic map of Assam for which recurrent ethnic violence between the local indigenous communities and the immigrant Muslims takes place from time to time. The recent spurt of ethnic clash between the Bodo-Kachari and the Muslims and between the Rabha and the Muslims is the major concern to the survival interests of the indigenous communities living here for a long time. To safeguard the interests of the local communities the leaders of various indigenous groups have drawn the attention to both the State and the Union Government by submitting various memoranda for implementation of various accords signed by the Govt. and the leaders of the movement.
11. In the late 1970s and 1980s, when the present author was in field in different tribal villages of Mechpara area of South Goalpara, Parbatjowar tract and Gossaingaon area of present Kokrajhar district, ruthless felling of *sal* trees was illegally done in connivance with forest officials by the unscrupulous contractors and timber merchants. The tribal people used to cut gigantic *sal* trees for fire wood and other purposes. This led to the disappearance of forests in different districts of lower Assam where forests and wildlife were once considered principal economic resource for the tribals and other local people.
12. The eviction of the tribal cultivators from forest lands found mention in secretary's reports and resolutions/minutes passed in various conferences of the All Rabha National Council (ARNC), All Rabha Students' Union (ARSU), Dudhnai Purbanchal and Paschimanchal Rabha Samajes, Mechpara Purbanchal and Madhyanchal Rabha Samajes and other Rabha organisations. Even in 1980s and 1990s, the activities of the Goalpara District Krishak Sabha, an affiliate of the Communist

Party of India (CPI), were mainly centered on the land and eviction issues that were strikingly noticed during *dharnas*, demonstrations and *gherao* programmes made before Dy. Commissioner's office, SDO and BDO offices, and so on.

13. The All Rabha Sahitya Sabha (ARSS) was established in a conference at Ghaksa village of then Kokrajhar Sub-division (now a separate district) on 8th April, 1973. Some students and educated youths of Koch section of Kokrajhar district were active in Sahitya Sabha. The Sahitya Sabha plays significant role in uniting different Rabha sections into a larger Rabha society and in promoting ethnic movement in different phases.
14. A Rabha students' convention was held in the premises of Goalpara College on 12th February, 1980 to form All India Rabha Students' Union (AIRSU) in order to look after various problems faced by the Rabha students studying at different levels. The AIRSU was renamed as the All Rabha Students' Union (ARSU) in its Debitola conference held on 12th February, 1981, which is also observed as its foundation day every year. It may be mentioned that some college and university educated youths namely Dr Kanta Ram Rabha, Sabya Shaci Rabha, Pranoy Rabha, Amitabha Rabha, Jibewar Koch, Rabin Koch, Majid Kumar Rabha and others were instrumental in forming this students' body. Contribution of the Rabha students' organisation is immense in bringing modernity to the Rabha ethnic movement.
15. The Rabha-Hasong Demand Committee (RHDC) was formed in a national convention of the Rabha leaders held at the Bishnu Rabha High School, Salapara near Krishnai, in 1992 and its executive body was formed with the prominent Rabha leaders of different socio-economic, socio-cultural and educational background who steered the Hasong movement with courage and responsibilities.

References

Anonymous, 1970. *Proceedings of the Dhupdhara Conference of All Assam Rabha Sangha* (AARS), 1970.

Anonymous, 2000. *Memorandum submitted to shri S.K. Sinha, Hon'ble Governor of Assam by the Rabha Hasong Coordination Committee*, Dudhnoi, Dist. Goalpara.

Anonymous, 2013. 'Assam Violence Toll Touches 19', *The New Indian Express*, Kozhikod Edition, 14.02.2013:7.

Anonymous, 2013. 'Curfew Clamped, Army Called out in Assam's Goalpara District', *The Hindu*, Hyderabad Edition, 30.04.2013:11.

Bagchi, Indrani, 2012. Indo-Bangla Boundary Pact to be Revised. *The Times of India*, Nagpur Edition, 28.7.2012:11.

Barbora, Sanjay, 2012. 'Identity of a Recurring Conflict', *The Hindu*, Hyderabad edition, 31.7.2012:6.

Bordoloi, B.N. (ed.), 1986. *Alienation of tribal land and indebtedness*. Guwahati: Tribal Research Institute, Government of Assam.

Chakravarti, Satis Chandra, 1966. *Brahmo Samaj. Depressed classes and untouchabilty* (second edition). Calcutta: Sadharan Brahmo Samaj.

Dholabhai, Nishit, 2012. 'Speed up Alien Detection, Delhi Tells Assam', *The Telegraph*, Calcutta Edition, 31.8.2012:6.

Pal, Surajit K. 2001. *The Rabha: a study of their agrarian social structure* (unpublished Ph. D. thesis, Chapter 3). Calcutta: University of Calcutta.

Pam, Ganapati, 1986. 'Dharmiya Sanskritir Prabhab' (in Assamese), in Charu Mohan Rabha (ed.) *Jilingani, A souvenir of the Dirma Jamat Sanmilan*, Chotamatia: Jilinguni Prakashan Samiti: 43-50.

Pam, Rabin, 1986. 'Atitar Jilingani' (in Assamese), in Charu Mohan Rabha (ed.) *Jilingani,* a souvenir of the Dirma Jamat Sanmilan. Chotamatia: Jilinguni Prakashan Samiti: 1-5.

Sarkar, Gobardhan Chandra, 1976. *Background history of origin of the Rabha National Council (RNC)*: *reminiscence* (in Assamese). Unpublished handwritten manuscript.

Sarkar, Hem Chandra, 1982. *The Religion of the Brahmo Samaj* (3rd edition). Calcutta: Sadharan Brahmo Samaj.

The Hindu, Editorial, 21.07.2000:12.

SECTION–IV

ETHNIC CONFLICT IN GUJARAT

14

Towards a Specialised Understanding of Ethnicity: Making of Everyday Borders and Identities in the Walled City of Ahmedabad

Aparajita De

Introduction

The understanding of ethnic identities and their constructions in social sciences have been primarily in terms of cultural differences and distinctiveness, as processes of delineation between the self and the other. Often, these processes have been examined through the processes of objectification of culture and construction of otherness. But 'space', I argue, as a category of analysis in these processes has been completely overlooked. Space, borders, boundaries and territorial enclosures share a unique relationship with the construction and practice of ethnic identities. The main focus of my paper is to explore this relationship and develop a specialised understanding of the processes of construction of ethnic identities.

The idea of space, spatial categories and scales is not new but is in fact central to discourses on ethnic identity construction, both in terms of theory and praxis. It has long been argued that the 'national space' of the nation-state provides a tightly bounded socio-spatial master frame for the formation of identities. Lately, in the context of globalisation and particularly in the light of time-space compressions in the globalising world the idea of space—and that of national space and nation-state—has been questioned. The world is envisaged as borderless or boundary-less, and a highly interconnected global space not restricted by space, border, boundaries and territorial enclosures of any kind, and particularly that of the nation-state. In other words, the globalised world is seen as a de-territorialised 'space of flows' undoubtedly freeing ethnic identities from being territorially or spatially bound. Yet, central to most ethnic movements across the globe are claims and counter-claims for 'separate spaces' as in nation-states to regions that underline how local cultures and collective ethnic identities rest in the idea of space, particularly local spaces.

Set in the background of the 2002 Godhra carnage and subsequent Hindu-Muslim riots throughout Gujarat, widely believed to be supported by the BJP (Bharatiya Janata Party), a Hindu right-wing political party-led government, my paper examines how boundaries of the nation are drawn, redrawn, and contested in the local spaces of the urban. The paper tries to understand how borders and homes on one hand and ethnic identities of Hindus and Muslims constructed in everyday lives in the walled city of Ahmedabad. The walled city is generally perceived as riot prone and a highly divided and bordered place where Hindus and Muslims have been living separately and in almost total segregation since the city was built by Sultan Ahmed Shah-I in early fifteenth century. In my paper I seek to examine these lines of separation or borders between the Hindus and Muslims, particularly the social and cultural processes through which these borders and homes are being produced and reproduced in everyday life-worlds (Newman and Passi, 1998; Thrift, 1999; Stuver, 2003; Newman, 2006).

Homes are idealised places that are social and spatial extensions of self and that of others. In other words, home is where the 'social and spatial are thoroughly imbued with each other's presence' and it is both 'material and ideological' (Cresswell, 1996: 11). Recent research theorises the location and making of borders where the places located beyond boundaries of home are seen as threatening that provokes anxiety among homemakers. Here home is an inside in opposition to an existing outside (Blunt and Dowling, 2006). Thus, borders that draw out home are symbolic of one's territory and identity and are not necessarily fixed nor are they natural lines between people and places. In fact, border-making is a dynamic process evolving from peoples' culture, politics, economy and history (Newman and Passi, 1998; Newman, 2006). Borders reflect a territorialised 'politics of belonging' differentiating those who belong and those who don't (Trudeau, 2006). Here within the scope of my paper, I try to explore these territorialised 'politics of belonging', that, I argue, are central to the construction of ethnic identities, by examining border narratives in the walled city of Ahmedabad.

Methodology

My paper adopts an ethnographic approach towards understanding border-making processes focusing on individual border narratives and experiences in order to capture its different meanings and notions, especially at the local micro-level. I particularly focus on the processes involved in creating the borders of homes and neighbourhoods, of self and others, of Hindus and Muslims in the walled city of Ahmedabad. The research for my paper is based on the many conversations, which also includes formal interviews, that I had conducted since 1996 with people living in and out of the *kot*, with Hindus, Muslims, Jains and Christians, with the young and the old, with people from all walks of life from shopkeepers, auto drivers to rich businessmen and factory owners, from clerks to high officials in the bureaucracy. The formal interviews were conducted in the six major residential localities of the *kot*, namely, Shahpur, Dariapur, Kalupur, Raikhad, Jamalpur and Khadia. The interviewees were from both the spatially dominant and non-dominant Hindus and Muslims living in that particular locality.[1] The other consideration that was taken into account was the internal heterogeneity within Hindus and Muslims along the lines of caste and *jamat* as identified by the interviewees. I conducted a total of twenty-four such detailed interviews, selected on the basis as already outlined, in 2004, which has been supplemented by the innumerable interviews and conversations I have had in the field since 1996. I have used narrative analysis as a textual method to comprehend the interviews and the imageries of the bordering processes involved in the making of homes.

Journeying through the Walled City of Ahmedabad

On a hot day in June, 2004, I got down in front of the old stock exchange in *Manek Chowk* and paid the auto driver. There waiting for me was Naresh Kaka to take me to his home, *Jagaseth ni pol* in Khadia. The casualness in Kaka's demeanor was not what I had anticipated, especially in the aftermath of the Godhra carnage and the subsequent riots. Perhaps, I had expected to hear an angry tirade of a Hindu demonising the Muslim other, of Hindu nationalism and how at long last the ghettoisation of Muslims is successfully complete. But none was forthcoming. Just like the kot's, many yet contradictory names that of the walled city and the city of gates—a closed yet open place, its people too appeared so.

In an attempt to understand these contradictions, let me retell the story put together from the many versions that I have read and heard. The walled city of Ahmedabad located on the eastern bank of river Sabarmati, was founded by Sultan Ahmed Shah-I in 1411 A.D. on its existing site, close to the older trading centre of Ashaval, Ashapalli or Karnavati (State Gazetteers, 1984; Gillion, 1968). Though the city was under the rule of the Muslim Sultans Hindus and the Jains were considered powerful. Later it emerged as an important trade centre known for its fine cloths, exported to West Asia, Europe,

South and South East Asia and various others parts of India. The textile industry was characterised by skilled Muslim weavers, Hindu and Jain financiers and merchants. In keeping with the mercantile ethos of the city the different communities enjoyed a relationship of cooperation and collaboration that brought great wealth and prosperity to it (Yagnik and Shah, 2005). People came to Ahmedabad to do business and the tone of the city was as much Hindu as it was Muslim. Over the years, the economy grew and diversified and so did the city and its people.

Structurally and historically, the city can be broadly classified into the *kot vistar*—the inner walled city and the *para vistar*—the outer suburbs. The *kot* is almost semi-circular, covering an area of two square miles defined by the fortified city walls, now demolished, and the twelve *Darwazas* or city gates (Jain, 2008). Planned according to the Indo-Aryan tradition the royal quarters, the citadel of Bhadra is at the heart of the *kot* with the main roads leading from or to the centre and subsidiary roads branching off to different localities (*ibid.*). The Bhadra fort is considered as the oldest part surrounded by a well-developed group of neighborhoods or residential localities also called *Paras* with Manek Chowk as the principal business and market area (State Gazetteers 1984). It was during the reign of Mahmud Begada (1459 A. D. to 1511 A. D.) that the *kot* was established with various *paras* like Shahpur, Dariapur, Kalupur, Khadia, Jamalpur and Raikhad (Mehta, 1948). Most of the *paras* were developed by Begada's Amirs (used as title for nobility, generals and high-level administrators) and named after them—Dariapur after Dariya Khan, Kalupur after Aba Haji Kalu popularly known as Kalu Miyan, Sarangpur after Malik Sarang etc. (*ibid.*).

Today the *pol* I am visiting is one of the innumerable residential micro-neighbourhoods that are found within these *paras*. Nareshkaka believes that these *pols* came into existence during the Mughal and Maratha rule (1573 A.D. to 1817 A.D.) due to reasons of insecurity and fear (Doshi, 1974). This he says is reflected in the *pol*'s structural layout—demarcated by a wall with a single *darwaza* or gate at its entrance, which was barred at night and other secret ones. *Pols* are usually characterised by compact housing clusters with dead-end main streets, and streets branching from it are too narrow for modern wheeled traffic. Structurally, it is almost physically insulated from the outside world and outsiders. Understandably, everyone within the *pol* not only knows each other but also knows of anyone entering it. At the same time it creates a tension of being watched, of being under constant surveillance that is associated with borders, particularly the crossing of borders.

Kaka informs me that '*there must be over a thousand pols in the kot and most of them have a distinctive social identity of their own based on religion, caste and occupation*' (De, 2002: 112-28). Historically, *pols* were mostly composed of a single caste group with few families from other serving caste groups like Brahmins, Suthar (carpenters) and Nai (barber), but have over time become more heterogeneous. But despite losing its so-called homogeneity and organisation one can find, even today, the dominance of particular caste group within a *pol* (*ibid.*). The entire *kot* at the macro *para* level depicts a social character similar to that found at the micro *pol* level. For example, Dariapur was mostly inhabited by Hindus and Patidars in particular; Jamalpur by Muslims; Kalupur by Jains and Vohras. Presently, Hindus mostly live in Khadia, and some pockets in Shahpur and Dariapur, Jains in Manek Chowk and particular neighbourhoods of Khadia and Shahpur and Muslims in Jamalpur, and in certain localities in Raikhad, Shahpur, Kalupur and Dariapur (De, 2002).

Naresh Kaka categorically points out to me that though the walls that separated the *kot* from the *para* have been demolished the *kot* remains conspicuous due to its distinct way of life, like a different society and a different place in comparison to the *para.* Many believe that the distinctiveness of the *kot* as a place lies in its warmth, which is unthought of in any modern city. Manubhai, whose family has been living in the *kot* for the past seventy years, says:

> [t]here are two things for which the *kot* stands out—one is *sangathan* (organisation) and the other is *shanti* (peace). You will not find either of these in the *para*. There people remain closed in their homes, too busy with their own lives or watching TV to show interest in other peoples' lives and their problems… It is not like that here. People there look down on us. They think that we are *desi* (rustic), *jabro* (aggressive) and that we will not be able to 'set' (adjust) with their so called superior ways.

In the same vein, Asfaqbhai, a resident of *Rajaji ni pol*, Shahpur, for more than 30-40 years, argues that the *kot* is unique as:

> Here only you will find *sath sahakar* (co-operation), which is unimaginable in the *para*. People will rush to your side at any point of time. In the *para* one has to be careful, even if somebody comes to your help he must be having some ulterior motive. And have you seen how people there behave? They have lost all sense… no values, no respect for elders. They know no one other than themselves … Here you will find that people know and understand what it is to be human—a good Muslim.

A *pol* is not only a defined area of jurisdiction spread over continuous houses that binds the families under certain rules and regulations[2] but also creates a sense of belonging (Newman 2006). No wonder, the *pol* residents till date believe it 'feels right' or it is the 'right place' in contrast to the *para vistar.* Thus, the questions that I seek to understand are—how does 'the sense of belonging' creates a sense of difference? How are these materialised and articulated through borders and homes? In other words, how do the processes of bordering create distinct idea/s of home, of self and others, of ethnic identities and *vice-versa?*

Spatial Mythographies of Homes and the Politics of Belonging and Difference

Lighting the *bidi,* Kaka tells me, '*you all and the media make too much of the dhamaal* (communal riots). *Kot vistar that is the area inside the 12 Darwazas, our own area, that is Hindu area is the safest. That is for us, hmm... For Muslims it is their areas that are the safest for them*'. Strangely, it reminded me of another conversation in a somewhat similar landscape. Leading from the crowded eateries of Karanj through the winding by lanes is the quiet neighbourhood of Chudi-Ol, with an eclectic mix of grand old houses and newer apartment buildings with high boundary walls and huge iron gates. In one such apartment, in the privacy of Naseerbhai's living room he confided:

> Our entire Mohollo is the safest in the entire *kot*. This area is completely safe even during your riots. It is a complete Muslim area. There are no Hindus living in this area…but Khadia is unsafe for us. It is a 'total' Hindu area and obviously safe for them.

It was clear to me that both were not only downplaying the significance of communal tensions but were deliberately trying to project to me, an outsider, an imagery of the *Kot* as a safe haven, particularly their homes and their areas. I immediately zeroed in on their choice of the word 'safest', 'total Hindu/ Muslim areas' and the concept of our homes and our areas being the safest for us and their homes and areas being the safest for them. I gleefully concluded that this feeling of security was not an absolute one and is in relation to how safe self feels or is 'at home' with respect to the Muslim or the Hindu other. Unfortunately, like the popular interpretations in the media I assumed that such divisions (Gregory, 2004) of 'our place' on this side of the border and 'your place' on the other side are a proof of communal discord and riots. But as I dug deeper I realised that the word safe had a much wider connotation than the apparent protection of self and the hearth from overt threats of violence posed by the other but encompassed within its borders the familiar world of self.

Kaka continued that he realised why outsiders found it difficult to understand and visualise life inside a *pol*—it was a world lost to us, the outsiders.

For 60 years I have lived here … Everybody knows me. In the area and around everybody respects me. I am fondly called by one and all—from the youngsters to the elders—as Naresh Kaka. Ask anybody and they will tell you who Naresh Kaka is, where he lives and what he does, and even what his father and his father did. Would you find this elsewhere?

In the meantime Manubhai and Hareshbhai joins us at Kaka's home for a discussion and Manubhai further adds:

> Here your neighbours are your friends … I think they are more than that; they are family. They are always there for you. I remember that my daughter had an accident and she required blood. Fifty men gathered here in no time to donate blood. Will you find this anywhere?

Hareshbhai, a quiet man in his early 20s and living in Garnala ni pol, Shahpur, not to be left out of the discussion elaborated:

> Not one but the entire *pol* will come to help you. There is no theft … Leave your house open for the entire day and nothing will happen…Hang your clothes outside and if it has been blown away by the wind your neighbor will go and collect it and keep it. If guests have come to your home and there is water shortage, you need not tell your neighbour to store water. He will do so on his own accord. And we would also do the same for him.

Let me for a moment take you to another setting—a *kitli* (tea shop) at the busy cross roads of a Masjid where I was meeting Mansukhbhai and Patel Chacha. On one side a group of young men in their 20s were sitting on their motorbikes and quietly chatting while on the other side a few boisterous kids stopped playing cricket to let a *burkha*-clad woman with her children pass. At the same time we could hear some kind of announcement being made in the Masjid's loudspeakers. Raising his voice above the din, Mansukhbhai informs me, 'when someone from our community passes away a man on a cycle with a loudspeaker announces it in the entire area. We immediately get to know what has happened and we at once go to his place and give him support when he requires it the most'. A rather garrulous Patel Chacha points out the reason for such humanness lies in the fact that:

> ….we do not differentiate within ourselves, we eat from one plate … and it does not matter whether we are rich or poor. In the eyes of the Allah we are all same so we treat each other with equal respect. This is how we live. We are one. During the riots or any other crisis we all come together and help each other.

Irrespective of religion, caste or class all my interviewees drew a picture of a separate world—a distinctive home and place on 'their' side of the border that was cocooned in warmth, where neighbours are not just friends but are family bonded together by their shared values. It is these simple values, that of mutual trust, respect and acceptance, which makes self unique and makes their homes the very essence of humanity, which cannot be found elsewhere. It is these values that distinguish self and 'my' place located on this side of the border from others and 'their' places on the other side (Welchman, 1996).

At this point I'd like to draw the readers' attention to imageries of elsewhere, particularly the other side of the border. Kaka rather carelessly remarks, 'They are parts, some ugly parts with which all of us live. Now take the 'M' class (Muslims) and their areas. Their area is dirty, so dirty that you will not feel like walking through. Along with people goats are also living. There is no difference between the two. It stinks. Then every two minutes you will come across a butcher's shop with dead remains of animals for display. Is that anything to display or decorate a shop with? Will you find such things here? No. Only there.'

Others were equally quick to point out that the squalor and stench actually indicated 'their' deeper malignancies, mainly their poverty of values. Understandably, the Muslim 'other' and their areas seem to represent the essence of moral degeneration, crime, violence and corruption:

> They are *Dada* (aggressive) type. You see all this areas are filled with *goondas* (criminals)—petty thieves to bootleggers, smugglers and underworld dons to international terrorists. And all are *topi-dariwalas* (refers to the practice of Muslims wearing head gear and keeping a beard), absolute *kattarwadis* (fundamentalists). They are always using abusive language for the Hindus... I have even heard that they ill-treat their own women—their mothers, wives and sisters. Some of them even beat them up. These people are cruel and merciless ... they don't spare anyone, not even their women.

Likewise the contending stories about the Hindu other are no different. Patel *chacha* tells:

> *Chyut-achyut* (untouchability), *bedhbhau* (difference)...this is all they know. This is 'their culture, their values. You can drink water from this person or eat in this persons house, this person can't enter the temple ... they do all this do their own. What kind of humans are they? Funny thing is they are always on a high moral ground. They of all people come to teach others of what is right and what is wrong. To them being a Hindu is right and all else is wrong, bad, dirty....*Unke to bache bache ko ay sab pata hai* (even their children know all this) such is the level of awareness.

Speaking of the level of consciousness of the Hindu and Muslim identities it would not be remiss to comment that these constructions of self and other are not simplistically derived from religious ideologies but from a more complex understanding of the different values and ways of life that symbolises self and the other. Interestingly, the border narratives evoke the spirit of the people and the place—the feeling of shared values and belongingness that one finds at home. And, it is these everyday experiences of shared values that constantly shape the complex understandings of self in relation to the other coinciding with the inside-outside borders of homes that are being constantly drawn and redrawn.

In Defence of Borders and Specialised Self and Others

When we speak of borders our imaginations seem to be dominated by borders that separate nation-states (Agnew, 1994). Not surprisingly, many argue that with globalisation on one hand and communication technology on the other have created a borderless world (Helliwell, 1998; Ohmae, 1990). Yet borders and border-making processes are an inherent part of our everyday life-worlds. Consciously and unconsciously, we continuously create, perpetuate and cross borders in our everyday life. These borders may not be visible in the manner we imagine them to be (Houtum, 2002)—guarded and controlled with barbed wires, border patrols and check points—yet we cannot deny their existence. In my paper, I have tried to explore these everyday borders with respect to homes that are being drawn and re-drawn and how they perpetuate and institutionalise sense of belonging and ideas of self at one hand and on the other difference and otherness.

In the context of the walled city of Ahmedabad, it appeared that borders of homes and neighbourhoods are primarily based on religious differences. Time and again the border narratives tell a story of how self and their homes are different and unique in sharp contrast to the others' areas and how 'safe' they feel here in their own homes. Predictably, the *kot*, the walled city, is a highly by ordered and divided places of Hindu/Muslim self *vis-à-vis* Muslim/Hindu others. Yet this may not necessarily indicate the construction of Hindus and Muslims as antagonistic binary opposites. Border narratives, I argue, infuse the spirit of the people, their feelings, shared values and belongingness in the borders. Thus, borders enclose 'inside' notions of self and their particular cultures—their ways of living, of seeing and understanding the world. The existence of borders of 'my place/places' ensures the survival of these particular cultures at one hand. On the other, the demarcation of borders of 'their place/places' suggests not the intolerance of the other but recognition of the other and its culture, albeit on the outside. Thus, a border emerges as an act of strategy that not only creates a distinct self from the other but ensures the survival of the self and the other.

References

Agnew, J., 1994. 'The Territorial Trap: The Geographical Assumptions of International Relations Theory', *Review of International Political Economy* 1, pp. 53-80.

Appadurai, A., 1997. *Modernity at Large: Cultural Dimensions of Globalisation*. Delhi: Oxford University Press.

Auge, M., 1995. *Non-Places. Introduction to an Anthropology of Supermodernity*. London: Verso.

Blunt, A. and R. Dowling, 2006. *Home*. London: Routledge.

Cresswell, T., 1996. In *Place/Out of Place: Geography, Ideology, and Transgression.* Minneapolis: University of Minnesota Press.

Dasgupta, M., 2002. '140 killed as Gujarat Bandh turns Violent', *The Hindu,* 1 March: 1.

De, A., 2002. *Spatial Structure and Social Interactions in the Core Areas of Indian Cities, The Case Study of Ahmedabad*, Unpublished Ph.D. thesis, Ahmedabad: Gujarat University.

Doshi, H., 1974. *Traditional Neighbourhood in a Modern City*. Delhi: Abhinav.

Gillion, K.L., 1968. *Ahmedabad: A Study in Indian Urban History*. Berkeley and Los Angeles: University of California Press.

Gregory, D., 2004. *The Colonial Present*. Oxford: Blackwell.

Hadjor, K.B., 1997, 'Race, Riots and Clouds of Ideological Smoke', *Race and Class*, 38 ; 15-32.

Haynes, D., 1991. *Rhetoric and Ritual in Colonial India: The Shaping of a Public Culture in Surat City, 1852 – 1928*, Berkeley and Los Angeles: University of California Press.

Helliwell, J., 1998. *How much do national borders matter?* Washington DC: Brookings Institution 1998.

Jain, K., 2008. 'Ahmedabad's Historic Core in 2001', in K. Jain and H. Khare (eds.) *Ahmedabad 2001 – Imperatives now Towards a New Metropolitan Management Strategy.* Ahmedabad: The Times Research Foundation.

Mehta, K.M., 1948. *Ahmedabad Sarvasamagraha*. Ahmedabad: Gujarat Publishers.

Nandy, A., 2001. *Time Warps. The Insistent Politics of Silent and Evasive Pasts*. Delhi: Permanent Black.

Newman, D. and A. Passi, 1998. 'Fences and neighbours in the post-modern world: boundary narratives in political geography', *The Progress in Human Geography* 22:, pp.186-207.

Newman, D., 2006. 'The lines that continue to separate us: borders in a "borderless world"', *The Progress in Human Geography* 30, pp. 143-161.

Ohmae, K., 1990. *The Borderless World*. New York: Harper Collins.

Perera, S. and J. Pugliese, 1997, 'Racial Suicide: The Reli-censing of Racialism in Australia'. *Race and Class*, 39, pp. 1-20.

Rediff.com, 2002. 'The Gujarat Riots', *Rediff on the Net*, http://www.rediff.com/news/godhra.htm, Accessed: April 2011.

State Gazetteers, Gujarat, 1984. *Ahmadabad District*. Ahmadabad: Government of Gujarat.

Stuver, A., 2003. 'Presenting Representation: On the analysis of Narratives and Images along the Dutch-German Border', in E. Berg and H. Van Houtum, (eds.) *Routing Borders between Territories, Discourse, and Practices*. Aldershot: Ashgate.

Thrift, N., 1999. 'Steps to an Ecology of Place' in D. Massey, J. Allen, and P. Sarre, (eds.) *Human Geography Today*. Cambridge: Polity Press.

Times of India, 2002. 'Violence Spreads like Wildfire in State', *Times of India*, 28th February: 1.

Trudeau, D., 2006. 'Politics of belonging in the construction of landscape: place-making, boundary-drawing and exclusion', *Cultural Geographies* 13:, pp. 421-443.

Van Houtum, H., and A. Struver, 2002. 'Where is the Border?' *The Journal of Creative Geography* 4, pp. 20-23.

Waldron, S.R., 1980. 'Within the Wall and Beyond: Harari Ethnic Identity and its Future', in G. Gmelch and W.P. Zenner, (eds.), *Urban Life: Readings in Urban Anthropology*. New York: St. Martin's.

Welchman, J.C., (ed.), 1996. *Rethinking Borders*. Minneapolis: University of Minnesota Press.

Yagnik, A., and S. Sheth, 2005. *The Shaping of Modern Gujarat: Plurality, Hindutva and Beyond*. New Delhi: Penguin Books.

Index